Meditations
For All the Days of the Year

VOLUME I

editations

For All the Days of the Year

VOLUME I

From the First Sunday in Advent to Septuagesima Sunday

"This day is born to you a Savior, who is Christ the Lord." - *St. Luke 2:11*

Meditations

For All the Days of the Year

FOR THE USE OF PRIESTS, RELIGIOUS AND THE FAITHFUL.

BY
REV. M. HAMON, S.S.,

Pastor of St. Sulpice, Paris, Author of "Life of St. Francis de Sales" and "Life of Cardinal Cheverus."

From the Twenty-third Revised and Enlarged Edition
BY
MRS. ANNE R. BENNETT,
(née GLADSTONE.)

WITH A METHOD OF USING THESE MEDITATIONS,
BY VERY REV. A. MAGNIEN, S.S., D.D.

VOLUME I

*From the First Sunday in Advent
to Septuagesima Sunday*

Originally published by:

NEW YORK, CINCINNATI, CHICAGO:
Benzinger Brothers
Printers to the Holy Apostolic See

Reprinted by Valora Media
Cover and layout by: Kenneth R. Henderson

Nihil Obstat

D. J. McMAHON, D.D.,

Censor Librorum
Imprimatur

MICHAEL AUGUSTINE,

Archbishop of New York

NEW YORK, July 14, 1894.

COPYRIGHT 1804 by Benzinger Brothers,
Printed in the United States of America

Printed in the United States of America.

Preface

To aid Christian souls better to know God with His infinite perfections and His adorable mysteries; better to love and serve Him, better to know themselves, their faults and their duties; better to reform themselves and to make progress in virtue: such is the end we have proposed to ourselves in writing this work. In this futile and frivolous age, in which hardly any one occupies himself with aught except external events, there are very few souls who seriously reflect upon these great and holy things; very few who carefully meditate every morning how much God deserves to be loved and served, how they can serve Him during the present day, and what they will do for His glory, for their own salvation, and their personal sanctification. As a remedy for this evil, we have believed it will be useful to make the very important exercise of meditation easy for souls of goodwill, by putting into their hands not a literary work which addresses itself to their minds, but a course of meditations which addresses itself to their hearts, and which should be read calmly, attentively, with reflection, with the object of entering into themselves and being awakened to a better life. May the reader thoroughly understand our design, meditate deeply and get to the bottom of each phrase, if we may so speak, penetrate himself with it and apply it to himself, by comparing what he is with what he ought to be, and deducing practical consequences for the reformation of his life, not in the distant future, but on the very same day. In the composition of his work, we have followed, step by step, if we can so say, the Roman liturgy, which has so admirably collected together the whole of religion within the course of the ecclesiastical year, and under the direction of such a sure guide we have meditated: first, upon the mysteries which are the basis of Christian virtues; second, the Christian virtues themselves, which are the edifice to be built upon this basis; third, the feasts of the most celebrated among the saints, whose life is virtue itself in action; and we have endeavored to present here these great subjects in a manner which will be equally suitable to the clergy and the faithful, so that our work may be useful to a greater number. The reader must not be astonished sometimes to meet with the same truth or the same virtue presented for meditation under different aspects. The soul needs to have the same truth often repeated to it, otherwise the impression would be effaced, until it became for us as though it had never been; it needs to reproach itself often with certain faults, otherwise it would lose sight of them, and would no longer take any care to correct them; lastly, it needs to be often raised up, because it often falls; hence our repetitions are anything but idle repetitions.

He must not be astonished, either, on the preceding evening, to find there the summary of the morrow s meditation. It is very important, in order to succeed properly in meditation, to fix precisely the subject on the preceding evening, and to arrive at the meditation of it already penetrated with what is about to occupy him. Hence, at the head of every meditation we have placed: First, an indication of the points of the meditation; Second, the enunciation of the resolutions which should be the practical consequence of it. We have added afterwards what St. Francis de Sales calls a spiritual nosegay; that is to say, a good thought which will be the sum total as it were of the meditation, and of which the perfume, embalming our heart during the whole day, recalls to us our morning meditation.

We have also placed at the beginning of each volume the usual morning and evening prayers, so that there may be no need to have recourse to another book to fulfill the daily duties of every Christian. Lastly, we have added to this third edition: First, several new meditations; second, a more careful and complete index; third, a plan of meditations for an eight day retreat; fourth, self examinations inserted in the greater part of the meditations; fifth, various developments op several subjects of meditation. May God, in His love for souls, deign to bless this new work and make it serve to His glory and to the sanctification of the elect!

☙ Contents ❧

Preface i
Morning Prayers 1
Evening Prayers 9
First Sunday in Advent 16
   Monday in the First Week of Advent 19
   Tuesday in the First Week of Advent 21
   Wednesday in the First Week of Advent 24
   Thursday in the First Week of Advent 26
   Friday in the First Week of Advent 29
   Saturday in the First Week of Advent 31
Second Sunday in Advent 33
   Monday in the Second Week of Advent 36
   Tuesday in the Second Week of Advent 38
   Wednesday in the Second Week of Advent 41
   Thursday in the Second Week of Advent 43
   Friday in the Second Week of Advent 45
   Saturday in the Second Week of Advent 47
Third Sunday in Advent 49
   Monday in the Third Week of Advent 53
   Tuesday in the Third Week of Advent 54
   Wednesday in the Third Week of Advent 56
   Thursday in the Third Week of Advent 59
   Friday in the Third Week of Advent 61
   Saturday in the Third Week of Advent 63
Fourth Sunday in Advent 66
   Monday in the Fourth Week of Advent 69
   Tuesday in the Fourth Week of Advent 70
   Wednesday in the Fourth Week of Advent 72
   Thursday in the Fourth Week of Advent 74
   Friday in the Fourth Week of Advent 76
December 25th - Christmas 79
   December 26th 82

December 27th	85
December 28th	87
December 29th	89
December 30th	91
December 31st	93
January 1st	96
January 2nd	98
January 3rd	101
January 4th	103
January 5th	105
January 6th	107
January 7th	109
January 8th	111
January 9th	113
January 10th	116
January 11th	118
First Sunday after Epiphany	120
Monday in the First Week after Epiphany	122
Tuesday in the First Week after Epiphany	124
Wednesday in the First Week after Epiphany	126
Thursday in the First Week after Epiphany	128
Friday in the First Week after Epiphany	131
Saturday in the First Week after Epiphany	133
Second Sunday after Epiphany	135
Monday in the Second Week after Epiphany	138
Tuesday in the Second Week after Epiphany	140
Wednesday in the Second Week after Epiphany	142
Thursday in the Second Week after Epiphany	144
Friday in the Second Week after Epiphany	148
Saturday in the Second Week after Epiphany	150
Third Sunday after Epiphany	151
Monday in the Third Week after Epiphany	153
Tuesday in the Third Week after Epiphany	155
Wednesday in the Third Week after Epiphany	157
Thursday in the Third Week after Epiphany	159

Friday in the Third Week after Epiphany 161
Saturday in the Third Week after Epiphany. 163
Fourth Sunday after Epiphany 165
   Monday in the Fourth Week after Epiphany 168
   Tuesday in the Fourth Week after Epiphany 170
   Wednesday in the Fourth Week after Epiphany 173
   Thursday in the Fourth Week after Epiphany 176
   Friday in the Fourth Week after Epiphany 178
   Saturday in the Fourth Week after Epiphany 180
Fifth Sunday after Epiphany. 182
   Monday in the Fifth Week after Epiphany 185
   Tuesday in the Fifth Week after Epiphany 188
   Wednesday in the Fifth Week after Epiphany 190
   Thursday in the Fifth Week after Epiphany. 193
   Friday in the Fifth Week after Epiphany. 195
   Saturday in the Fifth Week after Epiphany 197
Sixth Sunday after Epiphany 199
   Monday in the Sixth Week after Epiphany 202
   Tuesday in the Sixth Week after Epiphany 204
   Wednesday in the Sixth Week after Epiphany. 206
   Thursday in the Sixth Week after Epiphany 208
   Friday in the Sixth Week after Epiphany. 210
   Saturday in the Sixth Week after Epiphany 213

SAINTS DAYS

November 30th - St. Andrew the Apostle 215
December 3rd - St. Francis Xavier 215
December 8th - The Immaculate Conception, Meditation One. . . . 219
December 9th - The Immaculate Conception, Meditation Two. . . . 222
December 21st - St. Thomas, Apostle 224
January 17th - St. Anthony 226
January 25th - The Conversion of St. Paul. 229
January 29th - St. Francis De Sales 231
February 2nd - The Purification of Mary and the Presentation
   of Our Lord 234

Morning Prayers

In the name of the Father, + and of the Son, and of the Holy Ghost. Amen.

Place Yourself in the Presence of God, and adore His holy Name.

Most holy and adorable Trinity, one God in three Persons, I believe that Thou art here present: I adore Thee with the deepest humility, and render to Thee, with my whole heart, the homage which is due to Thy sovereign majesty.

ACT OF FAITH

O my God, I firmly believe that Thou art one God in three divine Persons. Father, Son, and Holy Ghost; I believe that Thy divine Son became man, and died for our sins, and that He will come to judge the living and the dead. I believe these and all the truths which the holy Catholic Church teaches, because Thou hast revealed them, who canst neither deceive nor be deceived.

ACT OF HOPE

O my God, relying on Thy infinite goodness and promises, I hope to obtain pardon of my sins, the help of Thy grace, and life everlasting, through the merits of Jesus Christ, my Lord and Redeemer.

ACT OF LOVE

O my God, I love Thee above all things, with my whole heart and soul, because Thou art all-good and worthy of all love. I love my neighbor as myself for the love of Thee. I forgive all who have injured me, and ask pardon of all whom I have injured.

THANK GOD FOR ALL FAVORS AND OFFER YOURSELF TO HIM

O my God, I most humbly thank Thee for all the favors Thou hast bestowed upon me up to the present moment. I give Thee thanks from the bottom of my heart that Thou hast created me after Thine own image and likeness, that Thou hast redeemed me by the precious blood of Thy dear Son, and that Thou hast preserved me and brought me safe to the beginning of another day. I offer to Thee, O Lord, my whole being, and in particular all my thoughts, words, actions, and sufferings of this day. I consecrate them all to the glory of Thy name, beseeching Thee that through the infinite merits of Jesus Christ my Savior they may all find acceptance in Thy sight. May Thy divine love animate them, and may they all tend to Thy greater glory.

RESOLVE TO AVOID SIN AND TO PRACTICE VIRTUE

Adorable Jesus, my Savior and Master, model of all perfection, I resolve and will endeavor this day to imitate Thy example, to be, like Thee, mild, humble, chaste, zealous, charitable, and resigned. I will redouble my efforts that I may not fall this day into any of those sins which I have heretofore committed (here name any besetting sin), and which I sincerely desire to forsake.

ASK GOD FOR THE NECESSARY GRACES

O my God, Thou knowest my poverty and weakness, and that I am unable to do anything good without Thee; deny me not, O God, the help of Thy grace: proportion it to my necessities; give me strength to avoid anything evil which Thou forbiddest and to practice the good which Thou hast commanded; and enable me to bear patiently all the trials which it may please Thee to send me.

THE LORD'S PRAYER

Latin

Pater noster, qui es in caelis, sanctificetur nomen tuum. Adveniat regnum tuum. Fiat voluntas tua, sicut in caelo et in terra. Panem nostrum quotidianum da nobis hodie, et dimitte nobis debita nostra sicut et nos dimittimus debitoribus nostris. Et ne nos inducas in tentationem, sed libera nos a malo. Amen.

English

Our Father, who art in heaven, hallowed be Thy name. Thy kingdom come. Thy will be done on earth as it is in heaven. Give us this day our daily bread and forgive us our trespasses as we forgive those who trespass against us. And lead us not into temptation, but deliver us from evil. Amen.

THE HAIL MARY

Latin

Ave Maria, gratia plena, Dominus tecum. Benedicta tu in mulieribus, et benedictus fructus ventris tui, Jesus. Sancta Maria, Mater Dei, ora pro nobis peccatoribus, nunc, et in hora mortis nostrae. Amen.

English

Hail Mary, full of grace, the Lord is with thee. Blessed art thou amongst women and blessed is the fruit of thy womb, Jesus. Holy Mary, Mother of God, pray for us sinners, now, and in the hour of our death. Amen.

THE APOSTLE'S CREED

Latin

Credo in Deum Patrem omnipotentem, Creatorem caeli et terrae. Et in Iesum Christum, Filium eius unicum, Dominum nostrum, qui conceptus est de Spiritu Sancto, natus ex Maria Virgine, passus sub Pontio Pilato, crucifixus, mortuus, et sepultus, descendit ad infernos, tertia die resurrexit a mortuis, ascendit ad caelos, sedet ad dexteram Dei Patris omnipotentis, inde venturus est iudicare vivos et mortuos. Credo in Spiritum Sanctum, sanctam Ecclesiam catholicam, sanctorum communionem, remissionem peccatorum, carnis resurrectionem et vitam aeternam. Amen.

English

I believe in God, the Father almighty, Creator of heaven and earth. I believe in Jesus Christ, His only Son, our Lord. He was conceived by the power of the Holy Spirit and born of the Virgin Mary. He suffered under Pontius Pilate, was crucified, died, and was buried. He descended to the dead. On the third day He rose again. He ascended into heaven and sits at the right hand of God, the Father Almighty. From thence He shall come to judge the living and the dead. I believe in the Holy Spirit, the holy catholic Church, the communion of saints, the forgiveness of sins, the resurrection of the body, and the life everlasting. Amen.

ASK THE PRAYERS OF THE BLESSED VIRGIN, YOUR GUARDIAN ANGEL, AND YOUR PATRON SAINT.

Holy Virgin Mother of God, my Mother and Patroness, I place myself under thy protection, I throw myself with confidence into the arms of thy compassion. Be to me, O Mother of mercy, my refuge in distress, my consolation under suffering, my advocate with thy adorable Son, now and at the hour of my death.

> Angel of God, my guardian dear,
> To whom His love commits me here,
> Ever this day be at my side,
> To light and guard, to rule and guide. Amen.

O great Saint whose name I bear, protect me, pray for me that like thee I may serve God faithfully on earth, and glorify Him eternally with thee in heaven. Amen.

LITANY OF THE MOST HOLY NAME OF JESUS

> O Lord Jesus Christ, who hast said: Ask, and ye shall receive; seek, and ye shall find; knock, and it shall be opened unto you; grant, we beseech Thee, unto us who ask, the gift of Thy most divine love, that we may ever love Thee with all our hearts, and in all our words and actions, and never cease from showing forth Thy praise.

Latin	*English*
Kyrie eleison.	Lord, have mercy on us.
Christe eleison.	Christ, have mercy on us.
Kyrie eleison.	Lord, have mercy on us.
Jesu aucli nos.	Jesus, hear us.
Jesu exaudi nos.	Jesus, graciously hear us.
Pater de coelis Deus,	God the Father of heaven,
...Miserere nobis	...Have mercy on us.
Fill, Redemptor mundi, Deus,	God the Son, Redeemer of the world,
Spiritus Sancte Deus,	God the Holy Ghost,
Sancta Trinitas, unus Deus,	Holy Trinity, one God,
Jesu, Fili Dei vivi,	Jesus, Son of the living God,
Jesu, splendor Patris,	Jesus, splendor of the Father,
Jesu, candor lucis aeternx,	Jesus, brightness of eternal light,
Jesu, rex gloriae,	Jesus, king of glory,
Jesu, sol justitiae,	Jesus, sun of justice,
Jesu, fili Mariae Virginis,	Jesus, son of the Virgin Mary,
Jesu amabilis,	Jesus, most amiable,
Jesu admirabilis,	Jesus, most admirable,

Jesu, Deus fortis,	Jesus, mighty God,
Jesu, pater futuri saeculi,	Jesus, father of the world to come,
Jesu, magni consilii angele,	Jesus, angel of the great council,
Jesu potentissime,	Jesus, most powerful,
Jesu patientissime,	Jesus, most patient,
Jesu obedientissime,	Jesus, most obedient,
Jesu, mitis et humilis corde,	Jesus, meek and humble of heart,
Jesu, amator castitatis,	Jesus, lover of chastity,
Jesu, amator noster,	Jesus, lover of us,
Jesu, Deus pacis,	Jesus, God of peace,
Jesu, auctor vitae,	Jesus, author of life,
Jesu, exemplar virtutum,	Jesus, model of virtues,
Jesu, zelator animarum,	Jesus, zealous for souls,
Jesu, Deus noster,	Jesus, our God,
Jesu, refugium nostrum,	Jesus, our refuge,
Jesu, pater pauperum,	Jesus, father of the poor,
Jesu, thesaurus fidelium,	Jesus, treasure of the faithful,
Jesu, bone pastor,	Jesus, good shepherd,
Jesu, lux vera,	Jesus, true light,
Jesu, sapientia aeterna,	Jesus, eternal wisdom,
Jesu, bonitas infinita,	Jesus, infinite goodness,
Jesu, via et vita nostra,	Jesus, our way and our life,
Jesu, gaudium angelorum,	Jesus, joy of angels,
Jesu, rex patriarcharum,	Jesus, king of patriarchs,
Jesu, magister apostolorum,	Jesus, master of apostles,
Jesu, doctor evangelistarum,	Jesus, teacher lists,
Jesu, fortitude martyrum,	Jesus, strength of martyrs,
Jesu, lumen confessorum,	Jesus, light of confessors,
Jesu, puritas virginum,	Jesus, purity of virgins,
Jesu, corona sanctorum omnium,	Jesus, crown of all saints,
Propitius esto,	Be merciful,
Parce nobis, Jesu.	Spare us, O Jesus,
Propitius esto,	Be merciful,
Exaudi nos, Jesu.	Graciously hear us, O Jesus.
Ab omni malo,	From all evil,
Ab omni peccato,	From all sin,
Ab ira tua,	From Thy wrath,
Ab insidiis diaboli,	From the snares of the devil,
A spiritu fornicationis,	From the spirit of fornication,

A morte perpetua,	From everlasting death,
A neglectu inspirationumtuarum,	From the neglect of Thy inspirations,
Per mysterium sanctse incamationis tuae,	Through the mystery of Thy holy incarnation,
Pet nativitatem tuam,	Through Thy nativity,
Per infantiam tuam,	Through Thine infancy,
Per divinissimam vitam tuam,	Through Thy most divine life,
Per labores tuos,	Through Thy labors,
Per agoniam et passionem tuam,	Through Thine agony and passion,
Per crucem et derelictionem tuam,	Through Thy cross and dereliction,
Per languores tuos,	Through Thy faintness and weariness,
Per mortem et sepulturam tuam,	Through Thy death and burial,
Per resurrectionem tuam,	Through Thy resurrection,
Per ascensionem tuam,	Through Thine ascension,
Per gaudia tua,	Through Thy joys,
Per gloriam tuam,	Through Thy glory,

Agnus Dei, qui tollis peccata mundi,
Parce nobis, Jesu.
Agnus Dei, qui tollis peccata mundi,
Exaudi nos, Jesu.
Agnus Dei, qui tollis peccata mundi,
Miserere nobis, Jesu.
Jesu audi nos.
Jesu, exaudi nos.

Oremus.
Domine Jesu Christe, qui dixisti: Petite, et accipietis; qiiaerite, et invenietis ; pul sate, et aperietur vobis, quaesumus ; da nobis peteu tibus divinissimi tui amoris affectum, ut te toto corde, ore et opere diligamus, et a tua nunquam laude cessemus.
Sancti Nominis tui, Domine, timorem pariter et amorem fac nos habere per petuum, quia nunquam tua gubernatione destituis quos in soliditate tuae dilectionis instituis. Qui vivis et reg. uas, etc. Amen.

Lamb of God, who takes away the sins of the world
Spare us, O Jesus.
Lamb of God, who takest away the sins of the world.
Graciously hear us, O Jesus.
Lamb of God, who takest away the sins of the world,
Have mercy on us, O Jesus*
Jesus, hear us.
Jesus, graciously hear us

Let us pray.
Make us, O Lord, to have a perpetual fear and love of Thy holy Name; for Thou never failest to govern those whom Thou dost solidly establish in Thy love. Who livest and reignest, etc. Amen.

THE ANGELUS DOMINI

Latin
V. Angelus Domini nuntiavit Mariae.
R. Et concepit de Spiritu Sancto.

> Ave Maria, gratia plena; Dominus tecum: benedicta tu in mulieribus, et benedictus fructus ventris tui Iesus. * Sancta Maria, Mater Dei ora pro nobis peccatoribus, nunc et in hora mortis nostrae. Amen.

V. Ecce ancilla Domini,
R. Fiat mihi secundum verbum tuum.

> Ave Maria, gratia plena; Dominus tecum: benedicta tu in mulieribus, et benedictus fructus ventris tui Iesus. * Sancta Maria, Mater Dei ora pro nobis peccatoribus, nunc et in hora mortis nostrae. Amen.

V. Et Verbum caro factum est,
R. Et habitavit in nobis.

> Ave Maria, gratia plena; Dominus tecum: benedicta tu in mulieribus, et benedictus fructus ventris tui Iesus.* Sancta Maria, Mater Dei ora pro nobis peccatoribus, nunc et in hora mortis nostrae. Amen.

V. Ora pro nobis, sancta Dei Genetrix,
R. Ut digni efficiamur promissionibus Christi.

> Oremus. Gratiam tuam, quaesumus, Domine, mentibus nostris infunde; ut qui, Angelo nuntiante, Christi Filii tui incarnationem cognovimus, per passionem eius et crucem ad resurrectionis gloriam perducamur. Per eumdem Christum Dominum nostrum.

R. Amen.

English
V. The angel of the Lord declared unto Mary.
R. And she conceived of the Holy Spirit.

Hail Mary, full of grace; the Lord is with Thee: blessed art thou among women, and blessed is the fruit of thy womb, Jesus.* Holy Mary, Mother of God, prayer for us sinners, now and at the hour of our death.

V. Behold the handmaid of the Lord,
R. Be it done to me according to Thy word.

Hail Mary, full of grace; the Lord is with Thee: blessed art thou among women, and blessed is the fruit of thy womb, Jesus.* Holy Mary, Mother of God, prayer for us sinners, now and at the hour of our death.

V. And the Word was made flesh,
R. And dwelt among us.

Hail Mary, full of grace; the Lord is with Thee: blessed art thou among women, and blessed is the fruit of thy womb, Jesus.* Holy Mary, Mother of God, prayer for us sinners, now and at the hour of our death.

V. Pray for us, O holy Mother of God,
R. That we may be made worthy of the promises of Christ.

Let us pray.

Pour forth, we beseech Thee, Lord, Thy grace into our hearts; that, as we have known the Incarnation of Christ, Thy Son, by the message of an angel, so by His Passion and Cross we may be brought to the glory of the Resurrection. Through the same Christ our Lord.

R. Amen.

Evening Prayers

In the name of the Father, + and of the Son, and of the Holy Ghost. Amen.

Come, O Holy Ghost, fill the hearts of Thy faithful, and kindle in them the fire of Thy love.

Place Yourself in the Presence of God and Humbly Adore Him.

O my God, I present myself before Thee at the end of another day, to offer Thee anew the homage of my heart. I humbly adore Thee, my Creator, my Redeemer, and my Judge! I believe in Thee, because Thou art Truth itself; I hope in Thee, because Thou art faithful to Thy promises; I love Thee with my whole heart, because Thou art infinitely worthy of being loved; and for Thy sake I love my neighbor as myself.

RETURN THANKS TO GOD FOR ALL HIS MERCIES.

Enable me, O my God, to return Thee thanks as I ought for all Thine inestimable blessings and favors. Thou hast thought of me and loved me from all eternity; Thou hast formed me out of nothing; Thou hast delivered up Thy beloved Son to the ignominious death of the cross for my redemption; Thou hast made me a member of Thy holy Church; Thou hast preserved me from falling into the abyss of eternal misery, when my sins had provoked Thee to punish me; Thou hast graciously continued to spare me, even though I have not ceased to offend Thee. What return, O my God, can I make for Thy innumerable blessings, and particularly for the favors of this day? O all ye saints and angels, unite with me in praising the God of mercies, who is so bountiful to so unworthy a creature.

Our Father. Hail Mary. I believe.

ASK OF GOD LIGHT TO DISCOVER THE SINS COMMITTED THIS DAY.

O my God, sovereign judge of men, who desirest not the death of a sinner, but that he should be converted and saved, enlighten my mind, that I may know the sins which I have this day committed in thought, word, or deed, and give me the grace of true contrition.

Here Examine your Conscience; then say

O my God, I heartily repent and am grieved that I have offended Thee, because Thou art infinitely good and sin is infinitely displeasing to Thee. I humbly ask of Thee mercy and pardon, through the infinite merits of Jesus Christ. I resolve, by the assistance of Thy grace, to do penance for my sins, and I will endeavor never more to offend Thee.

THE CONFITEOR

Latin

Confiteor Deo omnipotenti, et vobis fratres, quia peccavi nimis cogitatione, verbo opere et omissione: mea culpa, mea culpa, mea maxima culpa. Ideo precor beatam Mariam semper Virginem, omnes angelos et Sanctos, et vobis fratres, orare pro me ad Dominum Deum nostrum. Amen.

Misereatur nostril Omnipotens Deus, et dimissis peccatis nobis, perducat nos ad vitam aeternam. Amen.

Indulgentiam, + absolutionem, et remissionem peccatorum nostrorum, tribuat nobis omnipotens et misericors Dominus. Amen.

English

I confess to almighty God, and to you my brothers and sisters, that I have sinned through my own fault, in my thoughts and in my words, in what I have done and what I have failed to do. I ask blessed Mary ever Virgin, all the angels and saints, and you my brothers and sisters, to pray for me to the Lord our God. Amen.

May Almighty God have mercy upon us, and forgive us our sins, and bring us unto life everlasting. Amen.

May the Almighty and merciful Lord grant us pardon, + absolution, and remission of our sins. Amen.

PRAY FOR THE CHURCH OF CHRIST

O God, hear my prayers on behalf of our Holy Father Pope N., our Bishops, our clergy, and for all that are in authority over us. Bless, I beseech Thee, the whole Catholic Church, and convert all heretics and unbelievers.

PRAY FOR THE LIVING AND FOR THE FAITHFUL DEPARTED

Pour down Thy blessings, O Lord, upon all my friends, relations, and acquaintances, and upon my enemies, if I have any. Help the poor and sick, and those who are in their last agony. O God of mercy and goodness, have compassion on the souls of the faithful in purgatory; put an end to their sufferings, and grant to them eternal light, rest, and happiness. Amen.

COMMEND YOURSELF TO GOD, TO THE BLESSED VIRGIN, AND THE SAINTS

Bless, O Lord, the repose I am about to take, that, my bodily strength being renewed, I may be the better enabled to serve Thee.

O blessed Virgin Mary, Mother of mercy, pray for me that I may be preserved this night from all evil, whether of body or soul. Blessed St. Joseph, and all ye saints and angels of Paradise, especially my guardian angel and my chosen patron, watch over me. I commend myself to your protection now and always. Amen.

LITANY OF LORETTO

Latin	*English*
Kyrie, eleison.	Lord, have mercy.
Christe, eleison.	Christ, have mercy.
Kyrie, eleison.	Lord, have mercy.
Christe, audi nos.	Christ, hear us.
Christe, exaudi nos.	Christ, graciously hear us.
Pater de caelis, Deus,	God the Father of heaven,
...miserere nobis.	...have mercy upon us.
Fili, Redemptor mundi, Deus,	God the Son, Redeemer of the world,
Spiritus Sancte, Deus,	God the Holy Spirit,
Sancta Trinitas, unus Deus,	Holy Trinity, one God,
Sancta Maria,	Holy Mary,
...ora pro nobis.	...pray for us.
Sancta Dei Genetrix,	Holy Mother of God,
Sancta Virgo virginum,	Holy Virgin of virgins,
Mater Christi,	Mother of Christ,
Mater divinae gratiae,	Mother of divine grace,

Mater purissima,	Mother most pure,
Mater castissima,	Mother most chaste,
Mater inviolata,	Mother inviolate,
Mater intemerata,	Mother undefiled,
Mater amabilis,	Mother most amiable,
Mater admirabilis,	Mother most admirable,
Mater boni consilii,	Mother of good counsel,
Mater Creatoris,	Mother of our Creator,
Mater Salvatoris,	Mother of our Savior,
Virgo prudentissima,	Virgin most prudent,
Virgo veneranda,	Virgin most venerable,
Virgo praedicanda,	Virgin most renowned,
Virgo potens,	Virgin most powerful,
Virgo clemens,	Virgin most merciful,
Virgo fidelis,	Virgin most faithful,
Speculum iustitiae,	Mirror of justice,
Sedes sapientiae,	Seat of wisdom,
Causa nostrae laetitiae,	Cause of our joy,
Vas spirituale,	Spiritual vessel,
Vas honorabile,	Vessel of honor,
Vas insigne devotionis,	Singular vessel of devotion,
Rosa mystica,	Mystical rose,
Turris Davidica,	Tower of David,
Turris eburnea,	Tower of ivory,
Domus aurea,	House of gold,
Foederis arca,	Ark of the covenant,
Ianua caeli,	Gate of heaven,
Stella matutina,	Morning star,
Salus infirmorum,	Health of the sick,
Refugium peccatorum,	Refuge of sinners,
Consolatrix afflictorum,	Comfort of the afflicted,
Auxilium Christianorum,	Help of Christians,
Regina Angelorum,	Queen of angels,
Regina Patriarcharum,	Queen of patriarchs,
Regina Prophetarum,	Queen of prophets,
Regina Apostolorum,.	Queen of apostles,
Regina Martyrum,	Queen of martyrs,
Regina Confessorum,	Queen of confessors,
Regina Virginum,	Queen of virgins,

Regina Sanctorum omnium,
Regina sine labe originali concepta,
Regina in caelum assumpta,
Regina sacratissimi Rosarii,
Regina pacis,
Agnus Dei, qui tollis peccata mundi,
parce nobis, Domine.
Agnus Dei, qui tollis peccata mundi,
exaudi nos, Domine.
Agnus Dei, qui tollis peccata mundi,
miserere nobis.

V. Ora pro nobis, sancta Dei Genetrix.
R. Ut digni efficiamur promissionibus Christi.

Oremus.

> Concede nos famulos tuos, quaesumus, Domine Deus, perpetua mentis et corporis sanitate gaudere, et gloriosae beatae Mariae simper Virginis intercessione, a praesenti liberari tristitia, et aeterna perfrui laetitia. Per Christum Dominum nostrum.

R. Amen.

Queen of all saints,
Queen conceived without original sin,
Queen assumed into heaven,
Queen of the most holy Rosary,
Queen of peace,
Lamb of God, who take away the sins of the world,
spare us, O Lord.
Lamb of God, who take away the sins of the world,
spare us, O Lord.
Lamb of God, who take away the sins of the world,
have mercy upon us.

R. Pray for us, O holy Mother of God.
V. That we may be made worthy of the promises of Christ.

Let us pray.

> Grant, we beseech Thee, O Lord God, unto us Thy servants, that we may rejoice in continual health of mind and body; and, by the glorious intercession of blessed Mary ever Virgin, may be delivered from present sadness, and enter into the joy of Thine eternal gladness. Through Christ our Lord.

R. Amen

Meditations
For All the Days of the Year

VOLUME I

*From the First Sunday in Advent
to Septuagesima Sunday*

First Sunday in Advent

THE GOSPEL ACCORDING TO ST. LUKE, 21:25-36

"At that time Jesus said to His disciples: There shall be signs in the sun, and in the moon, and in the stars; and upon the earth distress of nations, by reason of the confusion of the roaring of the sea and of the waves, men withering away for fear and expectation of what shall come upon the whole world. For the powers of heaven shall be moved: and then they shall see the Son of man coming in a cloud with great power and majesty. But when these things begin to come to pass, look up and lift up your heads: because your redemption is at hand. And He spoke to them a similitude. See the fig tree and all the trees: when they now shoot forth their fruit, you know that summer is nigh. So you also, when you shall see these things come to pass, know that the kingdom of God is at hand. Amen I say to you, this generation shall not pass away till all things be fulfilled. Heaven and earth shall pass away, but My words shall not pass away."

SUMMARY OF TOMORROW'S MEDITATION

he holy season on which we have entered is intended on the part of the Church to make us meditate on the three great advents of the Savior upon earth: the first in the humility of the crib in order to save us; the second in the splendor of His glory at the last day in order to judge us; the third in the secret of our hearts by His grace in order to sanctify us. After having meditated on these three advents we will make the resolution: First, to enter upon a new life of recollection and prayer suitable to the season of Advent; second, to take particular care with regard to the perfection of every one of our ordinary actions, which will be the best manner of sanctifying this holy season. Our spiritual nosegay shall be the words of St. Paul: "Behold now is the acceptable time; behold now is the day of salvation." (2 Cor. 6:2)

MEDITATION FOR THE MORNING

Let us adore the Spirit of God inspiring the Church with the institution of Advent, to prepare us for the great solemnity of Christmas, of which the whole of this season is as the vigil, St. Charles says; a vigil, "remarks this holy Cardinal, which ought not to appear long to whoever rightly appreciates the excellence of the feast for which it prepares us" (Lit. S. Car., de Adventu). It is in this spirit that the holy Church cries to heaven: O God, send Thy all-powerful grace to dispose our hearts (Collect. Adventus), and that she exclaims in the epistle of to-day: Come forth out of your torpor; awake, children of men, prepare your hearts; the birth of the Saviour is at hand (Rom. 13:11). It is in this same spirit that she substitutes penitential vestments for her festal vestments, and special and longer prayers for her ordinary prayers; and that where she has it in her power she summons to her pulpits distinguished preachers, who may be able to touch the hearts of the faithful by the accents of a voice to which they are not familiar. Let us enter with our whole heart into the mind of the Church during this holy season.

FIRST POINT
✝ Why we must Meditate in a Special Manner during Advent on the Mystery of an Incarnate God

It is a proof of profound wisdom on the part of the Church not to introduce us at once to the crib of Bethlehem, but to point it out to us as it were with her finger a month in advance, that she may say to us, "Be prepared to meet thy God." (Amos 6:12). Reflect seriously on this great mystery which, after having been hid nine months in the womb of Mary, is about to reveal itself to the religion of the world on Christmas Day. Prepare for Him in your hearts, by meditation, to have a more lively faith in His greatness; a more profound devotion for the abasement of His majesty; a grateful love for His charity, which has descended so low from so great a height; a true humility, in order to honor Him in His low estate; a gentleness in character and in speech in harmony with His incomparable benignity; a spirit of penitence and recollection which will not form a contrast to the austerity of the crib and the holy occupations of the Divine Child. If you do not thus prepare your heart by a season's meditation on the mystery of the Incarnate Word, you will lose the graces attached to this great solemnity. Let us avoid such a misfortune by commencing from today to occupy ourselves with this mystery, and by entering upon a new life.

SECOND POINT
✝ Why we ought to Meditate in a Special Manner during Advent on the Coming of the Savior as Judge

Doubtless we ought every day of our lives to meditate on the great judgment with which the world will come to an end, and say, whilst performing every one of our actions: "After this the judgment." (Heb. 9:27) Nevertheless, the Church, believing this thought to be eminently useful to enable us to enter into the sentiments of fervor suitable to the holy season of Advent, summons us specially to meditate upon it through the recital of the last judgment which she causes us to read today in the Gospel. It is our duty to enter into her views; to conceive a lively faith in the coming of this great day, which will be so consoling for the good, who will then receive the recompense of their virtues, so terrible for sinners, who will then receive the punishment due to their vices; and to listen, like St. Jerome, to the voice of the trumpet which will summon us to it. May this voice resound in the bottom of our hearts during the whole of this holy season, in order to make us tremble at the mere appearance of evil, as well as to encourage us in the practice of good.

THIRD POINT
✝ *Why we ought to Meditate in a Special Manner, during the Holy Season of Advent, on the Coming of the Savior into our Hearts by Grace*

It is because this advent is the special means by which the graces of the mystery of Christmas are communicated to the soul. Jesus Christ, in this great feast, is not born corporally, as at Bethlehem, but He is born spiritually by His grace in souls which are well prepared to receive Him. He lives therein by His spirit, by the sentiments with which He inspires us, by His humility, His gentleness, His charity; in a word, by all His virtues which He communicates to us. O life of Jesus in us, how necessary art thou to us! Thou alone, O my God, canst render to our soul, disfigured by sin, its primary beauty (Hymn Laudum et Vesper, Brev. Paris); Thou alone art our salvation, our strength, our consolation; without Thee our poor soul would perish like a herb without water (Ibidem). We are the sick who cannot be cured save by Thee; men who have fallen and cannot be raised up again except by Thee. Show to us Thy divine graces, which ravish the souls of all; and then, enamored by Thy charms, we shall regain the lost flower of our innocence (Hymn Laudum et Vesper, Brev. Paris). We should obtain this birth and this life of grace first, through fervent prayers inspired by the feeling of the need which we have of it; second, by dint of vigilance in listening to grace, which asks but to speak to us; Third, through generosity in obeying it and by abandoning ourselves lovingly simply to its guidance. *Resolution sand spiritual nosegay as above.*

Monday in the First Week of Advent

SUMMARY OF TOMORROW'S MEDITATION

e shall meditate tomorrow on three means whereby to sanctify the season of Advent, that is to say: First, on the spirit of penitence and renewal of life; second, on holy desires for the birth of Christ in us: Third, on special devotion to the mystery of the incarnation. We will then make the resolution: First, to excite ourselves during every day of this holy season to lead a better life, and to ask of God by fervent prayers to enable us to do so; second, to think often and lovingly of the mystery of the Incarnation, above all when reciting the Angelus. Our spiritual nosegay shall be the prayer which the Church has borrowed from the prophet to invoke the reign of Christ in us: "Drop down dew, ye heavens, from above, and let the clouds rein the just." (Is. 45:8)

MEDITATION FOR THE MORNING

Let us adore with a deep fueling of love and gratitude the Incarnate Word dwelling during nine months in the womb of Mary, whence lie will issue forth on the most blessed night of Christmas to show Himself to the world. He bestows on us the holy season of Advent to dispose us to receive all the graces attached to the celebration of His birth. Let us thank Him for His goodness, and propose to ourselves richly to profit by it.

FIRST POINT

✝ **The Spirit of Penitence and of a Renewal of Life: the First Condition for Passing the Season of Advent Holily**

The season of Advent is, as we have already seen in one meditation, a series of holy and blessed days, destined to prepare us for the feast of Christmas by a better and more perfect life. It would, therefore, be in a way to profane it if we were to pass it in an ordinary manner. Formerly the Church sanctified Advent by abstinence, fasting, and long prayers. If we have not the courage of past days, we ought, at least, to sanctify it by a serious retrospect of ourselves, of the manner in which we perform our spiritual exercises, the employment of our time, the books we read, and our conversations, the detects of our character, our self-will and our self-love. We ought to examine ourselves in respect to all these things in presence of the crib, and taking as our judge the Child-God.

This serious examination will give birth in us to great sentiments of penitence for the past, strong resolutions for the future, and a firm determination to enter upon a new life. We have not a moment to lose. We have entered upon a holy season. We must set ourselves to work with our whole heart, and begin from this very instant with settling on some special defects to be corrected between now and Christmas.

SECOND POINT
✝ **Holy Desires for the Birth of Christ within us: the Second Disposition in which to Spend in a Holy Manner the Season of Advent**

In the same degree in which the patriarchs and prophets longed for the coming of the Messias, we ought also to long after His birth in our hearts by grace. For of what use would be the coming of the Messias upon earth if He did not come to be born and live in us; that is to say, if He did not come to animate us with His spirit, to inspire us with His grace, to fill us with His sentiments (Philipp. 2:5), since it is only on this condition that we are Christians, and that we can be saved (Rom. 8:9). Now Jesus Christ enters into the soul only if we desire Him, and according to the proportion in which we desire Him. He who does not desire Him does not appreciate Him, and renders himself, on that very account, unworthy to receive Him. We ought, then, during this holy season, to be men of desires (Dan. 9:23), to sigh as the patriarchs of old did for the coming of the Messias, and like the saints of the New Law after the reign of Jesus Christ in their hearts often repeating with them, "Drop down dew, ye heavens, from above, and let the clouds rein the just; let the earth be opened and bud forth a Savior." (Is. 45:8) "Oh, that Thou wouldst rend the heavens and wouldst come down." (Is. 64:1) "Come without delay, O Adonai! O Emmanuel! God with us! O King of peoples! Saint of saints! Expectation of the nations; the Desired of the eternal hills; Sun of justice; Splendor of glory. Come, O Lord, come!" (O Antiphon for Advent.) And these holy desires ought to be at once ardent and generous; ardent, that they may be in harmony with the excellence of the gift we ask for; generous to the point of sacrificing all which is displeasing to the Divine Host whom we desire should dwell in us. We cannot be ignorant of what displeases Him in us: our love of our own ease and of our well-being, our pride; in a word, everything which is a contrast to the humility, the suffering, and the poverty of the crib.

THIRD POINT
✚ A Special Devotion to the Mystery of the Incarnation: the Third Disposition Necessary for Spending Advent Holily

At all times this devotion ought to be eminently dear to the Christian soul; but the Church having instituted the season of Advent in order to lead us to honor and meditate upon this mystery, it is our duty to occupy ourselves with it in a special manner; to study the infinite love which has united the sublime nature of God to poor human nature; to thank, to love, to bless this great mystery; and in reparation of the past to live for nothing during Advent except the love and imitation of the Incarnate Word, who has condescended to render Himself the model of the life of a Christian. Happy he who will understand these truths, and who during the whole of this holy season will make it his study to bring them into practice; that is to say, to love and imitate the Word Incarnate. In so doing the whole of Christianity consists. Jesus Christ came down from heaven to earth solely to enkindle in all hearts the sacred fire of His love, and He did nothing more than show us by His example the line of conduct which we must follow during our sojourn upon earth. Let us thank Him for this double boon, and let us promise Him to profit by it. *Resolutions and spiritual nosegay as above.*

Tuesday in the First Week of Advent

SUMMARY OF TOMORROW'S MEDITATION

omorrow and the following days we will meditate on the second advent of the Savior coming to judge the world at the end of time, as the Gospel of Sunday last announced to us. We will, then, limit ourselves tomorrow to the consideration of the three preliminaries of the judgment; that is to say, First, the general resurrection; second, the separation of the good and the wicked; third, the descent of the Sovereign Judge, preceded by His cross. We will then make the resolution: First, to keep our bodies pure, so that they may rise glorious; second, to follow in all things the example set us by the saints, so that we may not be separated from them at the last day and driven back amongst the wicked; Second, to love Jesus Christ and His cross, which will be our joy in that great day if we have loved them during our life. Our spiritual nosegay shall be the words of the Apostle: "For we must all be manifested before the judgment seat of Christ." (2 Cor. 5:10)

MEDITATION FOR THE MORNING

Let us adore Jesus Christ, the Sovereign Judge of the good and of the wicked; of the good in order to recompense them, of the wicked in order to punish them. Let us hope in His goodness, saying with St. Teresa: What a consolation for me to have my best Friend for my judge! But let us also fear His justice, saying with St. Paul: After each action comes the judgment, which will discern between the good and the evil. (Heb. 9:27)

FIRST POINT
✝ The General Resurrection

God will prelude this great act by the burning up of the universe, which shall be reduced to ashes (2 Pet. 3:10). A heap of ashes behold that is all which will remain of the whole of this world in which the human race is in such a continual state of noisy agitation, and to which man attaches himself by so many ties! O children of men, therefore St Peter exclaims, what more is wanting to make you decide to be saints, detached and irreproachable in your conduct? (2 Pet. 3: 2-12) The scene of the judgment being thus prepared, the trumpet of the angels will make the four winds of heaven resound with the terrible words which caused Jerome to tremble in the desert: "Rise, ye dead, and come to judgment." The bodies and souls of all will obey instantly. The soul of the just will enter with joy into the body which it will animate, which formerly partook of its sufferings, and which is now about to partake of its recompense, which it even already shares: for it is glorious, impassible, immortal, agile like the spirits, brilliant like the sun. Oh, how glad will it then be to have crucified its flesh, given up its body to fatigue and to pain, and to have made of all its senses a pure offering to the Lord! The soul of the damned, on the contrary, will shudder with horror at the approach of the body which has ruined it, and desire to fly from it and be forever separated from it; but it is united to it by an invisible hand. O cursed body which has damned me, how mad I was to flatter thee, to spare thee, to caress thee! Why did I not immolate thee by penitential scourges! And whilst thus crying out, the poor soul cruelly feels the answer which the body would make, could it but speak: Thine alone is the fault! Thou ought to have led me and governed me; and thou made thyself my slave; thou didst plunge me into the mire, knowing that from thence I should fall into the flames. Let us here examine ourselves. What will the resurrection be to us? Will it be the sweet resurrection of the just, or the terrible resurrection of the wicked?

SECOND POINT
✝ The Separation of the Good and the Wicked

The human race having risen, a voice will make itself heard: Gather together His saints from all the quarters of the globe (Ps. 49:5). Immediately the angels will spread themselves amongst the assembled nations; they will gather together the elect; they will place them with honor on the right, and they will drive back the wicked to the left (Matt. 13:49). What a joy for the good to see themselves at last separated from the enemies of God, associated with all that is most venerable in heaven, with patriarchs and prophets, with apostles and martyrs, with even angels and princes of the celestial court! Oh, what ravishing society! How the heart will be at ease there, and what happiness to be reunited there forever! The damned, on the contrary, will shudder with rage at seeing themselves cast amongst all that the earth possesses of the vilest, of corruption the most infamous, of profligacy the most hideous, amidst all the devils! Oh, what frightful society, what despair at being associated with it throughout eternity! Oh, how deceived we have been; (Wis. 5.6) these wretched creatures exclaim. Behold those whose regularity, whose modesty, and whose piety we ridiculed: behold them shining with glory; and we, behold we are covered with ignominy as with a garment (Ibid. 3). Behold them ranged amongst the children of God, the princes of heaven (Ibid. 5), whilst we, who seemed to tread them under our feet, we are humbled, confounded, condemned to eternal torments! O my soul! let us avoid such great misery by means of a thorough reformation of our lives.

THIRD POINT
✝ The Descent of the Sovereign Judge, Preceded by His Cross

Then, says the Evangelist, shall appear in the air the standard of the Sovereign Judge, the cross, as the precursor of His coming being at hand (Matt. 14:30). A cry of happiness will burst from the just when they behold the sight. The cross was their delight when on earth; it was beneath its shade that they hid their merits, at its feet that they laid down their troubles, to its arms that they attached themselves by mortification and penitence. Behold wherefore the sight of it inundates them with such happiness! But how very different it will be with those who did not love the cross! They will tremble at the sight of it, because it will be their condemnation. It preaches nothing but privations, and they desired nothing but pleasures; it teaches nothing but humility and poverty, and they sought after nothing but glory and riches. What will the cross be for us at that great day? It is for us to decide. Meanwhile, after the cross will appear the Sovereign Judge; He will appear borne by the cherubim, surrounded by a thousand million of angels which form His court. The just will tremble with gladness at the spectacle. Oh, what reason we have to adore Him, to love Him, to fear Him, for how great He is, how amiable, how terrible! The damned, on the contrary, will be seized with fear; they will cry to the mountains to fall on them, they will call for death, and death will be deaf to their cries (Apoc. 9:6). What matter for serious reflection! *Resolutions and spiritual nosegay as above.*

Wednesday in the First Week of Advent

SUMMARY OF TOMORROW'S MEDITATION

e will meditate tomorrow on the last judgment, on the preliminaries of which we meditated this morning, and we shall observe: First, the severe examination which will then be made into the consciences of all men; second, the glory which will accrue to the good from it; third, the confusion into which the wicked will be cast. We will then make the resolution: First, to cite ourselves every evening to repair before the tribunal of Jesus Christ, and to ask ourselves what the Sovereign Judge will say of this present day; what He will say of the way in which I have employed it, of the words which I have uttered, of the thoughts in which I have indulged; second, to remind ourselves at every hour during the day of the words of St. Paul: "After this, the judgment." (Heb. 9:27)

MEDITATION FOR THE MORNING

Let us represent to ourselves the Sovereign Judge seated upon His throne. All nations are assembled before Him; the accused are cited to appear; let us suppose that it is ourselves. Let us humble ourselves and tremble.

FIRST POINT

✝ Examination which will be Made into the Conscience of all Men on the Last Day

I shall appear then before this terrible tribunal. There my cause will be taken in hand; the whole of my life will be revealed on that great day; the evil committed, and the good omitted, and the good ill-performed, and the graces fruitlessly received, and the same lost or badly employed, and every word and every action, and the motive which has made me act or speak, and each thought and mental reservation, and the confessions made without amendment, and the communions without love, and the prayers without attention (Matt. 10:6). You were a man, you were a Christian, you had the duties belonging to your state to fulfill, the Sovereign Judge will say to me. Render Me an account of the whole of your conduct in respect to these things. As man, I created you after My own likeness; where are the divine features that I impressed on your soul when I gave you life, the integrity, the probity, the moderation, the perfect decorum which characterize the good man created after My likeness? As a Christian, what conformity has there been between your life and the Gospel that law so chaste, so severe, so inflexible, of which there is not a single iota which ought not to find in you its accomplishment? As placed in a condition of life which involves responsibilities towards the Church, to society, to the family, in what manner have you fulfilled all your duties? Have you not neglected them in order to save yourself discomfort and constraint? Have you not placed pleasure before duty, enjoyment before conscience? What an immense field for examination! Let us judge ourselves now, in order not to be judged then. (1 Cor. 11:31)

SECOND POINT
✝ **The Glory which will Accrue to the Good from the Examination into their Conscience**

At that day God will render to every man the glory which will be his due (1 Cor. 4:5). He will reveal to the admiration of all nations all the merits of the just man, his virtue so pure, his intentions so upright, his sentiments so elevated and magnanimous, his gentleness so constant, his patience so persevering, his prayers so fervent, even to the most transient thoughts of his mind, the slightest movements of his heart, the most insignificant of his acts or words of charity (Ps. 36:6). All the people will applaud so edifying a recital; all those who will have been witnesses of so beautiful a life will relate in their turn all that they have remarked in it which was pious and meek and amiable. Oh, what a beautiful day of triumph for the just, what a beautiful feast at which they will vie with each other in honoring his conscience which he kept always pure: his parents, his friends whom he edified, Jesus Christ whose glory he procured. How great reason had St. Paul to exclaim in the midst of trials and tribulations: I suffer, but I am not confounded. I have laid all my troubles in the hands of my God, and He will compensate me at the great day of His justice (2 Tim. 4:8). How appropriate this thought is to console us in our troubles, to encourage us in our difficulties.

THIRD POINT
✝ **The Confusion into which the Wicked will be cast by the Examination into their Conscience**

This examination will overwhelm them with in describable confusion, first, at beholding in one of the scales of the balance of the Sovereign Judge all the graces received: exterior graces through sacraments, instructions, good examples; interior graces through good thoughts and pious impulses; and in the other scale, where so much holiness was required to maintain the equilibrium, nothing, or almost nothing; no solid virtue; far less than nothing, many sins. Confusion, secondly, at seeing their conscience revealed to the gaze of all nations, who will therein read so many secret sins, so many illicit thoughts and desires, so much self-love and proud pretensions, perhaps so many mysteries of iniquity. Confusion, thirdly, at hearing the cries of indignation bursting forth from so many souls, who, without having any other means of salvation, have raised themselves to a great height of virtue; so many others who, in a less favorable position, have preserved themselves pure in the midst of the contagion of the world, recollected amidst the distractions consequent upon business, humble and detached amidst grandeur and riches. He is guilty of death (Matt. 26:66), they will exclaim, and with these cries of reprobation will be mingled those of infidel nations, saying anathema to the despiser of graces; those of demons claiming him as their prey; those, above all, of his own conscience, which will tear him with remorse and will force him to exclaim, I see clearly all the evil I have done and I cannot deny it (1 Mach. 6:12). O God, preserve me from such terrible confusion; pierce my flesh with the fear of Thy judgments (Ps. 118:120). In order to avert it I am ready for everything. I will convert myself. *Resolutions and spiritual nosegay as above.*

Thursday in the First Week of Advent

SUMMARY OF TOMORROW'S MEDITATION

We will meditate tomorrow: First, on the sentence of the Sovereign Judge in favor of the good; second, His sentence against the wicked; third, the consequences of this double sentence. We will then make the resolution: First, to live holily that we may merit a place amongst the elect; second, with this view to watch over our actions, our words, our intentions, often asking ourselves: Is it thus that the saints would act, think, and speak? We will retain as our spiritual nosegay the prayer of the Church: "Remember, O good Jesus, that it was for me Thou earnest into the world; do not condemn me in the day of Thy justice." (Strophe of the Dies Irae)

MEDITATION FOR THE MORNING

Let us transport ourselves, in thought, to the last judgment, to that scene as consoling for the elect as it is terrible for the damned. Let us behold the just Judge seated on His throne; let us prostrate ourselves at His feet and render to Him our profound homage; let us listen reverently to Him pronouncing His sentence, from which there is no appeal.

FIRST POINT
✝ The Sentence in Favor of the Elect

We know what the sentence is: "Come, ye blessed of My Father, possess you the kingdom prepared for you from the foundation of the world." (Matt. 25:34) Come! How consoling is this word to the just soul! Come from labor to repose, from persecution to reward, from the miseries of earth to the joy of Paradise. Come to Me whom you have followed, desired, loved; to Me, your God, your last end, your sovereign good. "Come, ye blessed of My Father." You, My friends, My beloved; you have been, for My sake, hated, persecuted, cursed by man; you will now be the blessed of God; My Father blesses you; Heaven blesses you; you are blessed forever, and this blessing assures your happiness forever. "Take possession of the kingdom which has been prepared for you from the beginning." A kingdom prepared by a God; that is to say, sovereignty, glory, riches, pleasures for a king has all that; a kingdom prepared from the beginning; that is to say, O my God, that from all eternity Thou hast thought of me; from all eternity Thou hast loved me; Thou hast reserved me for the most magnificent of destinies, and it will be given to me one day to mount upon a throne, and thence to judge the nations. Thus, O my soul, those will be raised who are now humble; thus will be glorified those who will have counted as nothing in presence of duty the speeches and opinions of men, and as pure gold never shines with so much splendor as when it is withdrawn from the entrails of the earth in which it was buried, so they will appear in glory with Jesus Christ (Coloss. 3:4). Oh, how calculated these thoughts are to make us love humility, poverty, simplicity, obedience!

SECOND POINT
✝ The Sentence against the Damned

After the sentence in favor of the elect, the Sovereign Judge, turning towards the left, will cast upon the damned one of those terrible looks of which David was able to say: The earth trembled, its foundations shook because the Lord looked upon it. "Depart from Me, ye cursed!" He will say to them. O my God I whither will they go far from Thee; what will become of them without Thee; what will become of them cursed by Thee, cursed in their bodies, cursed in their soul and in all its faculties. "Depart into fire!" O my God, what a torment! Into everlasting fire! O my God, what despair! And this formidable sentence is without appeal; it is all over with these wretched men; their fate is fixed forever. Ah! if men only thought of it (Deut. 32:29). He who is not awakened by this clap of thunder, says St. Augustine, is not asleep: he is dead.

THIRD POINT
✝ Execution of the Double Sentence

The Sovereign Judge, declaring the session closed, takes His flight towards heaven. All the saints ascend with Him and form His glorious retinue. They rise triumphant and radiant, and make the air resound with their songs of victory and happiness (1 Thess. 4:16). Witnesses of this magnificent spectacle, the damned are filled with despair. Oh, what would they not give to follow so many relatives, friends, and acquaintances! But, O cruel separation! they must leave them leave them forever address to them a last and sorrowful farewell. Adieu, Christian parents, pious friends, whose lessons and examples I would not follow; adieu, beloved mother, whose society was so sweet, whose heart was so loving; adieu, holy angels; adieu, all ye saints; adieu, Mary, whom I was so often counseled to love and honor; adieu, Jesus, who did so much to save me; adieu, beautiful heaven, paradise of delight which was destined for me, and of which I rendered myself unworthy; adieu, Holy Trinity, my beginning and my end (St. Ephrem, Serm. de Jud.). Alas! he can no longer continue these sad farewells; the earth gives way beneath his feet, hell opens, he falls into it, and the abyss closes. Time is finished; eternity begins. Thus will pass the last day; thus will the world be brought to an end. O my God! what will be my fate on that great day? Of what shall I think, if I do not think of this? And where is my faith and my reason if I do not think of it and if I do not tremble at it, and if I do not correct myself, and if I do not become a saint? *Resolutions and spiritual nosegay as above.*

Friday in the First Week of Advent

SUMMARY OF TOMORROW'S MEDITATION

After having meditated upon the coming of the Savior at the end of the world, we will now meditate on His coming and His reign in our hearts by grace, and we shall see, First, that this reign is full of sweetness and of joy; second, that all the joys of the world are not to be compared to it. We will then make the resolution, first, to place all our delight in God alone, and our pleasure in His good pleasure; second, to maintain, by a habit of recollection, the reign of Jesus Christ in us; and we will beg of Him, by frequent aspirations, to live forever in our hearts. Our spiritual nosegay shall be the words of St. Paul: "Rejoice in the Lord always." (Philipp. 4:4), or else the words of St. Augustine: "May everything be bitter to me, that Thou alone may be sweet to my heart." (Solil. 22)

MEDITATION FOR THE MORNING

Let us adore Jesus Christ coming to bring true joy upon earth by His birth. "Behold, I bring you good tidings of great joy." (Luke 2:10), said the angel to the shepherds. Until then, men had placed their joy in the false possessions of the world; they sought satisfaction only in creatures, in the pleasures of life; and the greatest abominations were styled amusements and pleasures, but since His coming, they have learnt to rejoice in God (Ex. 32:6), and to place their happiness in the possession of God (Luke 1:47). Let us bless the Incarnate Word for the change which His coming has brought into the world.

FIRST POINT

✝ The Reign of Jesus Christ in us is Full of Sweetness and Joy

That which the prophet said of the advent of the Messias upon earth may very rightly be said of the coming of Jesus Christ into the Christian soul. Be comforted, O My people, God says in Isaias (40:1); rejoice and give praise, for the Lord comes to console His people (Is. 52:9). Happy, indeed, the soul in which Jesus comes to be spiritually born, in these blessed days, in order to live and reign there forever! It will taste how sweet the Lord is; how delicious are the joys inseparable from His presence in the midst of the heart. These joys will fill the soul entirely, and leave no void therein, no room for affliction, trouble, or uneasiness. It is because in God alone we find the happiness which can fully satisfy us; we find in Him the infinite; we possess Him, we taste Him, we enjoy Him; and it is, says St. Augustine, a foretaste of Paradise to such a degree that we can no longer take pleasure in creatures, and that all which is not God, or for God, is disgusting to us (Conf., lib. 10, 22). A single drop of this sweetness, the same Father continues, disgusts us with everything else (Solil. 22). These pure and holy joys have also this great advantage, that they cannot be taken from us (John 16:22). All other joys are transitory, and the fear of losing them often poisons the possession of them, but the joys which we taste in God nothing can deprive us of. No one can take God from me, said the old religious to those who asked him the reason of his continual joy. These are the joys which give repose during life, peace at the hour of death, paradise in eternity. O Jesus, King full of sweetness, come, then, to be born, to live, and to reign in me, with Thy beauty, Thy charms, and Thy sweetness, which fill the heart with consolation (Ps. 44:5).

SECOND POINT

✝ All the Joys of the World are not to be Compared to the Joys which Accompany the Reign of Christ in us

There are no joys in the world which completely satisfy the heart. Solomon, who had tasted them all, declares that he found nothing therein except vanity and vexation of spirit (Eccles. 1,2,14). I have been all that a man can be, said a Roman Emperor, and it has been of no service to me. These false pleasures stop at the surface of the soul; they only touch the flesh and the senses, and therefore they never satisfy. The more we have, the more we desire to possess; (Prov. 30:15 et seq.) and if we were to possess everything, we should not even then be satisfied: because Thou hast made us for Thee, O my God, and because our hearts, when not with Thee, are always ill at ease (Conf., lib. 1 cap. 1). The eye is not satisfied with seeing, nor the ear with hearing (Eccles. 1:8). Lastly, the joys of the world are something still worse; they dissipate and enervate the heart until it becomes incapable of all solid virtue; they plunge it into the senses, debasing it through their false sweetness; and, lastly, they cause it to be subject to bitter regrets, profound sorrow during life, despair at the hour of death, and torment throughout eternity (St. Bernard). Let us learn from these things no longer to seek happiness upon earth, but to seek it in God alone, for there only is it to be found. Are these our dispositions? *Resolutions and spiritual nosegay as above.*

Saturday in the First Week of Advent

SUMMARY OF TOMORROW'S MEDITATION

n order to prepare our souls for the birth of the Savior, we will consider, in our next meditation, that the most necessary preparation is: First, to renounce sin; second, to expiate sin by penance. We will then make the resolution: First, to watch over ourselves, so that we may avoid all sin; second, to accept, in a spirit of penance, all the troubles and annoyances which may befall us. Our spiritual nosegay shall be the words of Isaias: "Prepare ye the way of the Lord." (40:3).

MEDITATION FOR THE MORNING

Let us adore Jesus Christ, warning us, by His Holy Church, to prepare the way in our souls for His near coming. Let us thank Him for so useful a warning, and let us promise Him to put it in practice during the whole of the holy season of Advent.

FIRST POINT

✝ All Sin must be Renounced: the First Preparation for the Feast of Christmas

When a sovereign or some other great personage is about to make a sojourn somewhere, the first solicitude of the persons called upon to enjoy the honor of receiving him is to cleanse the apartment they have reserved for him, and to remove from it every stain which might displease his eyes. Jesus Christ, at the approaching feast of Christmas, is coming to dwell and reign within us. Himself directing our feelings and our conduct. It is for us, then, to banish from our hearts not only all sin, but all attachment to sin, above all, to certain favorite sins into which we have fallen so often for a long time past, and for which we are forever making excuses to ourselves, inspite of the complaints uttered by our conscience. It is our duty not only to weep over our voluntary distractions in themselves and in their cause; our uncharitable words, our falsehoods, our sensuality; but also to stifle the mischievous disposition which engenders these faults: the want of devotion, which causes distractions; the secret aversions, whence proceed so many faults against charity; the spirit of pride, which causes us to utter so many falsehoods in order to render ourselves of some account; the unbridled love of ourselves, which produces sensuality.

Blind as we are, we attack the branches and the twigs, and we leave the trunks and the roots, which produce fresh branches and fresh twigs. It is for us to separate ourselves from all occasions of falling, such as a certain kind of society which is a cause of dissipation for us; certain ties which entangle us; certain intercourse which ruins us.

SECOND POINT
✝ Sin must be Expiated: the Second Preparation for Christmas

Two things are required to expiate sin: a spirit of penitence and works of penance. First, a spirit of penitence. How could Our Savior enter within us if He did not behold in us true repentance for having offended Him; if the sighs of our heart, wounded with sorrow and love, did not prove to Him that we love Him, that we deplore our sad past, and that henceforth we desire to serve Him better? Is it really true that our sins afflict us that we feel an overwhelming grief for them, that is to say, greater than for all the misfortunes which might happen to us; a supernatural grief, produced by the Holy Spirit, and founded upon motives of faith; a universal grief, embracing all our faults, without exception? Do not our sins more often leave us as tranquil, as careless, as though we were innocent? Whence comes it, excepting that this regret is granted only to prayer, and that we either do not pray or that we pray badly; excepting, also, that we do not meditate enough on the horror sin deserves, the sufferings it caused Jesus Christ in His holy passion, and the evil it does to ourselves? If we knew that by sinning we should lose one of our eyes, or incur the disgrace or displeasure of one of our superiors, we should detest the fault, and we should regret it bitterly after having committed it. O Jesus, how little faith we have, thus to lose our soul, to incur Thy hatred, to displease Thee, O my God, as we do by sinning! Is not sin a greater evil than all imaginable misfortunes? O Lord, touch my heart; may I feel what misery it is to offend or displease Thee; may I weep over my faults, especially during this holy season. Second, if we have a real spirit of penitence, it will inspire us to perform acts of penance; for all sin, even when it is pardoned, must be punished either in this world or in the next. Now, penance in this world is much sweeter and more meritorious than the penalties of the life to come. For that it is sufficient to accept willingly, in a spirit of expiation, all the sufferings which may befall us, and to make of necessity a virtue; it is sufficient to mortify our will, our desires, our tastes, our disposition; to deprive ourselves of certain enjoyments which have only an insignificant effect upon the health; not to refuse to grant any of the sacrifices it may ask us for. And these penitential works, far from being painful, will fill the soul with consolation. We shall find incomparably more of sweetness than of bitterness in them. Let us here examine ourselves in the sight of God, who sees into the bottom of the heart, whether we have the spirit of penance, and if we perform penitential works. *Resolutions and spiritual nosegay as above.*

Second Sunday in Advent

THE GOSPEL ACCORDING TO ST. MATTHEW, 11:2-10

"Now when John had heard in prison the works of Christ, sending two of his disciples he said to Him: Art Thou He that art to come, or look we for another? And Jesus making answer said to them: Go and relate to John what you have heard and seen. The blind see, the lame walk, the lepers are cleansed, the deaf hear, the dead rise again, the poor have the gospel preached to them. And blessed is he that shall not be scandalized in Me. And when they went their way, Jesus began to say to the multitudes concerning John: What went you out into the desert to see? A reed shaken with the wind? But what went you out to see? A man clothed in soft garments? Behold, they that are clothed in soft garments are in the houses of kings. But what went you out to see? A prophet? Yea, I tell you, and more than a prophet. For this is he of whom it is written: "Behold I send My angel before Thy face, who shall prepare Thy way before Thee."

SUMMARY OF TOMORROW'S MEDITATION

e have seen this morning what is the first preparation for Christmas, which consists in purifying the soul in order to render it meet for the reception of the Incarnate Word. We will meditate tomorrow on how, after having purified it, we must ornament and embellish it; and we shall see that this ornament is composed: First, of holy affections towards the mystery of the Incarnation; second, of the acts of the Christian life, specially appropriate to the holy season of Advent. We will then make the resolution: First, to maintain ourselves in the habitual state of recollection which facilitates pious affections towards God; second, to practice the acts of virtue with which the spirit of God will inspire us. Our spiritual nosegay shall be today what it was yesterday, the words of Isaias: "Prepare ye the way of the Lord." (41:3)

MEDITATION FOR THE MORNING

Let us offer our homage to the Word Incarnate in the womb of Mary; let us adore Him as the Desired of the nations; let us admire Him as the Supreme Lord whom love has abased to a kind of annihilation (Philipp. 2:7); let us thank Him for having become incarnate in order to save us; and, by way of supplement to our powerlessness to thank Him as He merits to be thanked, let us offer Him the homage of Mary, of the holy angels, and of all the saints in heaven and on earth.

FIRST POINT
✝ Holy Affections towards the Mystery of the Incarnation

Holy affections are the aliment and the life of piety. They are the incense cast upon the fire; they maintain and increase the flame. They are the manna of the desert; they adapt themselves to all tastes, that is to say, to all the needs of the soul. They are as the savor of all the mysteries: they represent the essence and the grace of them, and they make them flow, as it were, spontaneously into the soul which reflects. How, for example, can we contemplate the Word Incarnate in the womb of Mary without speaking of it to the Three Divine Persons, and giving vent to our admiration and praise for the share which each one of them has taken in so great a mystery? How can we help saying to the Father: "O holy Father, how I congratulate Thee on this first Christian temple, which Thou didst form for Thy self in the womb of Mary, and where Thou didst receive the first adoration worthy of Thee; how I thank Thee for having given us Thine only Son and for having immolated the Innocent in order to save guilty men." How can we help saying to the Word Incarnate: "O eternal Son of God, with what delight I contemplate Thee in this living tabernacle where Thou dost come to receive our homage; on this throne where it pleases Thee to be adored and blessed; on this bed of justice where Thou loves to pardon; on this bed of repose where Thou wills to be congratulated; in this paradise upon earth where Thou wills to be loved. Ah, in presence of this sanctuary of love, I cannot speak to Thee but of love! I give myself to Thee forever. I deliver up to Thee all that I am, that Thou mayest do in me all that pleases Thee. I call down on myself Thy spirit to direct me, Thy heart to warm me, Thy holy life to be my life. I love Thee, but make me love Thee ever more and more; more love still, O Lord, and always still more love for I owe Thee everything; without Thee I was lost, with Thee I shall be saved, if I will." And how can we help saying to the Holy Spirit: "O Divine Spirit, who didst form this so pure a body, who didst unite to it a soul so beautiful, and didst unite the one with the other in unity of person; to Thee be glory, praise, and love for this mystery, which is Thy work."

How, lastly, can we help saying to Mary: "O Mother of God, how great thou art, how admirably in thee are concentrated all the splendors of the saints, all the perfections of the angels; thou dost participate in all the holiness of thy Son; He lives in thee and thou in Him. I admire in thee His humility, His gentleness, His goodness, His patience, His obedience, His continual prayer. Thou dost nothing except in Jesus and by Jesus. O my Mother, how happy it makes me to contemplate thy holiness, to praise it, to bless it." It is by means of these affections and others like to them that the soul prepares itself worthily for the great feast of Christmas.

SECOND POINT
✝ **Acts of the Christian Life Suitable to the holy Season of Advent**

In order to bring our life into harmony with so holy a season, we ought to apply ourselves to rendering all our actions perfect, to be more reserved in our words, more attentive in our prayers, and above all to the performance of the acts of virtue pointed out by the Prophet Isaias as means for preparing the way of the Lord, who is about to come. "Make straight His paths" (Is. 40:3), he says, that is to say, draw near to God in perfect integrity of heart, aspiring after nothing else but to please God alone. "Every valley shall be exalted, and every mountain and hill shall be made low" (Is. 40:4), that is to say, practice humility, simplicity, moderation; "and the crooked shall become straight."(Ibid.), that is to say, quit the ways of the world, which are nothing but duplicity and falsehood, in order to follow only the ways of God, which are ways of truth and justice; and the rough ways made plain (Ibid.), that is to say, correct the asperities of your character, the roughness of your manners, in order to be gentle and kind to all (Tit. 3:2). Uprightness and sincerity, gentleness and sweetness, such are the virtues by which we ought to prepare the way for Jesus Christ, if we wish that He should come into our hearts. This preparation will cause us great combats and sacrifices; but it will lead us to heaven; for Jesus walks before us, and He, the first, has done far more than He asks of us. The road is difficult only to the cowardice which shrinks from it; it is sweet to those who walk resolutely in it. The joy of a good conscience prevents our feeling any difficulty. Let us believe the saints who made experience of it. *Resolutions and spiritual nosegay as above.*

Monday in the Second Week of Advent

SUMMARY OF TOMORROW'S MEDITATION

In order better to appreciate the mystery of the Incarnation, the object of the devotion of this holy season, we will meditate tomorrow on all the love and goodness contained in the eternal decree: First, to redeem man after his fall; second, to redeem him by the Incarnation. We will then make the resolution: First, carefully to avoid all sin, since such is the gravity of sin, even if it be only venial, that it was not possible to expiate it, except by the Incarnation; second, not to neglect any means of salvation, however painful it may be, since God became man for our salvation. Our spiritual nosegay shall be the words of the Gospel: "God so loved the world as to give His only begotten Son, that whosoever believeth in Him may not perish, but may have life everlasting." (John 3:16)

MEDITATION FOR THE MORNING

Let us raise our souls to the utmost heights of the Most Holy Trinity; let us assist in thought at the Council held by these three adorable Persons, decreeing together what they will do with man after his fall. Let us prostrate ourselves in spirit before this august Council; let us adore, let us love, let us bless their decrees, so full of love and goodness.

FIRST POINT

✝ The Goodness of God Decreeing from all Eternity to Save Man after his Fall

There is in this decree of God a fathomless abyss of love. The angels fell before men; they remained without redemption, condemned forever to hell. Man sinned, and he is redeemed. Wherefore this difference? Man was unworthy of it in all respects; for his nature is very inferior to that of the angels. They are the eldest born of the creation; their nature is noble, excellent, incomparably superior to ours; and we, taken from the earth, are but a little clay made into the fashion of a man. The angels were guilty only of a proud thought, whilst we, enriched with the most beautiful gifts of God, spite of our baseness, revolted against our Benefactor, and that in a circumstance in which obedience was so easy and where the precept was given under such terrible threats. Wherefore, then, this preference of man over the angels? O mystery of love is the only answer we can make. Man, by the thousands of his sins which were clearly foreseen, appeared in the sight of God as nothing more than a being despoiled of the grace of original justice; an object of horror to divine justice, a criminal driven away from the terrestrial paradise, a creature condemned to death here below, and to eternal death in the world to come, if he were not redeemed; and it is such a being as this that God redeems in preference to the angels! Wherefore this? O mystery of love! That is the whole answer. And this being, favored by God with so marvelous a predilection, will not be grateful; God knows it well: he will have a hard heart, insensible to so much love; he will be a traitor who will recommence his offences, and will multiply them beyond the number of the hairs on his head; the majority of men will even refuse to accept redemption and will desire to damn themselves; there will be only a little number who will profit by this benefit. And yet, spite of all this, God decrees the redemption of man, preferably to that of the angels! Oh once more we exclaim, What a mystery of love to which we can only answer: God so loved the world, because He so willed it! It is for us to adore, to admire, to thank, to love, and to bless.

SECOND POINT

✝ **The Goodness of God Decreeing from all Eternity to Save Man through the Incarnation**

God had two means by which to save man; the first to pardon him gratuitously and without redemption; the second to furnish him with means whereby to pay the whole of his debt and to offer to the Divine Majesty whom he had offended a reparation equal to the offence. God did not will to avail Himself of the first means, because if it were a means of making His mercy shine forth, it did not cause either His holiness or His justice to shine forth on the enormity of sin. He therefore chose the second means; but the gravity of the fault being infinite, since the greatness of an injury increases in proportion to the superiority of the person offended, a reparation of infinite value was necessary: and where find such a reparation? It was not in Thee, O my God, since Thou couldst not abase Thyself or suffer, which were the two conditions necessary to the expiation of sin; it was not in a created being; it could not give to its abasements and sufferings anything more than a limited value, the value of a homage decreasing in proportion to the superiority of him who receives it over him who renders it; it could only then be in the hypothesis of the hypostatic union of the two natures, which once realized, human nature could be abased and suffer, and the divine nature communicate to these abasements and these sufferings an infinite value. God accordingly adopts this admirable plan, and the decree of the Incarnation is declared. O Holy Trinity, a thousand times thanks! Thy decree ravishes and transports me. It is the triumph of justice which is fully satisfied, the triumph of mercy which pardons, the triumph of goodness which sacrifices itself, the triumph of wisdom conciliating that which seemed incapable of being conciliated, the triumph of the power which unites in one sole person extreme greatness and extreme lowliness, the triumph of prudence which, showing man what it cost a God to expiate sin, teaches him on that very account to abstain from it. In my powerlessness to appreciate so great a benefit, I offer to Thee, O adorable Trinity, the praises of all creatures in heaven and on earth, begging them to bless and exalt Thee throughout eternity. I offer Thee the thanksgivings which the Man-God offered Thee in our name from the first moment of His Incarnation; and I conjure Thee through Him to pardon us our insensibility and our ingratitude for so great a mystery of love. I offer Thee my life, and in particular this day, which I desire to employ entirely in loving Thee. *Resolutions and spiritual nosegay as above.*

Tuesday in the Second Week of Advent

SUMMARY OF TOMORROW'S MEDITATION

It was already infinite goodness in God to have from all eternity decreed to save us, and that by means of the Incarnation; but behold now a very different marvel offers itself to our meditation. By what means will the Incarnate God save man? The Holy Trinity decides in its councils that it will be: First, by humiliation; second, by suffering; third, by death. After having meditated on these mysteries, we will make the resolution: First, to accept cheerfully all the humiliations and contradictions inflicted on our self-love; second, to submit to all the crosses and trials sent by Providence; third, to offer ourselves to God as victims worthy of death by reason of sin. Our spiritual nosegay shall be the words: "We were reconciled with God by the death of His Son." (Rom. 5:10)

MEDITATION FOR THE MORNING

Let us adore the Most Holy Trinity decreeing in its wisdom that the Word Incarnate upon earth should lead there a life of humiliation and of suffering which should be terminated by the death of the cross. Let us bless God for such a design. The world was sick with pride: it was necessary to confront it with the humiliation of a God; it was ruining itself through love of pleasure: it was necessary to oppose to it the sufferings of a God; it clung to life: the death of a God was necessary to detach it therefrom. Be Thou blessed, Lord, for this infinite goodness, which thus teaches man to humble himself, to suffer and to die; be Thou loved for Thine ineffable goodness, which, instead of the glory and splendor that belong to Thee, embraces for our sake humiliation, suffering, and death.

FIRST POINT

✝ On the Eternal Decree Determining that the Incarnate Word should Save the World by Humiliation

It would have been for the Eternal Word an incomprehensible abasement even to descend from the heights which He inhabits down to the choirs of angels, since the distance, even then, would have been infinite; it would have been a still greater abasement to have descended to us, even assuming the highest degree to which humanity can raise itself, and thereby to unite a nature infinitely rich with a nature infinitely poor, the Creator with the creature, being with nothingness, the Divinity with the clay of our flesh. Nevertheless, O Holy Trinity, Thou didst see in my proud heart so profound a repugnance to the humiliation which is, however, my due on so many accounts, that in Thy wisdom Thou didst deem it necessary to descend to the lowest degree of our poor nature, and Thou didst choose for Thy Word all that is most humble in our mortal condition: an obscure corner of the world; a poor cottage; instead of appearing at once in the form of a man, nine months hidden in the womb of a poor working woman without rank and at the end of these nine months a stable, the weakness and helplessness of a little child; and on issuing from infancy the condition of a poor artisan; and on quitting this condition, three years of a painful apostolate, pursued by calumny, contempt, hatred, even to the extent of being called a person possessed by the devil, an agent of Beelzebub, and even reputed to be worse than Barabbas, a thief and an assassin, down to being crucified between two thieves as the greatest of them; and after such a death the irreverence, the profanation, the infinite and continual abasement of the Eucharist. O God, how incomprehensible are Thy decrees! I adore and love them, since their object is to correct my pride, my pretensions, and my susceptibilities. Do not allow me to resist so powerful a lesson.

SECOND POINT
✝ On the Eternal Decree Declaring that the Incarnate Word should Save the World through Suffering

If we had been admitted into the councils of God we should doubtless have thought that the Word, taking a body like to ours, would exempt it from suffering and inundate it with enjoyment and happiness. The Holy Trinity judged very differently; it decreed that the Word should suffer, and that He should suffer more than all the martyrs put together; that His whole life should be a continual martyrdom, and that He should deserve by His sufferings to be called the King of martyrs. O heavenly Father, permit me to ask of Thee wherefore a decree so severe towards Thy beloved Son? Ah, I guess Thy answer. It is, Thou sayest to me, because I desire to teach the world that suffering is the penalty of sin, of which My Son has accepted the expiation; that suffering is the path to glory, the guarantee and the measure of eternal happiness for those who suffer as is meet; it is because I desire to comfort those of all ages by showing them that suffering is a blessing and a testimony of the love I bear towards souls. Lastly, it is because I desire to present to all men, in the person of My Son, a model of patience and resignation in the midst of trials. O God, how good Thou art! Thanks, a thousand thanks, for these useful lessons which cost Thy Son so much! How have I profited by them up to the present day? Have I loved suffering and the cross? Pardon, my God; I am ashamed of myself!

THIRD POINT
✝ On the Eternal Decree that the Incarnate Word should Save the World by the Death of the Cross

It was not necessary that the Eternal Word should die in order to redeem us a single drop of His blood would have been sufficient to expiate the sins of the whole world; but the Holy Trinity chose death as the most appropriate sacrifice for repairing the outrage offered to God by sin; as the most striking proof of divine charity towards us; lastly, as the most suitable example for encouraging the martyrs in their sufferings, and for teaching all Christians that death, the passage from exile to our true country, is more to be desired than feared. From amongst all kinds of deaths the Trinity chose the death of the cross, because, being at one and the same time the most ignominious and the most cruel of deaths, it teaches us better the value of our soul, the importance of our salvation, the horror of sin; it is the most calculated to raise our hopes, to reanimate our courage amidst difficulties and obstacles; in a word, to enable us to march with intrepidity along the road which leads to heaven. O my God, once more, how good Thou art! How nothing costs Thee aught when it has to do with my welfare! From the height of Thy cross draw the towards Thee, that I may live only for Thee! Render death pleasant to me, since Thou wert the first to taste of it. *Resolutions and spiritual nosegay as above.*

WEDNESDAY IN THE SECOND WEEK OF ADVENT

SUMMARY OF TOMORROW'S MEDITATION

e will meditate tomorrow on the glory accruing to God through the mystery of the Incarnation. The glory of God consists in the exterior manifestation of His infinite perfections. Now we shall see that the Incarnation shows forth marvelously: first, the power of God, allied to infinite wisdom and greatness; second, the mercy of God, allied to infinite justice and holiness. We will then make the resolution: First, often to ask God for an ever increasing knowledge of His perfections, so that we may love Him ever more and more; second, to honor His divine perfections by frequent acts of love, accompanied by deep religious feeling, especially in church and during prayer. Our spiritual nosegay shall be: "The Word was made flesh and we saw His glory." (John 1:4).

MEDITATION FOR THE MORNING

Let us adore God sending His angels to announce to the world the Incarnation of the Word in these beautiful words, "Glory to God in the highest" Let us repeat to ourselves these heavenly words in a spirit of love and conviction: for nowhere do the divine perfections shine forth more gloriously than in this mystery.

FIRST POINT

✝ How the Incarnation Makes the Alliance of Power, Wisdom, and Goodness to Shine Forth

What immeasurable power did it not require in God to unite in one person His supreme majesty and our lowliness; His sovereign independence and our servitude; the strength which can perform all things and the weakness which can do nothing! What power did it not require in order to consummate this union such as faith shows it to us, and to give to the Word our nature without changing His own, and the form of a slave without derogating from the form of God; to bring down the heights of the Divine Being as low as ourselves without its being less great; to despoil it without impoverishing it; to abase it without sinking it, and to render the Divinity visible without rendering it less adorable! Herein is contained, O Lord, the masterpiece of Thy omnipotence, or, rather, it is Thy chief work, compared with which all Thy other works are as nothing (Habac. cant. 2). And what is not less marvelous, to power is here united infinite goodness, which, in order to pardon us, conciliates the apparently incompatible rights of justice and mercy, and which, in order to cure us, opposes to our ills the most suitable remedies: to our pride, the humility of a God; to our sensuality, the sufferings of a God; to our horror of death, the death of a God. O divine wisdom, how I venerate thee in this mystery! (1 Cor. 2:17.) And yet the goodness of God shines forth in it more brightly still. Can there be a display of more marvelous goodness than that which makes a God descend to our lowliness? It is the monarch who comes and mingles with his servants, that he may render himself more beloved by them; it is the good father who humbles himself so far as even to lisp with his little children, that he may instruct them and form them to the life of a perfect man; it is the good shepherd who covers himself with the fleece of his sheep, in order to attract them to him. O Incarnate Word, Thou didst come in order to make Thyself one with us; to remain and converse with us, to live our life; humbling Thy greatness, to render it more familiar to us; contracting Thy immensity in order to communicate it still more to us. O divine goodness! O infinite goodness! what else can we say? Ah, Lord, I ought to die of love at the sight of so much love!

SECOND POINT

✝ How the Incarnation Shows forth the Holiness, Justice, and Mercy of God

What is holiness, unless it be the sovereign hatred of sin? Now, God nowhere shows better than in this mystery how much He detests sin. He pursues it even down to the shadow of it in His own Son, and that with unexampled rigor. This beloved Son He covers with wounds, with suffering, with ignominy; He drains all the blood out of His veins, and He makes Him die. He sees nothing in Him but an anathema, an object worthy of malediction, for the sole reason that He has made Himself to be the security for our sins, and He strikes Him without mercy. O God, how holy Thou art! How Thou dost detest sin and how much ought I not to detest it myself! For if Thou hast thus treated Thy Son, how wilt Thou treat me, who am a sinner by nature and through malice? (Luke 23:31.) O holiness of God, I tremble before thee! I should not tremble less in face of Thy justice, O Lord, if, by Thy Incarnation, Thou hadst not taken my debt upon Thyself; for, being obliged to make an infinite reparation for my sins,

I was evidently an insolvent debtor. But behold, by becoming incarnate Thou hast paid a superabundant price for my ransom; and Thy Father, in requiring it, has shown both heaven and earth that Thy justice is infinite, since it would not pardon me except by means of a satisfaction equal to the offence. O justice, higher than the mountains, more profound than the abysses, the blood of Jesus Christ has fully satisfied you; you have nothing more to demand, and even hell would be an infinitely less satisfaction. Herein is the work of Thy mercy, O my God: Thou wert the offended, and it is Thou who repairest the offence; Thou didst make Thyself a victim in my place, and Thou hast submitted to the punishment which was my due. O mercy! O justice! you give the kiss of peace the one to the other; you make an ineffable alliance together, which will make us exclaim from ago to age, in. an ecstasy of faith and of love: Yes, God is truly, infinitely great, infinitely merciful! How, then, O my heart, dost thou remain insensible in presence of so great a mystery; wherefore dost thou adore in so small a degree such justice as this, and show so little love for such mercy? *Resolutions and spiritual nosegay as above.*

Thursday in the Second Week of Advent

SUMMARY OF TOMORROW'S MEDITATION

We will continue tomorrow to meditate on the glory which accrues to God from the Incarnation of the Word, and, in order to rightly understand it, we will consider: First, that without the Incarnation the world could not render to God any glory really worthy of Him; second, that through the Incarnation the world renders to God infinite glory. We will then make the resolution: First, to keep ourselves united to Jesus Christ through confidence, through love, and through frequent elevations of the heart; second, to perform all our prayers and all our actions in union with Him. Our spiritual nosegay shall be the words of the canon of the Mass: "All through Jesus Christ; all with Jesus Christ; all in Jesus Christ."

MEDITATION FOR THE MORNING

Let us adore the Incarnate Word, incarnated as the centre of the world, which depends entirely upon Him as the soul and the life of every creature, as the essential mediator between heaven and earth. God has done all things for His glory (Prov. 16:4), but it is the Eternal Word that procures this glory for

Him in an infinite degree in all parts of the creation, upon earth as in heaven, amongst men as amongst angels. Let us then render Him, with this end in view, our praises and our thanksgivings.

FIRST POINT

✝ Without the Incarnation the World could not Render to God any Glory really Worthy of Him

The sole glory which is really worthy of God is an infinite glory. Now the material world is evidently incapable in itself of rendering to God this glory; it can only show itself to man in order to say to him after its manner: "Behold, how great is He who has created us, and how good is He who has done all for us. Honor and admire Him in our name and in yours." Man himself can only imperfectly fulfill this great mission; man, whose acts are only of extremely limited value, since he cannot even give birth, of himself, to one meritorious thought. What, then, O Lord, was to become of the design which Thou hadst proposed to Thyself, which was to procure for Thyself infinite glory, the only glory worthy of Thee? Evidently Thy design was on the point of becoming a failure and Thy work cut short if Thou couldst not give to creation an instrument more elevated than man, an instrument which would adore and love Thee as Thou meritest to be adored and loved, that is to say, if Thy Word did not become incarnate, since, without that, creation would have had but two results accruing from it: firstly, imperfect men and, consequently, men but little worthy of Thee; secondly, the eternal reprobation of the whole human race become sinful its actions without merit; its prayers without virtue; its existence without an object. Everything here below would have been sad without consolation, humiliating and discouraging; nothing would have remained for man but despair, and Thou wouldst have been able to repeat with added justice, "It repenteth Me that I have created them." (Gen. 6:7) O Word Incarnate, how necessary wast Thou then to the glory of God! Be always with us, since we cannot, without Thee, render to God, Thy Father, any glory worthy of Him.

SECOND POINT

✝ By the Incarnation we can Render to God Infinite Glory

The Word Incarnate, placed essentially by His dignity at the head of creation, there becomes the centre of it, the organ, the life, the religion of heaven and earth, the meeting place of all created beings, who, through Him, offer to God infinite homage, and address to the heavenly Father prayers of infinite value. Oh, how great, how beautiful, how divine, is the world thus united to the Word its Head! Material beings adore through man; man adores by Jesus Christ, who, sole worthy adorer, gathers together in His heart the homage of every creature, renders it divine in His Person by covering it with His merits, Hence results a magnificent concert of adoration, of thanksgiving, of love, of praise, and of prayer, which, rising all together, from all parts of the globe, forms before the throne of God, as it were, a universal and never interrupted hymn, as glorious to the Divine Majesty as it is profitable to man. For one single act of adoration of the Incarnate Word procures more glory to the Creator than the homage of a thousand worlds prolonged throughout eternity, even though it were to be supposed that these worlds were peopled by angels occupied solely in glorifying God. One only of these acts reconciles to God whoever desires to be reconciled (2 Cor. 5:19), merits all graces and all benedictions for the earth (Eph. 1:3). Hence it is that the Church in heaven adores God only by the eternal Amen which unites its adorations to those of the Word; and the Church on earth, following its example, offers its homage and prayers to God by Jesus Christ. What a consolation for us to be able thus to render to God infinite homage, and to address to Him prayers of infinite value, consequently all powerful over His heart! If we possessed a lively faith in this truth, we should obtain miracles (John 16:23). But, at the same time, what a duty is thereby imposed upon us of living and acting always in union with Jesus Christ, in perfect detachment from creatures and love of self, in order to be one with Him in all things! Is it thus that we act? *Resolutions and spiritual nosegay as above.*

Friday in the Second Week of Advent

SUMMARY OF TOMORROW'S MEDITATION

e will meditate tomorrow on the glory which accrues to man from the incarnation of the Word, und we shall see: First, that it raises man in Jesus Christ to the highest degree of greatness; second, that it places him in several respects in a better position than he was before his fall. We will then make the resolution: First, to respect our body and keep it always pure, seeing that the Incarnate Word has so greatly honored it; second, to grow every day in love to Our Lord, who has loved us so much, and to multiply acts of love day and night. Our spiritual nosegay shall be the words of the Church, "O happy fault which procured for us such a Redeemer!" (Bened. cer. pasch.)

MEDITATION FOR THE MORNING

Let us adore, love, and bless the infinite goodness of God, who is pleased to do good to men even after they have offended Him. Man had degraded himself by his sin, the Incarnate Word raises his fallen nature to the highest degree of greatness; man had despoiled himself of the gifts of grace and had debased himself below the devils, God raised him and placed him in a better state than in certain respects his primitive state had been. Let us pour out in His presence all our sentiments of gratitude and love.

FIRST POINT

✝ God has Raised Human Nature to the Highest Degree of Honor in Jesus Christ

Here a prodigy offers itself to our meditations which will be the eternal admiration of Paradise. The Word of God, uniting Himself with human nature in unity of person, has thereby raised it, not only above all angels, but to an equality with God Himself; for in virtue of the hypostatic union it will be everlastingly true to say that in Jesus Christ, man is God, and that this Man God has a right to the same homage as God Himself. From His first entrance into the world the angels are commanded to adore Him (Heb. 1:6). In the desert angels come and serve Him (Matt. 4:2). On the day of the ascension, God the Father makes Him sit at His right hand as His equal (Ps. 109:1; Heb. 8:1). It will be everlastingly true to say, when speaking of Jesus Christ: the soul of this Man is the soul of a God; His hands are the hands of a God; His body is the body of a God; His heart is the heart of a God; and this body will be adored by all the earth and in the heavens; this heart will be the object of the worship of all creatures in time arid throughout eternity. What an ineffable transformation of our poor natures from such a depth to be raised to such a height! But if God has so greatly honored human nature in His Word, let us learn to honor it in ourselves by always preserving it pure and holy, always guarded from everything that sullies and degrades, always adorned and embellished with all that is good, edifying, amiable, and honorable (Philipp. 4:8).

SECOND POINT

✝ God, by the Incarnation, has Placed us in Several Respects in a Better State than our State before the Fall

God, in fact, through Jesus Christ, was not contented with withdrawing us from the eternal abyss to which we were condemned, to redeem us from the slavery of the demon, and to obtain for us the pardon of our faults (Coloss.

1:14), but He restores us to His favor and to our heavenly rights, not only once, but every time that we lose them by our sins, however enormous, however multiplied they may be, on the sole condition of confessing them and repenting of them; so that, thanks to the incarnation, everyone who desires it may be saved: those only damn themselves who desire to be damned. This is not all. The Incarnation, through the assistance of the sacraments, makes us children of God, brothers of a God, members of Jesus Christ, and one and the same body with Him; it makes us share with Him the kingdom of heaven and His own throne (Apoc. 3:21; Eph. 2:6); it transforms us into temples of the Holy Ghost, who dwells in us (1 Cor. 6:19); into living sanctuaries of the divine Eucharist, by which Jesus Christ incorporates Himself in our body and makes of our heart a Paradise upon earth; lastly, it makes us the brothers and co-heirs of the saints, with whom we are destined to reign throughout eternity in glory. O my God! How true it is to say that Thy holy Incarnation has placed us in a better state than the state before the fall; and how great reason Thy Church has to exclaim, when speaking of the fall of Adam: "Happy fault which procured for us such a Redeemer!" But how do we appreciate so great a grace? Do we bless God for it every day? Do we love Him for it ever more and more? Do we love Him with more zeal? *Resolutions and spiritual nosegay as above.*

Saturday in the Second Week of Advent

SUMMARY OF TOMORROW'S MEDITATION

e will meditate tomorrow on the great blessings which accrue to us from the Incarnation of the Word, and we will consider the Word Incarnate: First, as our Consoler in troubles; second, as the charitable Physician who cures all our miseries. We will then make the resolution: First, to have recourse in all our troubles to Jesus Christ, as to our only real Consoler; second, no longer to attach ourselves to the false goods of this world, but to Jesus Christ alone. Our spiritual nosegay shall be the words of the Savior: "Come to Me, all ye that labor and are burdened, and I will refresh you." (Matt. 9:28)

MEDITATION FOR THE MORNING

Let us adore the Eternal Word drawn down to earth by His tender charity (Eph. 2:4), there to be the Consoler of the afflicted, the Help of those who suffer, the Strength of the weak, the Resource of the human race. Oh, how greatly He deserves, by all these titles, our homage and our love!

FIRST POINT

✝ The Incarnate Word is our Consoler in all our Troubles.

Let us consider, with a deep sentiment of devotion, the Incarnate Word choosing as His portion here below all the miseries of humanity, with the sole exception of sin, in order thereby to be more capable of consoling us, more disposed to have pity on our troubles (Heb. 4:15). If He had lived upon earth in the midst of enjoyment and pleasure, He would not have had grace to dry the eyes of those who weep and suffer. It would have been hard for the poor in their wretchedness to rejoice in His word if He had spoken it from the midst of opulence. Surrounded by glory and honors, how would He have been able to inculcate the love of poverty and humiliation? But, on the contrary, He is able to say to us, "You suffer, and I also have suffered, and suffered more than you. You are in need of many things, and I also was naked and despoiled of all in the womb of My mother, and since My birth I have had nothing all my life long except the food, the lodging, and the clothes of the poor. Obscurity and humiliation are revolting to you, and I hid My greatness from all eyes, and was looked upon whilst I was on earth as a man of nothing, a madman, an ignorant man possessed by the devil, a criminal." Then we shall understand how wrong we have been to complain; how, in deifying in His Person humility, poverty, and suffering, Jesus Christ has rendered them wholly worthy of our esteem and of our love: and we are consoled. It is a happiness for us to come and tell our sorrows to Him who was the first to suffer them, to address our sighs and confide our tears to Him who wept before us and for us. Oh, here indeed is the Consoler we needed, a Man-God, acquainted with infirmity (Is. 53:3), a Man-God, pure and humble (Heb. 2:17). Let us thank, let us love, the Word Incarnate, and have recourse to Him in our troubles.

SECOND POINT

✝ The Incarnate Word is the Charitable Physician who Cures all our Miseries

Our primary miseries are our sins, which tear us with remorse, take from us peace, sometimes even hope, and compromise our salvation. The Incarnate Word offers us the remedy for this primary evil. He makes for us a salutary bath of His blood, and purifies us therein from all our stains (Apoc. 1:5). When we again fall, He raises us up and pardons us, provided that we return to Him; if we fall once more, He again pardons us; if we are always falling, He still pardons us on the one condition of repentance (Matt. 9:2). Next to sin our passions are our second miseries; they tyrannize over us, and are always trying to make us fall. Here again, if we have recourse to the Word Incarnate, if we say to Him with confidence: "He whom Thou loves is sick" (John 11:3); "heal my soul, for I have sinned against Thee" (Ps. 40:5), He will reply to us: Receive My sacraments, meditate on My doctrine, be penetrated with My example, and you will triumph over your passions. Lastly, our third misery, the one which engenders all the others, is that deplorable error which makes us imagine that happiness consists in the enjoyment of external goods: honors, riches, pleasures false goods which may be taken from us at any moment by the caprice of man or of the elements. The Incarnate Word confronts this great evil by the example of His own person despoiled of external pomp. Around Him is nothing but poverty, humility, suffering, and hence He has excellently well said to whoever will listen to Him that there exists another greatness than that which strikes the senses, another glory than that of fame, another happiness than that of pleasures; that man is only happy by what exists within by peace of conscience, purity of heart, and that all which is outside us, not being ours, cannot render us either better or more honorable (Ps. 44:14). Have we as yet comprehended this divine language? Does not what we are in the opinion of others touch us much more nearly than what we are in the sight of God? Content to be taken for what we are not, do not we delight in the praises which we well know we do not merit? When we are unjustly blamed, do we not allow ourselves to be cast down as if public contempt changed us from that which we really are? *Resolutions and spiritual nosegay as above.*

Third Sunday in Advent

THE GOSPEL ACCORDING TO ST. JOHN, 1:19-28

"And this is the testimony of John: When the Jews sent from Jerusalem priests and Levites to him to ask him, Who art thou? And he confessed and did not deny; and he confessed: I am not the Christ. And they asked him: What then? Art thou Elias? And he said: I am not. Art thou the prophet? And he answered: No. They said, therefore, unto him: Who art thou, that we may give an answer to them that sent us? What sayest thou of thyself? He said: I am the voice of one crying in the wilderness, make straight the way of the Lord, as said the prophet Isaias. And they that were sent were of the Pharisees. And they asked him, and said to him: Why, then, dost thou baptize if thou be not Christ, nor Elias, nor the prophet? John answered them, saying: I baptize with water; but there hath stood One in the midst of you whom you know not. The same is He that shall come after me, who is preferred before me, the latchet of whose shoe I am not worthy to loose. These things were done in Bethania, beyond the Jordan, where John was baptizing."

SUMMARY OF TOMORROW'S MEDITATION

After having considered the excellence of the Incarnation in its affects, which are the glory of God, the glory of man, the consolation in our troubles and the remedy for our evils, we will now meditate on our duties in regard to this mystery. We will fix our thoughts tomorrow on the first of these mysteries, in order to study and understand it thoroughly; and we shall see, First, that there is no study more beautiful and more worthy of man; second, that there is none more useful. We will then make the resolution, first, often to reflect on this mystery, above all when we hear the angelus ring; and second, often to repeat lovingly St. Augustine's prayer, "Lord, grant me to know Thee, that I may love Thee," and these words shall serve us as our spiritual nosegay.

MEDITATION FOR THE MORNING

Let us unite ourselves with the apostle St. Paul on his knees before God the Father, to beg of Him, in favor of the faithful of Ephesus, an ever deeper knowledge of Christ and of His love, a knowledge which surpasses all science (Eph. 3: 14,16,19). Let us ardently desire for ourselves this divine knowledge, and let us ardently desire it from the bottom of our hearts. "Lord, grant me to know Thee, that I may love Thee."

FIRST POINT

✝ There is no Study more Beautiful and more Worthy of Man than the Study of the Mystery of the Incarnation

We find, in fact, in this mystery all the perfections of God and all the perfections of the creature united together, since, as consubstantial with His Father, the Incarnate Word is, like Him, infinitely perfect, and as consubstantial with us, He is beautiful with all the perfections with which God can enrich a creature. The Holy Trinity itself takes therein its pleasure and the whole of its delight (Mark 1:2). It finds therein in finite glory accruing to itself. Paradise finds there its joy, its pleasure, the subject of its most beautiful songs, and it exclaims, "Glory to God in the Highest!" (Luke 2:14.) Can there be anything more worthy of the study of the human mind? We delight to know illustrious men, and we should be ashamed to be ignorant of their origin, of their history, of their great deeds; and the Word Incarnate, the glory and honor of our nature, with which He has united Himself in unity of person He, our Redeemer and Savior, our King and our Master, and at one and the same time our co-heir sharing with us the kingdom of heaven, how little we study Him, how badly we know Him, and how greatly we deserve the reproach addressed by St. John to the Jews, "There hath stood One in the midst of you whom you know not." (John 1:26) If Moses said to himself, when speaking of the burning bush, "I will go and see this great sight" (Ex. 3:3), how shall we not much more say, I will study and apply myself more and more to understand this marvel above all marvels the marvel of God unchangeable in essence beginning to be that which He was not; the marvel of God remaining God without losing anything of His majesty and glory, although making Himself man and appropriating to Himself all man's weaknesses and miseries; the marvel of the supreme worship reserved until then for God alone, and now rendered to a Man-God not only by men, but also by even the angels, who adore in Him almighty weakness, the Eternal born in time, the Infinite limited within a little space, the Creator of the world descended to the rank occupied by His works, and become so small a part of the world. I will study and contemplate the Creator in His creature, heaven on earth, sovereign glory in ignominy, infinite riches in poverty, immortality in death, and, better than all that, the divine life in humanity, the perfections of heaven become visible on earth, the most profound humility in the most sublime elevation, the abnegation of self in the divinity, incomparable devotedness in Him to whom is due all devotedness. Now, shall we not imitate St. Paul, who made of Jesus Christ his sole study and his only science? To be wise in Jesus Christ as all his ambition (1 Cor. 2:2), and compared with this divine science all the rest appeared to him to be rather a loss than an advantage (Philipp. 3:8). Is it thus that we look upon the study and knowledge of Jesus Christ?

SECOND POINT

✝ There is no Study more Useful than the Study of the Mystery of the Incarnation

God has given us all in Jesus Christ (Rom. 8:32), and this mystery is an inexhaustible treasure of riches and spiritual blessings. But a treasure produces only in proportion as we draw upon it, and we cannot draw upon the mystery of the Incarnation except by studying it. By means of this study we learn to love God the Father, who has given us His Son; God the Son, who has given Himself to us; God the Holy Spirit, who performed this mystery in the womb of Mary; and Mary herself, who so divinely cooperated with it. The more we study this great subject, the more the heart is inflamed with love, and we desire to live only for love of God, who has so loved us. By studying this mystery we learn to judge wisely of all things, because we know the judgment and appreciation of Jesus Christ, infallible rules of the true; we learn to perform holily all things, because we have before our eyes the example of the Man-God, the adorable type of all that is holy. If we desire to adore God, we adore Him perfectly by uniting our homage to that of the Incarnate Word, who deifies them by presenting them to His Father, covered with all the dignity of His Person. If we wish to solicit graces, we lay our prayer in the heart of the Incarnate Word, who communicates to it the omnipotence of his intervention on the heart of God. Lastly, by studying this mystery virtue appears therein so beautiful, so ravishing, that the heart attaches itself to it with delight, and finds the practice of it as sweet as it is easy. For we say to ourselves, "My God does not ask anything of me which He has not first done Himself; can I then complain and feel that He asks too much of me?" Such are the precious advantages which the study of the mystery of the Incarnation presents. Have we profited by them up to the present time? Do we lovingly study it in the gospels, in the writings of St. Paul and the apostles, in pious works which describe its beauty and magnificence? *Resolutions and spiritual nosegay as above.*

Monday in the Third Week of Advent

SUMMARY OF TOMORROW'S MEDITATION

e will meditate tomorrow on our second duty towards the Word Incarnate, which is to love Him; and we shall see: First, what the love of the Incarnate Word is towards us; second, what our love ought to be towards the Incarnate Word. Our resolution shall be: First, often to repeat with love and admiration the words of the Gospel, "The Word was made flesh" (John 1:14). O ineffable mystery of love. Second, to perform all our actions from love of the Word Incarnate, and with the object of loving Him ever more and more. Our spiritual nosegay shall be the words of St. John: "Let us therefore love God because God first hath loved us." (1 John 4:19)

MEDITATION FOR THE MORNING

Let us adore the Divine Word dwelling front all eternity amidst the splendors of the saints, and out of the midst of so great glory lovingly accepting the mission given to Him by His Father to come and be incarnated in this world in order to save us. When St. Francis de Sales meditated upon this mystery, he fell into profound astonishment, and from thence into ecstasies of gratitude and love. Let us imitate this great saint, and say with all heaven: "The Lamb that was slain is worthy to receive power, and divinity, and wisdom, and honor, and glory, and benediction." (Apoc.5:12).

FIRST POINT
✝ What the Love of the Incarnate Word is for us

Four considerations serve to show forth the love of a benefactor: the excellence of the gift he makes us; the manner in which he makes it; the unworthiness of the person to whom it is made; and the reason for which it was made. Let us apply here four considerations to this subject: First, what is the excellence of the gift made us by the Incarnation? It is infinitely more than if God were to give us all the riches of heaven and of earth, even if He were to give us all the nine choirs of angels to do us service, since it is His own Son whom He gives us, the Word by whom all things were made, and who is God like unto Himself (John 3:16). Let us dwell in silence on this great gift, for it cannot be expressed in words. Let us consider, second, the manner in which this gift was made to us. The Eternal Word gave Himself to us by taking upon Himself all that is vilest in us, by making Himself flesh and clay like us. It only cost Him one word to create the world; but in order to save it He descends in person from His throne, and humbles Himself to the very lowest condition in this low world. O love, how ineffable thou art! And what is man, O my God, that Thou should love Him to such an excess? Third consideration: Man is only a small miserable creature, fallen through his sin from his primal dignity; he is a worm of the earth in insurrection, a sinner to whom nothing is due but vengeance; and yet, Thou, O my God! didst substitute Thyself in his place to bear the penalty which was his due, and God the Father accepts the exchange and delivers Thee up to death Thee, His innocent Son, to save guilty man! O love, how ineffable thou art! And wherefore, O my God, dost Thou thus act? Fourth consideration: Formerly the Jews asked the Savior why He, who was a man, made Himself God. And why did they not rather ask of Him why He who was God made Himself man? (John 10:33.) He might have answered them: It was because I loved you, and because I desired to be loved by you. I loved you with a gratuitous love, a love you had not deserved, a love superior to all ingratitude and to all outrages. I foresaw clearly that but a very small number would appreciate My love, and that the majority would disdain it; and yet I loved you, and I have come spite of all (Eph. 2:4-5). O mystery of love! How can I appreciate thee? How can I sufficiently thank thee?

SECOND POINT
✝ What ought to be our Love for the Incarnate Word

Alas! up to the present time, perhaps the habit of speaking about and of hearing this great mystery spoken of has rendered us, as it were, insensible to it. Every day we repeat the words which ought to make our hearts melt with love: "The Word was made flesh," and whilst saying it our hearts remain as cold as marble and as hard as stone. It must no longer be so with us hence forth. We must love Him who is so good a God, love Him with a strong, energetic love, a love which exclaims with St. John: "Let us love God, who hath first loved us." (1 John 4:19) Love Him with a generous love, which cries out with St. Bernard: The measure of divine love is to love without measure; love Him with a strong love which courageously embraces all kinds of sacrifices, whether they be those which we meet with in the accomplishment of duty, or those which Providence sends us, or those which the malignity of man imposes on us; love Him, lastly, with a practical love, which in all, as well as in every detail of our conduct, only proposes to itself the happiness of pleasing Him, and which carefully observes words, intentions, and acts in order to avoid even the smallest things which might be displeasing to Him. Oh, how far we are from having loved Him in this manner! *Resolutions and spiritual nosegay as above.*

Tuesday in the Third Week of Advent

SUMMARY OF TOMORROW'S MEDITATION

e will meditate tomorrow on our third duty towards the Incarnate Word, which consists in imitating Him, and we shall see: First, that the design of God in decreeing the Incarnation was to give us the Incarnate Word as our model; second, that the excellence of this model invites us to imitate it. We will then make the resolution: First, often to compare the sentiments of Christ with ours, particularly in regard to the love of the cross, of poverty, of preeminence; second, to enter within ourselves before every action and every resolution, in order to ask ourselves,

What would Jesus Christ do or think? Our spiritual nosegay shall be the words of the Savior: "I have given you an example that as I have done to you, so you do also." (John 13:15)

MEDITATION FOR THE MORNING

Let us adore the Son of God, descended from heaven to earth, not only to redeem us, but also to teach us the Christian life by His example. Before preaching His doctrine He began by practicing it (Acts 1:4). He observed His precepts and His counsels before giving them to us, so that we might have no pretext for neglecting them. Let us thank Him for so touching a condescendence, and let us excite ourselves to imitate Him.

FIRST POINT

✝ **The Design of God in Decreeing the Incarnation was to Give us His Incarnate Word to be our Model**

When God in His eternal councils decreed the Incarnation of the Word, He proposed to Himself to place Him before the eyes of men as the model of the new life which was destined to save them. As man, the Incarnate Word would show them the way; as God, He would guarantee to them the perfection of the model. His virtues would be capable of imitation, since they would proceed from a man, and they would be a sure rule, since they would proceed from a God. If, then, says St. Bonaventura, the Adorable Word made Himself visible upon earth, if He conversed familiarly with men, if He subjected Himself to the performance of even the most ordinary actions, it was for no other purpose than to give us an example in everything (De Inst. Novit. 32:1). I have given you an example, He Himself says, that I may offer to you in My person the rule of your conduct (John 13:15). "I am the way and the truth and the life," (John 14:6) the way you ought to follow, the truth you ought to hear, the life you ought to live. Lastly, St. Paul on his side declares to us that the predestination of the whole of the elect is on condition that they bear in themselves the semblance of Christ (Rom. 8:29). This is also the reason why St. Basil tells us that Christianity is nothing more than the imitation of Jesus Christ (Reg. Fus. Expl. 43); St. Gregory of Nyssa, that he alone deserves the name of Christian who shows forth in his life the life of Jesus Christ (De Perf. Christ.); St. Augustine, that Jesus Christ came upon earth there to be an example of a perfect life; St. Laurence Justinian, that the life of Jesus is the true model of perfection, the type of a good life, the teaching of religion, and the expression of all the virtues. Have we, up to the present time, well understood this fundamental truth, and striven to rule our life according to that of Jesus Christ?

SECOND POINT

✝ The Excellence of the Model set before us in Jesus Christ invites us to Imitate it

First, it is the most glorious of models: what is there that can be more honorable, more suitable to flatter a noble heart, than to be called upon to imitate a God, as St. Paul says? (Eph.5:1) Secondly, it is the most unexceptionable of all models: who is there that could find that painful to which a God was the first to submit, whilst promising us His grace to raise our weakness to His height? Thirdly, it is the most amiable of models: for if we strive to resemble the persons we love, if this resemblance causes us to be loved, then the imitation of Jesus Christ is at once an act of love towards Himself and a means of making ourselves to be more and more loved. Fourthly, it is the model the most within our reach: His life has not the austerity of that of St. John Baptist, which would have alarmed our weakness; He led a simple and ordinary life; He ate, slept, labored, like us; He suffered, wept, passed through all our trials, in order to serve us as an example in everything. Do we understand our happiness in having before our eyes so admirable a model? Do we strive to copy it, and to say to ourselves, Is it thus that Jesus Christ would act, would speak, would think? Is this His religion, His charity, His meekness, His modesty, His recollection, His spirit of sacrifice? Behold this is what we ought to say to ourselves every day and at every instant, so to speak. *Resolutions and spiritual nosegay as above.*

Wednesday in the Third Week of Advent

SUMMARY OF TOMORROW'S MEDITATION

In order that we may rightly fulfill the triple duty of studying, loving, and imitating the Incarnate Word, we will begin by meditating upon the life which He led during nine months in the womb of Mary, and we shall observe tomorrow that it was a life of imprisonment, solitude, and silence. We will then make the resolution: First, not to mix with the world without necessity; second, to love solitude and silence, as being more conducive to innocence of life and to the spirit of prayer. Our spiritual nosegay shall be the maxim of the Imitation: "It is in peace and silence that the soul makes progress." (1 Imit. 20:6)

MEDITATION FOR THE MORNING

Let us adore Jesus as a little child in the womb of Mary, which He willed to inhabit during nine months. He did not will to show Himself in the sight of the world all at once as a man. He preferred to follow the common condition of the human race, and to begin His life of the Incarnate Word in the womb of a woman. Let us admire, let us bless, this decree of His eternal wisdom, and let us beg of Him to enable us to understand it and to give us courage to imitate it.

FIRST POINT

✝ **The Life of the Incarnate Word in the Womb of Mary was a Life of Imprisonment**

Was ever prison darker? And yet how admirable it is that it was there He willed to remain during nine months, He who inhabits the splendors of the saints. It is there that, enclosing His immensity in the smallest possible space, abasing His omnipotence in the infirmity and His omniscience in the simplicity of a child, this gracious captive constituted Himself a prisoner for our crimes in order to spare us the dungeons of hell; a prisoner for our debts, because we were insolvent debtors; and He willed not to leave His prison until the hour and the day decreed by His Father. Moreover, it was to come into this world only to lead the life of the cross and of martyrdom, to die a cruel death, and to constitute Himself, until the end of all things, an obscure prisoner in the Most Holy Sacrament. O admirable and a thousand times amiable captive, render me a captive to Thy love, attaching me to Thy service by chains of love which nothing shall be able to break!

SECOND POINT

✝ **The Life of the Word Incarnate in the Womb of Mary was a Life of Solitude**

Jesus willingly remains in this solitude, so entirely unknown that no one save Mary is aware that He is there. And wherefore that, except to teach us that we ought not to seek either to see or be seen; that the entire world, if we could see it as a whole and in its details, would offer us nothing more than a vain spectacle; that it is far better to keep ourselves hidden, and to be taking care of our souls, than to attract observation by miracles, and, at the same time, to be neglecting ourselves; that it is more profitable to treat with God than with creatures; that God takes pleasure in the solitude of the heart, far from tumult; that the more we separate ourselves from the world and its vain frivolities, the more closely God will draw nigh to us, will speak to our heart, will make us enjoy the delight of His presence, the sweetness of His consolations, the more facility we shall find in preserving ourselves pure and keeping up a holy intercourse with heaven. O life of retreat, how precious thou art! How good it is to shut the gates of our hearts to creatures, and there to converse with Jesus! Nowhere do we find such peace; nowhere is one so much to one's self and to God. Do we esteem a life of retreat and of solitude in this manner?

THIRD POINT

✝ The Life of the Word Incarnate in the Womb of Mary was a Life of Silence

The Incarnate Word so greatly loves silence that during nine months He never spoke one word, and that for His birth He chose the night, when all creatures are silent (Wis. 18:14-15). Since His birth, down to the period when the generality of children begin to speak, He is silent; and from that moment down to His thirtieth year He still keeps silence, excepting when He utters words which are necessary or which propriety demands. During the three years of His mission He speaks because He is obliged to do so; but after His death, and until the end of all things, He keeps silence in the Eucharist. O wonderful silence, which teaches us that silence is the school of wisdom; that it is therein we educate ourselves and learn the great art of speaking and acting suitably, of acquiring a spirit of reflection, of faith, of recollection, and of prayer; that there is in the heart of man who keeps silence a treasure as precious as rests upon the lips of the wise man who speaks (Thomas a Kempis, Vallis Liliorum); that piety which is not under the safeguard of silence is not durable (Ibid); that too much speaking dissipates the mind (Ibid), and leads us to commit many faults (Prov. 10:19); lastly, that a religion which does not moderate the tongue is a vain religion (James 1:26). The more there is of silence, the more there is of innocence; if speaking dissipates the mind, silence brings it back. Before speaking, the wise man examines if what he is about to say is worth more than silence. Is it thus that we act? Do we find our happiness in keeping silence, and do we like better to hear others speak than to speak ourselves? *Resolutions and spiritual nosegay as above.*

Thursday in the Third Week of Advent

SUMMARY OF TOMORROW'S MEDITATION

e will continue to meditate on the life of Jesus in Mary, and we shall see: First, that it is the most humble of lives; second, the poorest of lives. We will then make the resolution: First, not to seek to parade ourselves, and never to say anything to our own advantage; second, to love poverty, and to employ our surplus in good works. Our spiritual nosegay shall be the words of the Imitation: "It is a great glory to serve Thee, O my God, and not to make account of anything which is not Thee." (3 Imit. 10:5)

MEDITATION FOR THE MORNING

Let us adore the Incarnate Word reduced in the womb of Mary to the most humble and most poor of conditions. Let us thank Him to have thus abased Himself in order to expiate our pride, thus to have impoverished Himself in order to correct our love of riches, and taught us thereby, at His own expense, humility and poverty, which are two virtues very dear to His heart, and which cost ours so much.

FIRST POINT

✝ The Incarnate Word in the Bosom of Mary Leads the Most Humble of Lives

He who has His throne in highest heaven humbles and lessens Himself to the extreme littleness of the body of a child in the womb of his mother. In the crib He will, at any rate, be visible to human eyes; the angels will sing His glory, the shepherds will adore Him, and the magi will prostrate themselves before Him; but here all is hidden, everything disappears: it is annihilation (Philip. 2:7). Hence the cry of astonishment littered by Holy Church: "Thou didst not abhor the Virgin's womb." (Hymn Te Deum) Worthy forecasts of His whole life, which will be nothing but a series of humiliations, of contempt and of opprobrium, and which only will allow to appear in His person, King of kings though He be, the last and most humble of men! What a lesson for our self-love! We are so sensitive when we are neglected, when we are not thought of by others and seemingly left on one side; obscurity and a hidden life are so revolting to our pride! Esteem and praise make such a sweet murmur to resound round about our heart. May the humiliations of the Word Incarnate make us blush to entertain such sentiments! When He who is so great makes Himself so small, it ill becomes us who are so little to desire to make ourselves great. When the Light is obscured it ill becomes darkness to wish to become light.

SECOND POINT
✝ The Word Incarnate in the Womb of Mary Leads the Poorest of Lives

He who has granted such magnificent riches to heaven and to earth might well have been possessed of them Himself: but He did not so will it. He despoiled Himself of everything in becoming incarnate, and made Himself poor for love of us (2 Cor. 8:9). He fell in love with poverty, and not finding it in the bosom of His Father, He came to seek it in the womb of His mother. There He is entirely naked, destitute of even the poor swaddling clothes which will envelop Him in the crib. There He enjoys the thought that He will be born poor, that He will live poor, that He will die poor; and that when He issues forth from the womb of His mother He will not be able, without the help of His creature, either to feed Himself or clothe Himself, or suffice for any of the needs of His life. Let us compare this state of the Word Incarnate with our dispositions. Jesus loves poverty so much, and we fear it. He seeks it and we fly from it. Everything is wanting to Jesus, and we desire not to want for anything; delicate and sensitive to the smallest privations, we take the greatest cafe to avoid them, and we are strangely uneasy when we meet with the most trifling inconvenience. Even what is necessary is not sufficient for us; we must have in surplus what is precious, luxury, and vanity. O Jesus, who didst canonize poverty (Matt. 5:3), who didst honor it with Thy choice and render it divine in Thy person, teach me to place my treasure in Thee alone. Make me comprehend that a man is rich when he possesses Thee; that to acquire so great a good he ought to leave all, and leave himself; that, on the contrary, he is very poor when he does not possess Thee, even though he were possessed of all the riches of the universe (2 Imit. 8:2). *Resolutions and spiritual nosegay as above.*

Friday in the Third Week of Advent

SUMMARY OF TOMORROW'S MEDITATION

e will meditate tomorrow on the mortified life led by the Word Incarnate in the bosom of His mother, and we shall admire how, in this state, He mortified, First, His senses; second, His will; third, His liberty. We will then make the resolution: First, to mortify our senses, above all our eyes and our tongue, even in things permitted to us, in order to teach ourselves to mortify them in things which are forbidden; second, to live by rule and under obedience, without ever yielding to caprice. Our spiritual nosegay shall be the words of the Apostle: "Christ did not please Himself." (Rom. 15:3)

MEDITATION FOR THE MORNING

Let us adore the Incarnate Word in the womb of Mary, submitting Himself there during nine months to a universal mortification, and there beginning the life of martyrdom and sacrifice which He was to continue to lead during the whole of His sojourn upon earth. Everything is mortified in Him; His senses, His will, His liberty. Let us bless the great example which He gives us, and beg of Him grace to imitate it.

FIRST POINT

✝ **The Incarnate Word Mortifies His Senses in the Womb of Mary.**

In point of fact His eyes do not enjoy the light, nor His tongue the use of speech, nor His limbs the power of moving. He passes nine months in the greatest darkness, cramped in the whole of His body. Other children, who are not at that time possessed of reason, do not feel the painfulness of such a position; but with a reason perfectly developed, to find oneself bound in captivity and darkness, how severe a mortification it must be! What a universal privation! To these exterior sufferings are added those of the interior senses, of the mind and the imagination, which keep continually present to His thoughts His death as ignominious as painful, and the eternal loss of so many souls which will not accept the salvation He comes to bring them, and the future sufferings of His mother, and the torments of the martyrs, and the tears and persecutions of all the saints. All these sorrows weigh down immensely upon His soul, and he bears the weight with resignation. What a great heart in so small a body! What excess of charity in a God towards His creatures! But, also, what an example for us! Jesus does not pass a single moment without suffering for our love, and we will suffer nothing in His service; He mortifies His eyes, and we will grant everything to ours; He crucifies His senses, and we desire to flatter them; He suffers extreme interior pain, and we revolt against what we suffer. Let us blush at our cowardice, which will suffer nothing for a God who has suffered so much for us.

SECOND POINT
✝ **The Incarnate Word in the Womb of Mary Mortifies His Will**

Jesus remains nine months in the womb of Mary through obedience to His Father. He does not measure the time by His own desires, but He accommodates His desires to the decrees of His Father, neither retarding nor advancing it, even by a single moment. As Incarnate Wisdom, He had a right Himself to direct and rule His actions, but He renounces the use of this right, and leaves His will to the disposal of obedience. He not only obeys the will of His Father, but also the will of His mother, who carries Him wherever she wishes to go; the will, also, of the Roman Emperor, of St. Joseph, of all those to whom Mary was subject. And what He did at the commencement of His life He did unto the end (John 8:20); and after having led all His days a life of complete obedience, He will die from obedience (Philip. 2:8). Let us learn from this henceforth never to take our own will as the rule of our conduct and our determination, but ever to will, like Jesus Christ, what God wills (Luke 22:24), and to will it firmly from the bottom of our hearts, entirely and without reserve. Let us learn henceforth to regulate the employment of our time according to the order of God's good pleasure, to perform every action in its proper place, not giving to business the time set apart for prayer, amusement the time set apart for labor, and to conversation the time set apart for silence. O Lord, Thou who art God didst renounce Thy will, and I, a worm of the earth, I desire to follow mine; Thy pleasure is to obey, and I desire to command. What blindness is mine!

THIRD POINT
✝ **The Incarnate Word in the Womb of Mary Mortifies His Liberty**

Not only does the Incarnate Word interdict Himself from following His own will, but He also denies Himself all power; He takes on Himself all the weaknesses of infancy, and suffers by choice all the powerlessness to which children are subjected through necessity; He who by a single word created all that exists makes Himself mute and unable to utter a single word, in order to teach us to be silent, not to murmur or complain at discomforts; not to argue with others, as though we always wanted to have the upper hand, but to yield modestly, as though we had no answer ready; to restrain our tongue under the influence of passion, as though we had lost all use of it. He by whom all things move can make no other movement than that of children in the womb of their mothers, in order to teach us to be content with inaction when our bodily infirmities reduce us to it, to repress the movements of corrupt nature, to act only under the influence of obedience and grace. Lastly, He who in the bosom of His Father is sovereignly independent, depends upon Mary for His life, His food, His preservation. He has a being and human life only through dependence upon Mary; He has no other aliment than the blood of her heart, whilst waiting until He can draw milk from her breasts, and His preservation depends solely upon her. He cannot of Himself defend His little, feeble, delicate body; the least imprudence on the part of His mother would occasion His death. O God, so under subjection, so powerless, so dependent, teach me to repress the spirit of independence, the child of my pride, that license of the tongue which does not know how to be silent when it ought to be, and that desire to do whatever is pleasing to myself. *Resolutions and spiritual nosegay as above.*

Saturday in the Third Week of Advent

SUMMARY OF TOMORROW'S MEDITATION

e will apply ourselves tomorrow to meditate upon the occupations of the Incarnate Word during His sojourn in the womb of Mary. The first of these occupations was continually to render to God four great duties: First, adoration, second, love, third, thanksgiving, fourth, praise. After having meditated upon these different kinds of homage, we will make the resolution: First, often to utter, by means of the salutary practice of ejaculatory prayers, acts of adoration and love, of gratitude and praise; second, to offer our actions to God with one or another of these different kinds of homage in view, and thereby to encourage ourselves to perform them very perfectly. Our spiritual nosegay shall be the words of the Psalmist: "The Lord is great and exceedingly to be praised" (Ps. 47:2;95:4;144:3).

MEDIATION FOR THE MORNING

Let us adore the Incarnate Word, making a true paradise within the womb of Mary, where He renders to God His Father the most perfect homage which can be given Him. In the same degree that it pleases Him to render it, it pleases God to receive it. Let us rejoice at seeing God so perfectly honored, and let us bless the Incarnate Word who procures such glory for Him.

FIRST POINT

✠ Duties of Adoration which the Incarnate Word Renders to God in the Womb of Mary

Adoration proceeds from the knowledge of God and of oneself. The more we are aware of the excellence and grandeur of the Divine Being, the more we humble and annihilate ourselves, and the more we are overpowered with respect in His presence, the more, also, we know ourselves; the more little we feel ourselves to be in the sight of God, the more deeply do we descend into our own nothingness. O holy Father, the world does not know Thee (John 17:25), and it does not know itself: hence it adores Thee so little and so ill. Ah, if men but knew what Thou art, and what Thou wilt be to them throughout eternity, how reverent and humble they would be before Thee at church, in prayer, everywhere and always! How they would bury themselves in the abyss of their nothingness and of their sins, in presence of Thy Divine Being, the abyss of all being and all good! This is what the Incarnate Word did in an excellent manner. Perfectly knowing the immense distance which separates the creature from the Creator, He humbled Himself in the presence of His Father with the most profound respect, with the most humble adoration, and with all His strength He glorified the infinite majesty of God. Then was seen what had never before been seen, a God adored and a God adoring, a God rendering to God homage which honored Him in the measure which His infinite grandeur deserves; all heaven, filled with astonishment at this marvel, exclaiming Amen to this sublime adoration and rivaling one another in singing, Holy, Holy, Holy is the Lord, the God of hosts. Benediction and honor, and glory and power forever and ever (Apoc. 5:13). Is it thus that we adore God? Alas! how little we know how to humble ourselves with reverence in presence of His greatness, and to be confounded by the sense of our own littleness in presence of His holy majesty.

SECOND POINT

✝ **Duties of Love which the Incarnate Word Renders to God in the Womb of Mary**

The soul of Jesus, which entered into the state of beatitude from the first moment of its existence, enjoyed from that moment the clear vision of God, allowing Himself to be seen for the first time by mortal eyes. This view inflamed it with the most perfect beatific love; it plunged with ecstasy into this ocean of all good; it possessed it, it enjoyed it, it was ravished by it. Its personal union with the Word giving it a sight superior in clearness to all the light of the angels, gave it, for that very reason, a love which neither the cherubim nor all the angelic choir put together can approach to. To love God is its passion, its life, its incessant occupation. Do we rejoice that there exists in the world a heart which so perfectly loves God and repairs all the offenses committed against Him? But, at the same time, let us learn from hence that God alone is everything for the heart of man; that all which is not God cannot give us happiness. O Lord, may I die in order to see and love Thee! (St. Augustine) I love Thee so little in this life! At least, I will, from today, strive to love Thee better; I will multiply my acts of love as much as is possible for me to do.

THIRD POINT

✝ **Duties of Thanksgiving which the Incarnate Word Renders to God in the Womb of Mary**

Jesus, seeing all the good things which God has given Him, and those which He has given and will always give to all creatures, of which He, the Incarnate Word, is the head and representative, dilates all the powers of His soul, that He may worthily thank the Lord for them (John 6:41; 17:10). He is filled with admiration at the sight of these blessings, so magnificent, so multiplied, so continuous, and, at the same time, so gratuitous, unmerited, without interest as well as without reserve. These considerations inspire Him with ineffable and incessant acts of thanksgiving. O God, may I associate myself with these divine thanksgivings for all the good things I have received from Thee; may I say to Thee from the bottom of my heart: Thanks be to Thee, O Lord our God! I will delight myself in repeating it often by day and night.

FOURTH POINT

✝ **Duties of Praise which the Incarnate Word Renders to God in the Womb of Mary**

The soul of the Incarnate Word does not consider God only in His benefits; He considers Him still more in Himself as the center of all beauty and of all perfection: as an immense ocean whence flows, at every moment, all that is good in heaven or on earth. From this point of view, it is a song of praise, filling the whole of His soul a song which infinitely rejoices the heart of God and which nothing can interrupt. Let us unite ourselves to this divine song, saying with the Psalmist: "Bless the Lord, O my soul and let all that is within me praise His holy Name" (Ps. 102:1); or with St. Thomas: "Praise God as much as thou canst, O my soul, because He is so infinitely above all praise that we can never praise Him sufficiently" (Hymn Lauda Sion). The duty of the creature is wholly to spend himself in praising his Creator, from whom he has everything and for whom alone he exists. How do we fulfill this duty? Do we take pleasure in the perfections of God, and do we delight to praise them, to admire them, to bless them? Are we not of the number of those who hardly ever think of them, or who never think of them at all? *Resolutions and spiritual nosegay as above.*

Fourth Sunday in Advent

THE GOSPEL ACCORDING TO ST. LUKE 3:1-6

"Now, in the fifteenth year of the reign of Tiberius Caesar, Pontius Pilate being governor of Judea, and Herod being tetrarch of Galilee, and Philip, his brother, tetrarch of Iturea and the country of Trachonitis, and Lysanias tetrarch of Abilina, under the high-priests Annas and Caiphas: the word of the Lord was made known unto John, the son of Zachary, in the desert. And he came into all the country about the Jordan, preaching the baptism of penance for the remission of sins, as it was written in the book of the sayings of Isaias, the prophet: A voice of one crying in the wilderness: Prepare ye the way of the Lord, make straight His paths. Every valley shall be filled, and every mountain and hill shall be brought low: and the crooked shall be made straight, and the rough ways plain. And all flesh shall see the salvation of God."

SUMMARY OF TOMORROW'S MEDITATION

n order to conform ourselves to the Gospel of the day, which cries out to us to prepare the way of the Lord, who is about to be born in our hearts, we will meditate tomorrow: First, on the obligation of preparing ourselves in a more special manner for the feast of Christmas; second, on the manner of making this special preparation. We will then make the resolution: First, to spend the days which separate us from Christmas in a more perfect state of recollection and with a more sustained

attention to the better performance of our ordinary actions; second, heartily to make to God all the sacrifices with which His grace may inspire us, and to express frequent desires, by means of ejaculatory prayers, for the life of Our Lord within us. Our spiritual nosegay shall be the words of the Gospel: "Prepare ye the way of the Lord, make straight His paths." (Luke 3:4)

MEDITATION FOR THE MORNING

Let us adore the Incarnate Word in the womb of Mary sighing for the moment of His appearance upon earth in order to save it (Symb. Nic.). Let us admire this great mystery of love and of goodness, which appeared so evidently in the flesh with which a God clothed Himself in order to expiate our sins; a mystery which the Holy Spirit attested by so many miracles; a mystery which had the angels for witnesses, which has been preached to the nations, believed in the world, raised to heaven in glory (1 Tim, 3:16). Is it not very just and right to prepare ourselves in a very special manner to celebrate such a mystery when its great solemnity is at hand?

FIRST POINT

✝ **The Obligation we are under to Prepare Ourselves in a more Special Manner for the Feast of Christmas**

In like manner as God, in times past, deputed the angels to announce to the shepherds the birth of the Savior, He has deputed the Church from the beginning of Advent to say to us, "Prepare yourselves to receive the Lord, who is about to come" (Invit. Adv.). Today the Church renews her entreaties. "We are drawing near to the solemn moment," she exclaims to us; "prepare yourselves still more perfectly" (Ibid). How, in fact, shall we worthily honor the Infant Jesus, if we do not become more recollected in proportion as the feast approaches? Our senses perceive in the crib nothing but littleness and poverty, they see nothing there to touch or cause emotion. It is necessary for that to have an entirely fresh provision, if I may so express it, of faith and love which will teach us to discover in this little Child the Eternal Son of God engendered before the aurora in the splendors of the saints; He who is seated at the right hand of the Father, He whom the angels adore, whom the prophets call Emmanuel, God with us, whom the apostles call the Word by whom all things have been made, He who bears all by the virtue of His Word, and who is the splendor of glory. The Infant Jesus, who comes to be born for us, has a great desire to be born in us, but He will only do it in proportion to the measure of our preparation during these blessed days. To hearts well prepared He will give abundantly of the peace promised to men of good will: peace with God, peace with our neighbor, peace with ourselves and our consciences; He will give a spirit of humility and meekness, of poverty and simplicity, of obedience and abandonment to the guidance of God: precious graces suitable to the mystery of Christmas; but to hearts that are ill-prepared He will close His heart and His hand. Let us fear this misfortune.

SECOND POINT
✝ **The Manner of Preparing Ourselves for the Feast of Christmas**

There are three means of doing so: recollection, holiness of life, and the frequent use of ejaculatory prayers. First, recollection, nothing removes God from a heart so much as dissipation, which causes the soul to occupy itself wholly with outward things, absorbs it in a world of thoughts and idle imaginations, and thereby troubles and agitates it (3 Kings 19:2). In proportion to the approach of the great day, we must therefore more carefully keep our heart from all which may dissipate it; we must think oftener of the mystery of Christmas, of the love of God in the crib, of the pious sentiments and resolutions which we ought to offer Him in return for His love and His goodness. Second, with recollection we must unite holiness of life. We must, during the whole of these days, watch more carefully over ourselves, that we may avoid all sin, consecrate all our actions to the love of the Child Jesus, and with this object in view perform them as perfectly as possible; we must offer to Him everyday some sacrifice for example, the sacrifice of a desire, of an impulse, of a repugnance, of an expression of self-love or of bad temper, and make of all these sacrifices a nosegay of myrrh, as it were, to offer to the Infant Jesus; above all, we must pray the Holy Spirit Himself to form in us the tender and fervent spirit of piety which Mary and Joseph, the shepherds and the Magi, brought to the crib, and which so many holy souls bring there at the present day. Third, the practice of ejaculatory prayers, that is to say, of the holy desires which bring the Savior God into the soul, will complete our preparation. The Church furnishes us with the touching expression of them in the sighs which she borrows from the patriarchs and prophets: "Drop down dew, ye heavens, from above, and let the clouds rain the just" (Is. 45:8). "Oh, that Thou wouldst rend the heavens and wouldst come down" (Is. 64:1). "I beseech thee, Lord, send whom Thou wilt" (Ex. 4:13). "Show us, O Lord, Thy mercy, and grant us Thy salvation" (Ps. 84:8). "Show forth Thy wonderful mercies, Thou who saves them that trust in Thee" (Ps. 16:7). The beautiful antiphons of the great O's of Advent will furnish us with still further similar sighs. Let us often repeat them, and let us add to them the sigh of St. John in his Apocalypse: "Come,

Lord Jesus" (Apoc. 22:20). Are we firmly resolved to prepare ourselves for the approaching feast, by the three means on which we have been meditating? *Resolutions and spiritual nosegay as above.*

Monday in the Fourth Week of Advent

SUMMARY OF TOMORROW'S MEDITATION

e will consider tomorrow Jesus in Mary constituted priest of the human race by God, His Father, and under this title burning with zeal, first, for the glory of God, and second, for the salvation of men. We will then make the resolution: First, to refer all our actions to the greater glory of God, and with this object in view to perform each one of them with the greatest possible perfection; second, to do all that is in our power for the salvation of our neighbor. Our spiritual nosegay shall be the words of St. Ignatius: "To the greater glory of God!"

MEDITATION FOR THE MORNING

Let us adore the Word Incarnate in the womb of Mary as our High-Priest, established in this dignity by God, His Father (Heb. 5:56). Let us admire the zeal He shows in this quality for the glory of God and the salvation of men. Let us thank Him for a zeal so full of love for God and for us, and let us beg Him for a share in it.

FIRST POINT

✝ **The Zeal of the Incarnate Word in the Womb of Mary for the Glory of God**

The Word, in becoming incarnate in the womb of Mary, had only one aim: namely, that of procuring the glory of God, by making Him to be known, loved, and served, and this thought never quitted Him; it preoccupied Him during the day, it preoccupied Him during the night. To it were referred all the beatings of His heart, all His prayers, all His sufferings. He did not take any thought about Himself, or His interests, or His glory. "I seek not My own glory," He said. "I honor My Father" (John 8:49-50). What admirable zeal! What purity of love! Let us approach this sacred fire, to purify our intentions, which are so often mixed with human aims, which take away the merits of our works, and in order to kindle our zeal, which is so often cold and careless in regard to the great interests of the glory of God. Let us learn from the Incarnate

Word to do nothing, to say nothing, to desire nothing from self-love, for the sake of praise and reputation, but to refer all to God and His glory. Happy those who understand these holy things and conform their lives to them!

SECOND POINT

✝ The Zeal of the Word Incarnate in the Womb of Mary for the Salvation of Men

The Incarnate Word mingles together in one and the same love the glory of God and the salvation of men, the children of God, destined to bless Him and love Him in time and throughout eternity. He therefore desires the one and the other with equal ardor. He burns with an immense desire to come and save all men, to do them good, to teach them all truth; to preach to them all virtues by His example and His words, to employ His miraculous power to the solace of their misery, His wisdom to show them the path which leads to heaven, His grace and the merits of His blood to enable them to walk therein. If apostolic men suffer a kind of martyrdom when they are frustrated in their designs for the salvation of men, what must the Incarnate Word not have suffered, detained in the womb of His mother, and from the first moment of His life always being urged by the desire to immolate Himself in order to save us (Luke 12:50). How, then, after that, can we have so little zeal for our salvation; so little ardor to advance towards perfection; so little preoccupation for the conversion of the sinners who surround us? Let us beg Our Lord to communicate to us some of the flames of the sacred fire which consumes Him. *Resolutions and spiritual nosegay as above.*

Tuesday in the Fourth Week of Advent

SUMMARY OF TOMORROW'S MEDITATION

e will meditate tomorrow: First, on the life of prayer which, as our High-Priest, the Word Incarnate leads in the womb of Mary. Second, on the sweet obligation under which all of us are equally to lead a life of prayer. We will then make the resolution: First, better to perform our ordinary prayers; second, often to ask God for the spirit of prayer, which of all graces is the one most necessary for our salvation. Our spiritual nosegay shall be the words of the Savior, "Pray always" (Luke 18:1), or the words of the apostles, "Lord, teach us to pray." (Luke 11:1)

MEDIATION FOR THE MORNING

Let us adore Jesus continually at prayer, as our High Priest, in the womb of Mary. This and the homage He renders to God are His constant occupation. Oh, what a beautiful, fervent prayer is His! How it glorifies God! How it brings down graces upon all future ages, which the great Pontiff of the New Law embraces in His supplications! Oh, how greatly does this divine Suppliant merit all our thanks, all our praises, and all our love!

FIRST POINT

✝ The Life of the Word Incarnate in the Womb of Mary was a Life of Prayer

The holy soul of Jesus was no sooner created, than raising immediately His eyes to God, He saw in Him the ocean of all good, beyond which nothing good exists (Ex. 33:19). Ravished by this spectacle, and knowing, on the one hand, that, in the ordinary course of things, graces are given only on condition of being asked; and, on the other hand, that the mission of a priest is to address these petitions to Heaven, He enters into prayer for Himself and for the whole world from the first moment of His existence. And who can tell how perfect was this prayer? It was fervent, because the graces which He asked for, being of infinite value, deserved to be in finitely desired; it was continual and persevering, because at every moment the creature has need of the help of his Creator; it was humble, because His holy soul profoundly felt that the creature is nothing, and that God alone is all; it was full of confidence, because the Word who spoke by this prayer rendered it divine, and because a God, asking of a God, cannot be refused. Let us here examine ourselves. Do we pray, first, with joy at honoring God by our prayer; second, with the double sentiment of the need in which we stand of His aid and the necessity of asking for it. Third, with a high esteem of the spiritual blessings which we ask for, and a hearty desire to obtain them. Fourth, with perseverance, not allowing ourselves to be discouraged if we are not heard immediately and answered. Fifth, with humility, humbling ourselves exceedingly in the presence of God, through the consideration of His greatness and our lowliness. Sixth, with confidence, resting upon the words of Our Lord; "Amen, Amen, I say to you, if you ask the Father anything in My name, He will give it you!"(John 16:23) Alas, we pray and we do not obtain, because we pray ill. (James 4:3)

SECOND POINT
✝ **The Life of Prayer is a Duty for every Christian and the Secret of Happiness**

First, it is a duty; for all the examples set us by Jesus Christ are precepts. Now Jesus, our model, led a life of prayer; we ought therefore ourselves to lead a life of prayer. Besides, our needs are so great, so continuous, that we can no more cease to pray than the beggar can cease to ask the alms, without which he would die. Lastly, if we do not lead a habitual life of prayer, we shall perform our obligatory prayers badly; they will only be a continual distraction; we shall be incessantly preoccupied with news, with affairs, with happy or unhappy events, with imaginations and useless thoughts. Experience sufficiently proves this to us. Second, a life of prayer is the secret of happiness. Is there anything sweeter than to live in the society of the three Divine Persons; to pour our hearts into the heart of the Father who has created us; of the Son who has redeemed us, and who prays for us without ceasing in the tabernacle as in heaven; and of the Holy Spirit who pursues us with His love and His holy inspirations? Can there be a more noble, a more delicious occupation for the soul than that of holding communion with its God? Whatever may be our troubles, let us come to Him and tell Him of them, and we shall be consoled. Whatever may be the difficulties we may meet with on our path, let us come and ask His assistance, and we shall be helped. A life of prayer will make of our exile a Paradise, it will be for us the beginning of heaven. Let us believe in the experience of it. Those who do not pray are full of sadness, whilst souls which pray bear upon the features of their face a sweet and amiable serenity which is the reflection of their internal happiness. *Resolutions and spiritual nosegay as above.*

Wednesday in the Fourth Week of Advent

SUMMARY OF TOMORROW'S MEDITATION

We will consider tomorrow that the bosom of Mary is not only a temple wherein the Incarnate Word displays His zeal and pours out His soul in prayer, but that it is also an altar on which He immolates Himself. We shall therefore meditate: First, on the life which Jesus leads as a victim in the bosom of His mother; second, on the life which we ought to lead ourselves as victims. We will then make the resolution: First, to sanctify the day by frequent acts of love towards Jesus, our victim, in

the bosom of Mary; second, to labor after our own spiritual amendment, by the sacrifice of our tastes and of our wills. Our spiritual nosegay shall be: "Jesus Christ hath loved us, and hath delivered Himself for us." (Eph. 5:2)

MEDITATION FOR THE MORNING

Let us adore the Incarnate Word offering Himself to God His Father in the womb of Mary, as a victim upon the altar of sacrifice. Oh, how adorable is the victim! How amiable He is! The Father takes pleasure in Him (Mark 1:2), the earth finds in Him its salvation, the angels the subject of great joy. Let us render our homage to so august a victim.

FIRST POINT

✟ The Life of a Victim Led by the Incarnate Word in the Womb of Mary

According to the testimony of St. Paul (Heb. 10:5), Jesus Christ from the moment of His entrance into the world said to His Father, "Sacrifice and oblation Thou wouldst not, but a body Thou hast given Me; I offer it to Thee and I offer it to replace the ancient sacrifices." Let us respectfully consider this adorable victim in the womb of Mary, which was His first altar. How cheerfully He offers Himself to His Father to be our salvation and the price of our ransom. He takes upon Himself the heavy burden of our sins, of our ingratitude, of our cowardice, of our weaknesses; and in order to expiate them He submits Himself to nine months of imprisonment and discomfort, of humiliation, of poverty, and of suffering. O adorable victim of the sins of the world, how can we sufficiently bless and thank Thee? My heart melts with love at seeing Thee in this state laboring for my salvation: First, with so much promptitude: without a moments delay or inaction, Thou dost set Thyself to work from the first moment of Thy existence; second, with so much fervor: Thou dost there employ all Thy soul, Thou dost expend the whole of Thy body, all Thy strength, and Thou dost give to each one of Thy acts all the perfection possible. Third, with so much constancy: not a moments relaxation or diminution in Thy zeal. Such as was the beginning of Thy life, such it will be to the end! Oh, how great reason had St. Paul to exclaim, "We have not a High Priest who cannot have compassion on our infirmities." (Heb. 4:15) Jesus pities us so much that, in order to save us, He gives us all that He has; He gives Himself wholly, and lives only to be our victim. O love, how admirable Thou art! How amiable! How can I help loving Thee a little!

SECOND POINT
✝ All Christians are Called to Lead the Life of a Victim

We are all of us called to this life: First, because we ought all of us to imitate Jesus Christ: He is our model, we ought to be copies of Him. We are Christians only on this condition. Second, because we have many sins to expiate and a great penance to perform. O days ill-employed! O years lost! How I regret you! O sins committed, how I deplore and detest you! It is, indeed, nigh time to begin for good and all to perform penance by the immolation of our whole self to Our Lord. Third, because if we have not courage to immolate our character to God with all its bursts of ill temper; our will with its caprices; the love of our own ease with that effeminacy of life which leads us to seek ourselves in everything, we shall infallibly fall again. The least difficulty will stop us; the least disgust will disconcert us, the least pleasure will lead us astray; inconstancy and frivolity will render our resolutions of no effect and the graces of God sterile. There is then no salvation for us, unless we lead the life of a victim; that is to say, of renunciation of ourselves, in order alone to follow the path of duty and that which we believe to be most agreeable to God. Let us have this courage, and we shall find in this practice consolation and sweetness, happiness in time and in eternity. *Resolutions and spiritual nosegay as above.*

Thursday in the Fourth Week of Advent

SUMMARY OF TOMORROW'S MEDITATION

We will conclude our meditations upon the life of the Word Incarnate in the bosom of Mary by considering, First, the merits which He acquired during nine months; second, the share that He will give us in these merits. We will then make the resolution: First, to put our confidence in the merits of Jesus Christ, and to combat, through this consideration, every thought of discouragement and mistrust; Second, to render all our actions meritorious, by offering them to God, and uniting them with the like actions in Jesus Christ. Our spiritual nosegay shall be the words of the Psalm: "In Thee, O Lord, have I hoped; let me never be confounded." (Ps. 30:1)

MEDITATION FOR THE MORNING

et us adore the Word Incarnate in the womb of Mary accumulating merits upon merits, in His quality of priest and of victim, and making of all these spiritual riches an immense treasure, by which all generations will benefit down to the end of time. He imitates the good father of a family, who amasses a large fortune for his beloved children. Let us glorify Him for such riches, let us bless Him for allowing us to share in them, and let us invite the saints and angels to thank Him with us. (2 Cor. 9:5)

FIRST POINT

✞ The Immense Merits which the Incarnate Word amasses during Nine Months in the Womb of Mary

Everything concurred together to increase the merits of the Child-God in the bosom of His mother: on the one hand, His soul was enlightened with the purest light, and His will with the utmost energy tended towards good; on the other hand, His humanity, raised by grace to the highest degree of holiness, was hypostatically united to increased holiness, and His soul, although in a glorious state, was capable of suffering in a passable and mortal body. With so much aptitude for meriting, and in such favorable conditions, the Incarnate Word did not lose a moment, He began to merit at the very moment that He began to live; He continued with incessant ardor to merit always more and more, and of all His actions there was not one which was not infinitely holy, there was also not a single one which was not infinitely meritorious. He merits in His prayer, He merits in His repose, and even in His sleep; He merits by every good thought, every pious sentiment or good desire: and this life of merit was only the prelude of the merits which He will continue to accumulate from His birth down to His death, and at every moment of His existence, meriting thereby the salvation of the world, heaven for the elect, grace for all. In presence of so many merits, let us regret the many opportunities of meriting which we have allowed to slip by, so many actions which we have performed mechanically without reflection, or from purely natural motives, so much time lost, so many graces rendered fruitless; and let us propose to ourselves to repair all these losses: First, by henceforth seizing every opportunity of meriting, and never refusing God any sacrifices, whether they be little or great, which His grace may demand from us; second, by performing all our actions from love; third, by suffering cheerfully all crosses; fourth, by never losing our time.

SECOND POINT
✝ The Share which Jesus Christ gives us of His Merits

All the merits amassed by Jesus Christ are ours: He transmits them to us as an inheritance or a patrimony, for all the possessions of the father of a family are the patrimony of his children; and He says to us what He said to His Father: "All My things are thine, and Thine are Mine." (John 17:10) "Amen, I say to you, if you ask the Father anything in My name" that is to say, in the name of My merits, "He will give it you." (John 6:23). It was by virtue of these foreseen merits that the Blessed Virgin was preserved from original sin, and conceived wholly pure; that the saints of the Old Testament received all their graces; it was by virtue of these acquired merits that the saints of the New Testament were and still are every day sanctified; that the Church triumphs over so many trials, and that the whole of society receives so many graces. We are free to benefit at our pleasure by this inexhaustible treasure; prayer is the key which opens it to all; the sacraments are the channel by which this immense ocean pours its spiritual riches upon our souls. If we confide in ourselves we are worth nothing, and can do nothing; we remain in our poverty and misery; but if we confide in Jesus Christ, if we but say to Him with humility and confidence: "Lord, I only ask Thee for one drop of Thy blood, one tear from Thine eyes, one sigh of Thy heart; I shall be rich if Thou dost deign to apply to me the merit of it," our confidence will not be deceived, either during life or at death, and we shall be saved. *Resolutions and spiritual nosegay as above.*

Friday in the Fourth Week of Advent

SUMMARY OF TOMORROW'S MEDITATION

After having meditated on the life of Jesus in Mary, we will meditate tomorrow on the life of Mary united to Jesus, and we shall see that it was a life: First, wholly interior; second, entirely of love; third, wholly of imitation. We will then make the resolution: First, to watch over our soul and not allow it to be occupied with outward things which will tend to dissipate it, such as idle news, frivolous conversations, vain amusements, useless thoughts; second, to unite ourselves often to God by acts of love and by applying ourselves to imitate Jesus Christ. Our spiritual nosegay shall be the words of Mary: "My spirit hath rejoiced in God my Savior." (Luke 1:47)

MEDITATION FOR THE MORNING

Let us adore the Incarnate Word residing in Mary as in His tabernacle. Let us unite ourselves to the angels, who adore Him there; let us unite ourselves still more closely to Mary, who better than all the angels put together offers Him her praises with her love, and honors Him by the most holy life that has ever been led and that ever will be led by a pure creature.

FIRST POINT
✝ The Life of Mary United to Jesus was a wholly Interior Life

Man, here below, has to choose between two kinds of life the exterior and the interior life. The first is one wholly outward, spent in perpetual dissipation, which is nourished at one time by serious affairs, grave interests, the course of events; at another time by curiosity for idle news, frivolous conversations, vain amusements, unprofitable reading. The second, shut up within the soul, occupies itself with its sanctification, with the perfection of its ordinary occupations, and attaches more value to an act of love to God than to all earthly treasures. The Blessed Virgin, possessing the Incarnate Word in her womb, did not hesitate between these two kinds of life. What did the world signify to her with its dissipation, its foolish joys, its preoccupations with perishable things? God, whom she bore within her, was everything to her soul, and all the rest was nothing (Imit.). If it be true that the heart of man is there where his treasure is, the heart of Mary could be nowhere but in Jesus, because Jesus was really and in truth her treasure, her riches, her joy, and her all. The whole of her happiness consisted in thinking of Jesus, in loving Jesus, in pleasing Jesus, and she lived more in this dear Son than in herself. Oh, how poor and miserable the world appeared to her; how unworthy of occupying an immortal spirit, of attaching a heart created for the Infinite, and which nothing could satisfy except infinite good! And I, where am I with regard to this interior life, this life of the presence of God? God is with me by His immensity which fills all, by His providence which governs all, by His love which follows me everywhere; and I am so rarely with Him, I so often forget Him who never forgets me! I take my pleasure in thinking of everything else, in earthly frivolities, often even in vain imaginations; recollection seems to me to be a burden and without attraction; and I do not love to keep myself in the secret of my heart, in the company of God, who is the delight of Paradise. Oh, when will God alone be everything for my heart and when, content with Him alone, shall I be wholly His, only His?

SECOND POINT
✝ The Life of Mary in Jesus was a Life wholly of Love

The interior life of Mary embraced in an eminent manner the practice of all the virtues in their most perfect degree, but at the same time love was the dominating sentiment. If nothing be comparable to the love of a mother for her child, who can have any idea of the height to which Mary ascended in her maternal love for a Son so amiable, the most beautiful among the children of men (Ps. 44:3), for a Son in whom were united all the perfections proper to human nature and the infinite perfections of the Divinity which kept the angels in heaven in a state of perpetual ecstasy? It was a love continually new, produced by the ever new admiration with which she was inspired at the sight of such greatness reduced to so low a point, of so much loftiness abased, of so much immensity restricted by a marvel of charity, of which her heart was the scene. It was a love borrowing its flame from the very focus itself of divine love, which caused the Incarnate Word to descend from amidst the splendors of the saints into her poor soul, and which, consequently, surpassed incomparably all other kinds of love, even though it were the love of the seraphim and the most burning of the cherubim. It was a practical love, which gave up the whole of her person and the whole of her faculties to the guidance of her beloved Son, and that to such an extent as to allow herself to be ruled by Him in all her acts, in all her words, in all her thoughts, and all her sentiments. Jesus spoke to her heart, inspired her with all His designs; and Mary, attentively listening, was not less prompt to obey and generous to execute. O holy life, perfect life, life of the complete reign of divine love in a soul! How far am I from leading this life of love! It is indeed high time for me to endeavor henceforth to lead it, and at least to approach it as nearly as possible.

THIRD POINT
✝ The Life of Mary in Jesus was a Life wholly of Imitation

Amongst the marvels which Mary contemplated in the Word Incarnate she studied above all those which she could imitate; for she knew that one of the principal ends of the descent of the Divine Word upon earth was to offer to men the model of a perfect life, and that Jesus loves nothing better than to see Himself living again in men. To resemble Jesus was therefore all her ambition; to be humble like Him, poor and mortified like Him, gentle and loving like Him, was the subject of her continual aspirations. She questioned Him within herself; asked Him what He would do, what He would say, what He would think in the different circumstances in which she found herself; and the Divine Child made her to hear the answer in the bottom of her heart, and she strove to act, to speak, to think like this adorable model of all the elect. Thus Mary acted, and thus ought we ourselves to act. Do we do so? *Resolutions and spiritual nosegay as above.*

December 25th - Christmas

THE GOSPEL ACCORDING TO ST. LUKE 2:1-14.

"And it came to pass that in those days there went out a decree from Caesar Augustus, that the whole world should be enrolled. This enrolling was first made by Cyrinus, the Governor of Syria. And all went to be enrolled, every one into his own city. And Joseph also went up from Galilee out of the city of Nazareth into Judea, to the city of David, which is called Bethlehem, because he was of the house and family of David, to be enrolled with Mary, his espoused wife, who was with child. And it came to pass that when they were there, her days were accomplished that she should be delivered. And she brought forth her first-born Son, and wrapped Him up in swaddling clothes, and laid Him in a manger: because there was no room for them in the inn. And there were in the same country shepherds watching and keeping the night-watches over their flock. And behold an angel of the Lord stood by them, and the brightness of God shone roundabout them, and they feared with a great fear. And the angel said to them: Fear not, for behold I bring you good tidings of great joy, that shall be to all the people: for this day is born to you a Savior, who is Christ the Lord, in the city of David. And this shall be a sign unto you. You shall find the Infant wrapped in swaddling-clothes, and laid in a manger. And suddenly there was with the angel a multitude of the heavenly army, praising God and saying: Glory to God in the highest: and on earth peace to men of goodwill."

THE GOSPEL ACCORDING TO ST. LUKE 2:15-20.

"And it came to pass, after the angels departed from them into heaven, the shepherds said one to another: Let us go over to Bethlehem, and let us see this word that is come to pass, which the Lord hath showed to us. And they came with haste: and they found Mary and Joseph, and the Infant lying in the manger. And seeing, they understood of the word that had been spoken to them concerning this Child. And all that heard wondered:

and at those things that were told them by the shepherds. But Mary kept all these words, pondering them in her heart. And the shepherds returned, glorifying and praising God, for all the things they had heard, and seen, as it was told unto them."

SUMMARY OF TOMORROW'S MEDITATION

e will meditate tomorrow on the mystery of the day, and we will consider Jesus Christ in the crib: First, as our Savior; second, as our Master; third, as the delight of our hearts. We will then make the resolution: First, to keep ourselves often in spirit, during this holy day, on our knees before the crib, between Mary and Joseph, as between two cherubims, in order there to render our homage to the newborn Child, and to dedicate ourselves forever to His service; second, to honor His sufferings by the cheerful endurance of all the discomforts of the season, His nakedness by our love of poverty, His humiliation by taking care to say or do nothing from self-love. Our spiritual nosegay shall be the words of St. Bernard: "The more He humiliates Himself for me, the more I love Him."

MEDITATION FOR THE MORNING

Let us transport ourselves in thought to Bethlehem, in the society of Mary, who seeks a shelter wherein to give birth to the Word Incarnate, and finds nothing but a stable (John 1:2).

FIRST POINT
✝ Jesus at His Birth Shows Himself to be our Savior

During the space of four thousand years, the world had awaited the Savior, the patriarchs and prophets had called for him by their sighs and their tears; for if He had not come we should all of us have been lost. He descends at last to His crib, and there His first care is to save us by satisfying for our sins (Luke 2:14). If, in His little cradle, He raises His little hands to heaven, it is in order to soften the justice of His Father; if He sheds tears, it is in order to wash away our stains, and extinguish the fire of divine anger; if He utters sobs, it is in order to call down the divine mercy upon us. His voice is heard. O admirable spectacle! Jesus is in the crib, satisfying for us, and God is in Jesus accepting these satisfactions in payment of our debts. Jesus is in the crib, poor and humiliated, and God is in Jesus accepting these humiliations and this poverty in expiation of our pride and our love of riches. Jesus is in the crib, suffering, gentle, obedient, and God is in Jesus, accepting these sufferings, this gentleness, this obedience, in expiation of our pleasures, of our impatience, and of our rebellions (2 Cor. 5:19). It is thus that from His first entrance into the world the Man-God hastens to suffer and to perform penance in our stead. O first tears that my Savior shed over my sins, I adore and revere you; first cries that He made His Father listen to for me, as the prelude of that great cry by which He Was destined, at His death, to consummate His sacrifice and our redemption, may you re sound in the very bottom of my soul, touch it, move it, and make me take my salvation more to heart!

SECOND POINT

✞ Jesus at His Birth Shows Himself to be our Master (Tit.2:11-12)

The wisest philosophers of Athens and of Rome only stammer in comparison with this Divine Child, and their most erudite lessons become pale in presence of the crib. There Jesus preaches wisdom, not by words, but by deeds (St. Bern., de Nativ.). He who could have procured for Himself all the enjoyments of life feeds Himself with His tears, reposes upon a board, trembles with cold, and yields His delicate limbs, so sensible to impressions of suffering, especially at that age, to the severity of the season. It is thus that He teaches us not to humor our senses, not to seek our ease; not to flatter our sensuality and our tastes, and not to be impatient at privations. He who, as master of heaven and earth, could have been born in the bosom of opulence is born in extreme poverty, during the difficulties of a journey, where those who are able to take the most precautions still need many things, in the midst of the night, in an abandoned stable. It is thus that He teaches us not to be so greedy after riches; to tear out of our heart the passion for amassing, the cause of so much injustice. Lastly, He, the King of glory, humbles Himself to the lowest degree of humiliation, and seems to find it difficult to discover a place low enough for Him to make His entrance into the world. He thus teaches us not to allow ourselves to be led astray by the desire to be honored and esteemed, by the wish to make an appearance, and to accept scorn and contempt when they present themselves. O Jesus, how admirable are Thy lessons! Who, in presence of Thy crib, could wish for pleasure, riches, or glory?

THIRD POINT

✞ Jesus at His Birth Shows Himself to be the Delight of our Heart (Tit. 3:4)

When I contemplate, said St. Bernard, the Son of God in the bosom of His Father, I am seized with respect, and I tremble with astonishment in presence of His incomparable majesty; but when I see Him in the crib I cannot fear Him, I can only love Him (St. Bern., de Nativ.). I love Him concealing the majesty which alarms, veiling the glory which dazzles, abasing the loftiness which astonishes, in order to allow only love which attracts to appear, and the goodness which takes possession of us. It is a little newborn Child; who shall be afraid? (Luke 2:10). We have only to draw near to Him and to love; to approach Him and to be touched. The tears of a little forsaken child, even if he were a stranger and un known, would touch our hearts; how much more, then, ought we to be moved at the sight of this Child God, the tender victim which surfers and weeps in our stead, which stretches forth lovingly His little hands to ask us for our heart, and to say to us with His eyes, as He is unable to speak, "My son, give me thy heart." (Prov. 13 26) Who is there that would dare, by his baseness and lukewarmness, to grieve this Divine Child, and draw from His innocent eyes fresh tears? Ah, rather let us go to the altar to receive Him with the utmost love; let us press Him to our breast, pray to Him to come and be born in us, and make of our heart His cradle. From the altar as from the crib we can say, "In His littleness how amiable He is! " And yet in what manner have we loved Him up to the present? How do we love Him now? O my heart, love at last a God so amiable; breathe nothing now but love for the God of the crib, and may the great feast of Christmas inaugurate in thee a life full of love. *Resolutions and spiritual nosegay as above.*

December 26th

SUMMARY OF TOMORROW'S MEDITATION

e will tomorrow honor St. Stephen, teaching us, first, love of our neighbor; second, zeal for the salvation of souls, which is love to our neighbor in its highest sense; third, Christian fortitude based upon hope. We will then make the resolution: First, to pardon our neighbor all his offences against us, and always to render good for evil; second, to labor with all our strength for the salvation of our brethren; third, often to raise our courage in the midst of trials by the hope of heaven. Our spiritual nosegay shall be the words of St. Stephen: "I see the heavens opened and the Son of Man standing on the right hand of God." (Acts 7:55)

MEDITATION FOR THE MORNING

Let us adore the Son of God in two very different states: infinitely abased in the crib, wherein the whole of this octave presents Him to us, and sovereignly raised in glory in heaven, where St. Stephen, whose feast it is today, beheld Him. These two states recall to us the order of things established by God: that is to say, that we must suffer upon earth with Jesus Christ, that we may rejoice in heaven with Him; combat here below. In order to triumph in the kingdom above; humble ourselves in this world, in order to be exalted in the world to come. Let us thank the Incarnate Word for this admirable economy of His Providence, and let us pray to Him to impress it deeply on our souls.

FIRST POINT
✝ St. Stephen Teaches us to Love our Neighbor

Let us heartily admire St. Stephen, tenderly loving all men, and, above all, those of whom he had to complain the most, those who had persecuted him and who had sworn to kill him. Far from bearing them malice, far from being enraged against them or desirous to revenge himself, he loves them with his whole soul, and if he reproves them it is only in order to make them better. If for all reply to his discourse they stone him, he continues to love them; he prays for those, who are killing him, he prays on his knees, begging forgiveness, grace, and mercy for them: "Lord, lay not this sin to their charge." (Acts 7:59) and by the fervor of his prayer he obtained the conversion of Saul, and merits that his persecutor on earth should be his companion in glory in heaven. It is thus that he meets injuries with benefits, hatred with charity, anger with sweetness, malice with loving kindness, and that he puts in practice the maxim of his Master: "Pray for them that persecute you, do good to them that hate you" (Matt 5:44). May this beautiful pattern teach us in admirable manner not only never to allow ourselves to yield to aversion, to bitterness, to annoyances, but to pardon all injuries, to bear with all defects, to render good for evil, and to show ourselves in all circumstances gracious and amiable to all without exception.

SECOND POINT
✝ St. Stephen Teaches us Zeal for the Salvation of Souls

It was not enough for St. Stephen to love his enemies; he thirsts for them, he will at all costs gain them over to Jesus Christ and save them. In order to do so, he preaches to them, with all the vehemence of zeal and the authority of miracles, the divinity of Jesus Christ whom they have crucified (Acts 6:8). They do not give heed to his words; he is not discouraged, and confounds his adversaries, who cannot resist the spirit of wisdom which speaks by his mouth (Acts 6:10). Men falsely zealous for the law, uniting themselves with doctors and the princes of the nation, raise up the people against him; they accuse him of blasphemy at the supreme tribunal of the Jews, uttering cries of rage and calling for his death; and these false witnesses denounce him as sinning against the temple and the law of Moses. Stephen, happy at meeting with so favorable an opportunity for preaching Jesus Christ, presents himself before his judges with a modest exterior which reveals him to be in his person rather an angel of heaven than a mortal man (Acts 6:15). Then beginning to speak, he establishes by the Holy Scripture the divinity of the Savior Jesus. He receives no other answer from his judges than the furious anger of self-love cut to the heart (Acts 7:54); they utter great cries, they stop their ears, so that they may not hear him (Acts 7:56); they throw themselves upon him, they cast him out of the city in order to stone him, and the holy deacon does not cease to preach to them until he has ceased to live. Can there be zeal for souls more admirable, more intrepid, more generous? Alas! What relation is there between us and the holy preacher. We behold souls being lost, and we are so little touched, and we do so little to save them! Let us at last kindle the sacred fire of zeal within us.

THIRD POINT
✝ St. Stephen Teaches us Christian Strength Based upon Hope

Our present life is nothing but a continual martyrdom: a martyrdom of the body through infirmities and sickness, a martyrdom of the soul through the deceptions of self-love, losses and reverses, ill-will and hatred, weariness and disgust. Let us learn from our holy deacon to have Christian strength, which, founded upon hope, is invincible in face of all trials. St. Stephen under the rain of stones cast on him by his enemies raises his eyes to heaven; he there sees the glory of God into which he is about to enter; the glory of Jesus Christ who is about to crown him; and triumphs delightedly and is thrilled with joy at the sight. "I see" he says, "the heavens opened and the Son of Man standing on the right hand of God." (Acts 7:55). With such a spectacle before him, death seemed to be happiness. Exhausted by loss of blood and ready to expire, he yields his soul with joy into the arms of Jesus Christ, who introduces him into Paradise (Acts 7:58). Thus is accomplished the oracle of the Holy Spirit so well suited to sustain us under trial: A little patience and in return happiness (Ecclus. 1:29). How is it with us in regard to Christian strength founded upon hope? We are cowardly under trial; the least suffering discourages and casts us down. One glance of faith directed to heaven will render us strong, and we shall be invincible. *Resolutions and spiritual nosegay as above.*

December 27th

SUMMARY OF TOMORROW'S MEDITATION

n our next meditation we will learn from St. John: First, to love Jesus Christ; second, to love our neighbor; third, specially to love the Blessed Virgin. We will then make the resolution: First, to perform all our actions from love to God; second, to love our neighbor with the generous love which bears and pardons; third, to reanimate our love towards the Blessed Virgin. Our spiritual nosegay shall be the title which St. John gave to himself: "He was the disciple whom Jesus loved." (John 13:23)

MEDITATION FOR THE MORNING

Let us adore Jesus Christ, loving St. John with a love of predilection, and in return beloved by St. John with an incomparable affection. Let us also honor Mary as the adopted mother of St. John; and let us congratulate this happy disciple to have had such tender and intimate relations with Jesus and Mary.

FIRST POINT

✝ St. John Teaches its to Love Jesus Christ

First, he offers to us in his whole life one of the most beautiful examples of this love. If he writes his Gospel, we feel when reading it that it is love which has held the pen: each page breathes nothing but love. If he writes his Epistles, charity itself seems to have dictated them; they may be summed up in these words: let us love God, let us love Jesus, let us love our neighbor. If he composes his Apocalypse, love overflows it on every side and inspires it down to the last line, which is a sigh of love: "Come, Lord Jesus" (Apoc. 22:20). His acts as well as his writings are nothing but inspirations of his love. To this love is due within his beautiful soul innocence of life and simplicity of manners, and in his exterior candor and modesty, within, a virginal purity which is the delight of Jesus, the true friend of virgins, the king of virgins; in his exterior life, evangelizing travels, first through the cities of Israel and the fields of Samaria, then after Pentecost, across Asia, where he founds churches, consecrates bishops, combats heretics, and when the frosts of old age prevent him from walking he has himself carried to church to preach love and to say to the faithful, "My little children, love one another." His love, superior to all fear, had led him on the night of the Passion into the midst of the raging people to seek there his beloved, and the very day of the Passion to the foot of the cross, there to console Jesus, if he could not defend Him; but after the death of Jesus love made him brave exile, and martyrdom, and boiling oil, and the fury of tyrants. Could there be a more fervent love? Alas! What is ours in comparison? Let us rouse ourselves and excite ourselves to love this amiable Jesus. Second, St. John exhibits in his life the great blessings which love procures for him who loves. We see by him that he who loves Jesus is sure to be loved in the same proportion. Because St. John loved much, Jesus heaps upon him all the favors of which He gave the others only a share: He makes him at one and the same time an apostle, an evangelist, a bishop, a doctor, a martyr, a confessor, a virgin, a patriarch, and a founder of the churches in Asia; at the Last Supper He receives him upon His heart, and He inundates him with treasures of holiness and of light; he raises his eyes up to the bosom of the Father, there to contemplate the generation of the Word, and there to write his Gospel, there to read in the future and behold the triumphs of the Church and its trials, the fall of idolatry, and the events of the latter days. Oh, how good it is to love Jesus, and how magnificently He recompenses those who love Him! O my soul, open thyself to the love of Jesus, and henceforth live only to love Him!

SECOND POINT
✝ St. John Teaches us to Love our Neighbor

The other Evangelists only indicated the precept of charity, to St. John it was given to develop it in all its beauty. It is he who teaches us that evangelical charity is a really new commandment, because of the perfection to which it ought to rise (John 13:34); that it is the distinctive character of the Christian (Ibid. 35); that it ought to be modeled upon the very love itself which Jesus Christ felt for men to the extent of forgiving all wrongs and meeting ingratitude and coldness with nothing but love (Ibid 34); that it ought to take its model higher still, in the union of the three Divine Persons amongst themselves (John 7:22). Such is the sublime doctrine which he preaches all his life long; and when the weakness of age does not allow him to deliver long discourses, he knows how to repeat in the assembly of the faithful: "My little children, love one another." But wherefore always repeat to us the same words? He was asked. Because, he replied, such is the precept of the Savior, and if we observe it, that suffices (St. Jerome, in Epist. ad Galatas). Is it thus that we understand charity?

THIRD POINT
✝ St. John Teaches us to Love the Blessed Virgin

He did indeed love her as the mother of Jesus; this title was all sufficient for the disciple whom Jesus loved; but he also loved her as his own mother, given as a legacy to his love by the dying Jesus. "Behold thy mother" (John 19:27), the Divine Savior had said to him. And on account of this double title he felt towards her all that nature puts of what is most loving into the heart of a son, and all that grace, from which he held this sonship, can add to nature. He was her guardian angel, her consoler, her support, her refuge. After the death of the Savior, he received this afflicted widow, this desolate mother, into his house, he lavished on her his services and his tenderness, and as long as she lived he provided for all her wants. Oh, how profitable for St. John were these good offices which he performed for Mary! What benefit to his soul he received from the holy examples of piety, of humility, of gentleness, of modesty, and charity which he had constantly before his eyes, in his heavenly intercourse with the mother of a God, in the good counsels, the touching exhortations which he received from her, and above all in the prayers by which she drew down blessings from heaven upon him and upon the whole of his apostolic labors! Oh, how good it is to love Mary, to be wholly devoted to her, and how many graces are attached to this devotion! Do we thoroughly understand it, and do we endeavor every day to increase in our love for Mary? *Resolutions and spiritual nosegay as above.*

December 28th

SUMMARY OF TOMORROW'S MEDITATION

We will consider tomorrow in our meditation: First, what happiness it was for the Holy Innocents to die for Jesus Christ; second, what happiness it is for every Christian to suffer, although he be innocent. We will then make the resolution: First, to esteem the troubles of this present life as the guarantee of happiness to come and cheerfully to accept such a portion of the cross as it shall please God to send us; second, often to recall to ourselves the words of the Apostle: "For that which is at present momentary and light of our tribulation, worketh for us above measure exceedingly an eternal weight of glory" (2 Cor. 4:17). Our spiritual nosegay shall be the words of St. Peter: "If you suffer anything for justice sake, blessed are ye." (1 Pet 3:14)

MEDITATION FOR THE MORNING

Let us adore Jesus Christ who came into the world to save us, and pursued by the world which desires to put Him to death. What a contrast of good and evil! Let us bless Him for this goodness; let us ask pardon of Him for this malice, and let us say with a loving and humble heart: How good God is, and how worthless is man!

FIRST POINT

✝ What Happiness it was for the Holy Innocents to Die for Jesus Christ

First, to die in place of Jesus Christ, to shed their blood in order that His might be spared to who is there that does not comprehend all the glory which accrued thereby to the Holy Innocents, and with how much honor they would be received by the just of the Old Law, when they went to announce to them the coming of the Messias, awaited so long? Second, to give testimony to Jesus Christ, not by words, but by blood, as the Church says; above all, to be the first to render Him this testimony; the first in the career of martyrs; the first victims immolated like tender lambs, to celebrate the birth of the Lamb without spot, who had come to wipe away the sins of the world; the first flowers of the harvest of martyrs, the first-born of the Church which the Savior had come to found who can understand so much happiness? Second, to triumph over the world before having known it, to have received life only to sacrifice it, and to conquer, so soon after their birth, a blessed immortality was not that also a great happiness? If the Holy Innocents had lived longer, perhaps, instead of being numbered amongst the blessed, they would have been among those who crucified Our Lord, and who were afterwards eternally damned. Their mothers, who knew nothing of this mystery of grace, were inconsolable. Thus do we act ourselves, in certain circumstances which are, however, only the effects of divine mercy. Let us learn from hence to abandon ourselves with confidence and love to Providence, who, knowing better than we do what is best, knows how to draw good out of what seems to us to be evil, and disposes everything for the greatest good of His elect.

SECOND POINT

✝ What Happiness it is to Suffer, being Innocent

When, in a life which is without reproach, we suffer with calmness and resignation, we share in the happiness of the Holy Innocents; we attest, not only our faith in Jesus Christ, the head and model of suffering souls, but also the power of His grace, which sustains human weakness under the weight of the cross; the excellence of the religion which alone makes strong and great souls; the magnificence of our hopes beyond the tomb; lastly the truth of those evangelical doctrines which the world has so much difficulty in believing: "Blessed are they that suffer;" (Matt. 4:10)

"Blessed are they that mourn;" (Ibid. 5) "If you partake of the sufferings of Christ, rejoice;" (1 Pet. 4:13) "That which is of the honor, glory, and power of God rests upon you." (Ibid 14). It is by suffering whilst innocent that the Holy Innocents obtained eternal happiness, and no Christian can obtain it otherwise. To be innocent and to suffer is the character of the predestinate; it is the guarantee of the love which God bears the soul, and the measure of the happiness which He destines for it in Paradise; it is the most perfect feature of resemblance to Jesus Christ, and the surest guarantee of heaven. Oh, how we deceive ourselves, then, when we hate or fly from suffering, when we look upon it as being an abandonment by God, or when we bear it with an ill grace, which takes from it all its merit. Is not this our history, and do we not too often fall into this error? *Resolutions and spiritual nosegay as above.*

December 29th

SUMMARY OF TOMORROW'S MEDITATION

We will meditate tomorrow upon the angels at the crib, and we will consider: First, the homage which they render to the Child-God; second, their zeal in drawing others thither; third, the song which they chant in His praise. We will then make the resolution: first, often during the day to bless, in union with the angels, the Child-God, the heavenly Father who gave Him to us, and the Holy Spirit who formed Him, lovingly repeating, "Glory to God in the highest." (Luke 2:14) Second, to do all we can to love and to cause others to love a God so loving, so amiable, and to perform all our actions with a view to pleasing Him. Our spiritual nosegay shall be the chant of the Church: "Glory to God in the highest!"

MEDITATION FOR THE MORNING

Let us transport ourselves in spirit before the poor crib of Bethlehem, in which is laid the treasure of heaven, the ransom of the world, the joy of men and of angels. Humbly prostrate at the feet of the amiable Child, let us adore Him as our God; let us offer Him all that we have and all that we are; let us give up ourselves wholly to Him, and let us pour forth in His presence all the love of which our heart is capable. Ashamed at being able to offer Him so little, let us rejoice at the homage rendered to Him by the angels.

FIRST POINT
✝ The Homage which the Angels Render to the Child-God

How beautiful was the stable at Bethlehem at the moment in which the Infant Jesus was born! It shone with a splendor more beautiful than that of any palace; it became a paradise. Docile to the order given them by the heavenly Father (Heb. 1:6), the angels descended there immediately, to adore their Savior and their King under the form of a little child! The more they see their great God abased, the more they adore Him and recognize His infinite grandeur under the veil of so much abasement; they confess that in comparison with His perfections their light is but darkness, their strength only weakness, their virtues only defects, and in addition that all the excellencies of nature, of grace, and of glory which are in them come from His munificence: it is a gift for which they are indebted to Him. They thank Him for it with a heart full of gratitude, and they proclaim that to Him alone belongs all honor and all glory, all praise and all benediction in time and in eternity. Let us rejoice at this homage rendered to the Infant Jesus; let us desire to have the hearts of the seraphim in order to honor Him in the same manner, and may the angels at the crib be the pattern of our adoration in church, during prayer, everywhere.

SECOND POINT
✝ The Zeal of the Angels in attracting Adorers to Jesus Christ

The heavenly spirits do not limit themselves to love the newborn Infant; they burn with the desire to make Him loved. It is not enough for them alone to enjoy the mystery of the crib, they long that it should be enjoyed by man also; and in consequence they wing their way towards the shepherds, who, at half a league's distance from Bethlehem, watch over their flocks. Gabriel, appearing in the air, in a human form, from out the midst of a dazzling light, which fills them with terror, says to them: Fear nothing, I bring you glad tidings which shall be an occasion of great joy to all the people; for this day is born to you a Savior, in the city of David. And this is the sign whereby you shall know Him: you will find a child, wrapped in swaddling-clothes lying in a manger (Luke 2:10-12). As soon as the heavenly messenger had ceased speaking, a great host of angels joined themselves with him and made the air resound with the praises of the Child-God. It is thus that when we love God we have it at heart to make Him loved by others. Where there is no zeal there is no love, but where there is great zeal there is great love. Let us judge ourselves by these rules.

THIRD POINT
✝ Song of the Angels at the Birth of the Savior

Glory to God in the highest, and on earth peace to men of good will," thus the angels sang; let us meditate upon their song. "Glory to God" that is to say: may God be glorified by the angels in heaven, for the Incarnation of the Word which procures for Him infinite glory. May God be glorified by men on earth, for the abasement of this same Word, who abases Himself only in order to exalt God and procure His glory by saving men. May God be glorified in all our acts, in all our projects, in all our intentions; and may we never have any other aim. May God be glorified at the expense of our own abjection, at the expense of all sufferings and of all privations. "Peace on earth to men of good will," the angels added, that is to say: peace with God, in virtue of the merits of Jesus Christ; for although the treaty of peace will have, later on, to be signed with His blood, and sealed with the seal of His cross, the acceptance of it is given from today; peace with our neighbor, by the spirit of charity and meekness which the cross preaches; peace for each individual with himself, through purity of conscience and the calm of an irreproachable heart, the fruits of the birth of the Savior; a triple peace, but only for men of goodwill; that is to say, for those who, loving God frankly, are ready to make Him all the sacrifices which duty demands. Let us examine ourselves and see whether we are of this number. *Resolutions and spiritual nosegay as above.*

December 30th

SUMMARY OF TOMORROW'S MEDITATION

e will meditate tomorrow upon the shepherds at the crib, and we shall see: First, the appeal which Jesus Christ made to them at the crib; second, the manner in which they replied to this call. We will then make the resolution: First, to esteem poverty more than we have ever done before, together with simplicity and all the duties belonging to our state; second, to bring to our prayers more respect and more love; third, promptly to obey the inspirations of grace. Our spiritual nosegay shall be: "Let us go over to Bethlehem and let us see this word that is come to pass which the Lord hath showed to us." (Luke 2:15)

MEDITATION FOR THE MORNING

Let us adore Jesus Christ in the crib, surrounded by the shepherds, who, prostrate at His feet, offer Him their most fervent homage. Let us unite our hearts with theirs, and let us pour forth before this Incarnate God all the sentiments of gratitude and love of which we are capable.

FIRST POINT

✝ The Appeal which Jesus Christ made to the Shepherds at the Crib

Here two questions present themselves to our meditation: wherefore and how did Jesus Christ call them? First question: Wherefore? First, because the shepherds are poor: Our Saviour desires to testify how little He esteems riches and greatness, which are often nothing more than the price of injustice and baseness, the food of ambition, the aliment of cupidity, the triumph of pride, and how He prefers to them poverty, as being more favorable to humility, to moderation in our desires, to meekness, to all the virtues. Second, because they are simple and upright souls, and such souls are dear to Him. (Prov. 3:32) Third, because they are laborious men who, not content with working during the day, watch also during the night: God hates the idle who lose their time. Fourth, because they are men who apply themselves to the duties of their state: God wills that each one should fulfill the duties of the state in which he is placed on earth. Let us examine ourselves, and see whether we bear in ourselves these four characters, which were the means of obtaining so much happiness for the shepherds: are we poor in heart, perfectly detached from the goods of this world? Are we simple and upright, without any other desire in this world than that of pleasing God? Do we love work, and are we careful not to lose our time? Are we diligent in performing the duties incumbent on us, and do we watch night and day over those who are confided to us by God? Second question: How did Jesus Christ call the shepherds? He surrounded them with a dazzling light which impressed them with a religious fear, because a profound respect, seizing the soul with fear before the divine majesty, is always the commencement of the operations of God in a soul. To fear He makes joy succeed. "Fear not" the angel said to them, "for behold I bring you good tidings of great joy! For this day is born to you a Saviour". (Luke 2:10) All other joy would be but vanity, but the coming of so good a Saviour is a subject for holy joy. Have we this respect for God and this joy in God?

SECOND POINT

✝ Manner in which the Shepherds Responded to the Call of the Savior

First, they answered it with promptitude. Hardly had the angels announced to them the good tidings, than they cried, "Let us go over to Bethlehem, and let us see this word." (Luke 2:15) And they left their flocks there, and they themselves set out at once, inspite of its being night. Oh, why are we not as prompt in following the inspirations of grace, which like so many celestial messengers call us to Jesus Christ! Do we not allow these divine inspirations to grow cold by our delays, after which they die out and remain without effect? O divine inspirations return to me! I will no longer be unfaithful to you; my soul sighs after you; it opens to you its bosom, disposed to receive you with respect and love. Second, the shepherds, having arrived at Bethlehem, enter into the stable, and who could express with what faith and with what devotion? In this Child so abased they adore the great God of eternity; in His littleness they revere His humility, in His swaddling clothes His poverty, in the hardness of His couch His mortification, and these three virtues appear to them to be beautiful and glorious as being the livery of the King of kings. They admire in this Divine Infant the true treasure of heaven; they permit themselves to offer to Him little presents, in harmony with their humble condition, and their hearts give vent to and overflow with sentiments of gratitude and love. Third, after having rendered their homage the shepherds return full of holy joy, glorifying and praising God for all they had heard and seen (Luke 2:20). Thus ought we to do ourselves when we quit our meditations and communions, our visits to the Blessed Sacrament, our spiritual readings, our sermons and instructions. From each one of these services we must bring away with us an ardent desire to become better, a burning zeal to glorify God and to publish His praises, a zeal such as St. Francis Xavier possessed when he exclaimed, "Who will give me the happiness, O Lord, to die for Thee and to make Thee known and loved in every part of the universe?" *Resolutions and spiritual nosegay as above.*

December 31st

SUMMARY OF TOMORROW'S MEDITATION

We will meditate tomorrow: first, on the devotion of the Blessed Virgin at the crib; second, on the sentiments which we ought to borrow from her in order to pass, in a holy manner, the new year which is about to dawn. We will then make the resolution: first,

frankly to resolve to live a better life during the year which is drawing nigh; second, to sanctify the last day of the year by the double sentiment of gratitude and of contrition: of gratitude to God for the blessings received during this year, and of contrition for the evil we have committed. Our spiritual nosegay shall be the words of St. Augustine: "How I regret, O my God, all the days of this year in which I have loved thee."

MEDITATION FOR THE MORNING

Let us return today to the crib, the source of light, the furnace of love, the paradise of delight. Let us prostrate ourselves in spirit before the Child-God, between Mary and Joseph, and let us offer to Him, at least in spirit, all that these two first adorers of the Incarnate Word offered Him of what is most pious, most loving, most devoted.

FIRST POINT
✝ Devotion of Mary at the Crib

The devotion of Mary in these circumstances was a mixture of joy, of sorrow, of holy reflections. It was an ineffable joy for her to look at the Divine Child, to caress Him, to be caressed by Him, and to say to herself: "This is my God, my God with His infinite treasures of holiness and grace, my God with His ineffable beauty which ravishes Paradise; and this God is my Son, my only Son, mine only. He is the Savior of the world, who will convert all nations and whom all nations will adore. He is the King of Paradise, and there He keeps for me in reserve the most beautiful of thrones. He is my treasure, He is my love, He is the joy of my heart. "Oh, why have we not more faith, why do we not love more; we should then enjoy something similar in meditation, in communion, and in visiting the Blessed Sacrament. In the midst of these joys it was an inexpressible sorrow for the heart of Mary to think, when fixing her eyes on the head of this blessed Child, that the day would come when it would be crowned with thorns; when gazing on His face, that it would be bruised with blows, covered with blood and spittle; when kissing His blessed hands, that they would be pierced with nails; when wrapping Him in swaddling clothes, that He would one day wear garments of ignominy; when laying Him in His cradle, that the cross would be His death-bed. She could not see a lamb, a dove, or any of the animals offered in sacrifice, without thinking of the adorable Victim of which they were figures. She could not read the Holy Scriptures, the oracles of the prophets, the story of Abel put to death, of Isaac immolated, of Joseph sold, of David and Jeremias persecuted, of the brazen serpent, of the paschal lamb, without seeing in all these things the sufferings and the death of her dearly beloved Son, and what anguish did not her maternal heart suffer in consequence! At the same time in the midst of these sorrowful previsions which the prophetic spirit, possessed by her in a very perfect degree, rendered certain, she was calm, resigned, and desired nothing but the will of God, an admirable model of tried souls. Amidst these sorrows and joys, she nourished her piety with the most holy reflections, kept, preciously in her soul all that she heard the shepherds and angels say (Luke 2:19), and which was so edifying, and all that the Holy Spirit said to her upon so much littleness in a God so great, so much poverty in a God so rich, upon exchanging heaven for a stable, the splendor of glory for poor swaddling clothes, the eternal throne for the crib; and these considerations threw her soul into a state of ravishment, into sweet transports, into loving ecstasies. She took the Divine Child in her arms, and offered Him to the Eternal Father, saying, "Behold God, our protector, and look on the face of Thy Christ." (Ps. 83:10) May we partake of the sentiments of Mary towards the Word Incarnate.

SECOND POINT

✝ In Order to Pass in a Holy Manner from one Year to Another, we ought to Borrow from Mary the Sentiments which we have Considered in Mary.

We must rejoice, with a great feeling of gratitude, in the goodness of God who has granted us, during the year which is about to end, so many benefits in the natural order and in the order of grace. In the natural order He has preserved our life, He has guarded us from a thousand dangers, He has provided for all our wants, whilst He has not treated thousands of persons in so gracious a manner in the order of grace, what sacraments, what instructions, what good examples, what holy inspirations which He has not granted to so many others. Thanks be to God for all these benefits! Second, we must be afflicted, and we must regret that we have abused so many graces, lost and ill-employed so many moments, humored our defects so greatly, left fruitless so many means of salvation; what matter is there herein for contrition! O God, have mercy on us! Third, we must reflect seriously, what does there remain to me of the year which is about to end? There remains to me a sweet and consoling remembrance of the trouble which the good I have done cost me; the trouble is past, the remembrance endures. There remains to me a bitter remembrance of the satisfaction I have felt in my effeminate and sensual life; the satisfaction is past; but the bitter remembrance endures. There remain to me the good and the evil which I have done, and which are destined to be placed in the balance of the divine justice, the one in the scale of recompenses, the other in the scale of punishments. Which will be found wanting? If I continue to lead the same life in the new year which I have done in the old, can I hope for heaven at the end of my course? Was it by living in this manner that the saints were saved? Just God, I understand, it is imperative on me to change my life. It is done, I will be converter. (Ps. 76:11) *Resolutions and spiritual nosegay as above.*

JANUARY 1ST

THE GOSPEL ACCORDING TO ST. LUKE 2:21

"And after eight days were accomplished that the Child should be circumcised, His name was called Jesus, which was called by the angel before He was conceived in the womb."

SUMMARY OF TOMORROW'S MEDITATION

e will consider tomorrow in our meditation the circumcision of Our Lord, first, as a mystery of love; second, as a mystery of mortification. We will then make the resolution: First, to commence the new year in a spirit of love towards Jesus Christ, and to perform all our actions with a very determined intention of pleasing Him; second, cheerfully to suffer for love of Him all the crosses sent us by Providence, and to offer Him as New Year's gifts some special acts of mortification. Our spiritual nosegay shall be the words of the Scriptures: "Behold I make all things new." (Apoc. 21:5)

MEDITATION FOR THE MORNING

Let us adore Jesus Christ, granting us a new year in which to labor for our salvation, but at the same time without promising to let us see the end of it, so that we may always watch vigilantly. Let us thank Him for presenting to our piety, at the beginning of this year, the mystery of the Circumcision, as being eminently suited to make us begin it holily.

FIRST POINT

✝ The Circumcision of Our Lord is a Mystery of Love

Hardly eight days had passed since His birth, when the Divine Infant, impatient to make His blood flow in order to wash away our sins and purify our stains, said, not with His lips, for He kept them mute, but from the bottom of His heart: "And I have a baptism, wherewith I am to be baptized, and how am I straitened until it be accomplished." (Luke 12:50) In the ardor to suffer for us which consumes Him, He submits to be placed beneath the knife of circumcision; the incision is made, and the blood flows, the blood of which a single drop would have sufficed to expiate the sins of a thousand worlds, and yet on the first effusion of which He looks as being but the first fruits and the engagement of the more abundant effusion which He will make on Calvary. O Jesus, when Thou givest me so touching a proof of Thy love, could I be as ice towards Thee, or love Thee only with an idle love, lukewarm and without energy? No, it is not possible. I will then begin to love Thee with a wholly new love; with a practical love which will give life to all my works; with a strong love which nothing will repel; for nothing costs us aught when we love, or, if it costs us something, we rejoice to suffer.

SECOND POINT
✝ The Circumcision of Our Lord is a Mystery of Mortification

This mystery preaches to us at once mortification in our enjoyments, in our self-love, and in our attachments. From the first moment of His descent into the crib, the Child Jesus preached this doctrine to us by His little body trembling with cold and stretched upon straw; but today the lesson is a great deal more severe, for the suffering is far more cruel. The knife of the circumcision tears His flesh and makes His blood flow. Would it be possible for Him to speak more eloquently to the world that we can only be saved by suffering, that unhappy are those who enjoy, blessed those who suffer; that at least we ought cheerfully to bear all the crosses Providence sends us, suffer without complaining the severity of the seasons, and the contrarieties received from our neighbor, and exterior or interior troubles, and the violence which sometimes the accomplishment of duty imposes on us? At least we ought not any longer to refuse in any degree or in any manner to endure discomfort and suffering; we ought not to be constantly seeking our own ease with a delicacy little worthy of a Christian soul. Second, the mystery of the Circumcision preaches to us the sacrifice of self-will; for the Incarnate Word, by causing Himself to be circumcised, imprinted on His body the character of a slave and of a sinner: the character of a slave because it was the practice of the master to impress on the body of his slaves a mark which made their dependence and their servitude recognizable; the character of a sinner, because it recalled to mind that original sin was propagated by way of generation; that in this way the Jews were all born sinners; whence it followed that the witnesses of the ceremony could say of the Child-God: Behold a slave, behold a sinner! What a humiliation for a God! Who after that could desire to be esteemed and honored to be ambitious for glory and reputation? Third, the mystery of the Circumcision preaches to us the sacrifice of our attachments, that sacrifice which St. Paul calls the circumcision of the heart, and which is the great object of Christian morals. This circumcision of the heart has been substituted by the Gospel for the circumcision of the flesh; it consists in the retrenchment of all the ties which draw us towards the earth, towards the flesh and the senses; towards that egotistical me, a monstrous mixture of self-love and its caprices, of the temper and its brusqueness, of the character and its fits of anger, of idleness and its negligences, of our judgment and its foolhardiness. It is in this that true virtue consists, much more than in exercises of piety and frequentation of the sacraments, good and holy things as they doubtless are, but only as means for attracting grace, which gives courage to take in our hands the knife of mortification, to make the incision down to the quick, into the bad strata which all of us bear within ourselves. *Resolutions and spiritual nosegay as above.*

JANUARY 2ND

SUMMARY OF TOMORROW'S MEDITATION

e will consider in our next meditation that the name of Jesus, which was given to the Child-God the day of His circumcision, is: first, a name of greatness and majesty which commands respect: second, a name of mercy and salvation which inspires confidence; third, a name of sweetness and tenderness which calls for all our love. We will then make the resolution: first, always to pronounce this divine name with respect, and love, and often to repeat it in the manner of an aspiration; second, to pay special attention to the name of Jesus, which enters into the conclusion of all our prayers, remembering that from it our prayers derive all their value; third, not to speak of Our Lord in ordinary language by other names, such as the Christ, the Master, but to call Him by His true name (Matt. 1:21). Our spiritual nose gay shall be the words of St. Bernard: "O Jesus, be Jesus to me," that is to say, Savior.

MEDITATION FOR THE MORNING

Let us adore the Incarnate Word taking the name of Jesus on the day of His circumcision. Let us render to Him the homage of our praise, of our gratitude and our love. Let us beg Him to enable us to realize the excellence of this sacred name, which is the joy of heaven, the consolation of earth, the terror of hell.

FIRST POINT
✝ The Name of Jesus is a Name of Greatness and of Majesty which Commands Respect

O Lord my God, how admirable and great is Thy name! It is, in the opinion of St. Paul, a worthy recompense for all Thy humiliations and sufferings. On hearing it pronounced every knee should bow in heaven, on earth, in hell, and every tongue ought to confess that Thy glory is incomparable. (Philipp. 2:9) Thy name is great on account of its origin; it is from heaven that it comes to us; an angel received it from the mouth of the heavenly Father, and brought it to earth. It is great because of its signification, for it signifies Savior, that is to say, a person infinite in charity to the extent of sacrificing Himself for our salvation, and infinite in majesty, giving to this sacrifice an infinite value, alone capable of paying such a debt! It is great in heaven, where it appeases divine justice, and changes the lightnings of heaven into showers of grace. (Ps. 134:7; Jer. 51:56) It is great upon earth, where it works miracles and sanctifies the elect. It is great in hell, where it enchains the fury of the devils. It is great everywhere, and so great that it is above all names, above even the name of Jehovah, for the name of Jehovah only represents to me God as Creator of heaven and of earth; but the name of Jesus designates the Author of a better world: of a supernatural world, of the world of grace. The name of Jesus raises me high above the order of nature; it makes me behold, issuing from the bosom of the Father, an adorable Victim, ineffable sacraments, inestimable graces; it enables me to see man redeemed and sanctified, the universe repaired and changed; a Man-God, consecrated by His Father as Eternal Priest, King immortal throughout the ages; it enables me to behold in one and the same person the perfections of God and of man, grandeur joined with goodness abasing itself to my condition; mercy united with justice, meekness and divine benignity rendered visible upon earth. O Lord, may all nations confess the greatness of Thy name, because it is so holy and venerable that it makes us tremble with awe (Ps. 98:3), and has nothing in common with ordinary names, which only excite indifference and coldness in our souls.

SECOND POINT
✝ The Name of Jesus is a Name of Mercy and Salvation which Inspires Confidence

St. Paul has said: "Whosoever shall call upon the name of the Lord shall be saved;" (Acts 2:21) it is through Him that we obtain salvation; (Acts 4:12) Jesus Christ Himself said so to His apostles: My name renders prayer all powerful (John 16:23), and the Church teaches it to us by her practices. It is in the name of Jesus that she prays, that she administers the sacraments, that she blesses us from the cradle to the grave. The history of centuries confirms it; it shows to us all the miracles worked in the name of Jesus. By this name the disciples perform greater wonders than their Master; in the name of Jesus the lame walk, lepers are cured, the blind see, the deaf hear, the dumb speak, the paralytics recover the use of their limbs, death gives up its victims, heaven is opened to the sinner who is converted by this divine name. In the name of Jesus devils are put to flight; lions, forgetting their ferocity, respect the martyr who has the name of Jesus on his lips. In the name of Jesus, chains fall from the hands of the captive, the gates of prisons open, the elements obey, the raging sea is calmed, and the earth transports mountains. Oh, who would not have confidence in this divine name; who would not invoke it in time of need? "Our help is in the name of the Lord;" (Ps. 123:8) "Blessed is the man whose trust is in the name of the Lord." (Ps. 39:5) In temptations and trials, in sickness and infirmities, in anxiety and fears, it is the name of Jesus we must invoke, says St. Bernard.

THIRD POINT
✝ **The Name of Jesus is a Name of Sweetness and Tenderness which Exacts Love**

He who says "Jesus," says everything that is most amiable, most loving, most sweet, most perfect. He who says Jesus, says the most generous, the most disinterested of friends, to the extent of devoting Himself wholly for those whom He loves, the Friend who lives only for His friends, who ceaselessly watches over their interests, intercedes for them with the Father as their Mediator and Pontiff, pleads their cause by the voice of all His wounds, as their charitable advocate. The oftener we repeat Jesus, the more we find therein of charm and amiability, the more we appreciate it, and the more the heart is filled with love. Therefore the saints were never tired of repeating it, and of enjoying the savor of it. St. Paul repeats it as often as 243 times in his fourteen epistles. St. Augustine has not enough words to say what he finds of sweetness in this divine name. The sweetness of the name of Jesus, says St. Bernard, throws me into a kind of ecstasy; all is insipid to me without the name of Jesus; Jesus is honey in my mouth, melody in my ears, jubilation in my heart. Is it thus that we appreciate this divine name? Let us never pronounce it except with respect and confidence, with love and delight. *Resolutions and spiritual nosegay as above.*

January 3rd

SUMMARY OF TOMORROW'S MEDITATION

e will consider in our next meditation how the holiness of St. Genevieve was: first, eminent; second, fruitful in good works. We will then make the resolution: first, not to seek ourselves, but God alone, in our acts and our projects; second, heartily to embrace all the good works compatible with the duties of our station. Our spiritual nosegay shall be the maxim of the Holy Spirit: "The simplicity of the just shall guide them." (Prov. 11:3)

MEDITATION FOR THE MORNING

Let us adore Jesus Christ, choosing St. Genevieve, a simple and ignorant girl, weak and having no influence, a humble shepherdess belonging to the lowest ranks of society, in order to make of her a great saint, the wonder of her century, the patroness of France and of the Church. Let us praise Him for this marvel (Ps. 67:36), and let us ask of Him a share in the virtues of this saint.

FIRST POINT
✝ How Eminent was the Holiness of St. Genevieve

Two features characterize the eminent holiness of St. Genevieve: her life was a life of death to herself, and of union with God. First, was a life of death to herself. Subject to continual infirmities, she was not satisfied courageously to bear only that one cross; she added to it long fasts combined with all the austerities of penance; then all kinds of interior mortifications, bearing silently and meekly the bad treatment of an ill-tempered mistress, and, some years later on, calumnies and persecutions inflicted on her by those to whom she had done nothing but good. Second, was a life of union with God. From the age of seven, enlightened by a supernatural illumination on the excellence of Christian perfection, upon the lofty wisdom of detaching ourselves from everything in order to belong to God alone, she consulted St. Germain of Auxerre and St. Lupus of Troyes. Following their advice, she made the vow of perpetual virginity, and received from her bishop the sacred veil of religion. Thenceforth, separating herself as much as possible from inter course with her fellows, she gave herself up to pious exercises, spent in prayer a portion of her days and nights, and when not engaged in prayer she raised herself to God by means of all that met her eyes, by the aspect of the skies and of the fields, even by the sight of her flock, of which she was the shepherdess. These intimate communications with God, soon followed by raptures and ecstasies, enlightened her with such a profound knowledge of divine things that she spoke of them like an angel come down from heaven, that people came from all parts to consult her as though she were an oracle, and that the most intelligent teachers had recourse to her counsels. What admirable effects of the union of prayer with mortification! We perform our prayers so badly only because we do not mortify ourselves, and the reason of our not being mortified is because we perform our prayers so ill. Mortification, by detaching the heart from the creature, disposes it for union with God; and union with God, enabling it to comprehend that all which is not God is nothing, renders mortification easy to it. Have we, up till now, well understood this double truth: no prayer without mortification, and no mortification without prayer?

SECOND POINT

✝ How Fruitful in Good Works was the Holiness of St. Genevieve

The soul which is empty of creatures and of itself, but full of God, is precisely the instrument of which God loves to make use for great works. Let us admire in St. Genevieve the truth of this principle. The saint, burning with zeal for the glory of God and the salvation of souls, visits prisons, hospitals, the huts of the poor, consoling the afflicted, solacing the unfortunate, instructing the ignorant, converting pagans and sinners. The care of virgins and widows is confided to her; she forms them in virtue and teaches them the duties of their state. Sick people attacked by incurable maladies are brought to her: her prayers cure them. Attila, King of the Huns, besieges Paris with a formidable army: the prayer of Genevieve puts him to rout. Childeric, the father of Clovis, comes in his turn to besiege Paris; the city is about to die of famine, Genevieve sends for victuals as far as Champagne; and if she did not prevent the taking of Paris, at least she obtains from the prince many acts of clemency, and from Clovis, his son, the liberty of several prisoners. Later on, she saves the Capital from the miseries of a fresh siege, from inundations of the Seine, from conflagrations which threaten to reduce it to ashes, from war and from famine. Lastly, it is not only Paris, but Meaux, Laon, Troyes, Orleans, and Tours which are made to feel the happy effects of the gift of miracles granted to this holy soul. Her great works carry her name to the most distant regions, and from the interior of Asia St. Simon Stylites recommends himself to her prayers. After her death, her sepulcher becomes more glorious than even her life; crowds visit it from all parts, and numerous miracles are obtained there, amongst others, the cessation of the scourge styled des ardents, in 1129. Even at the present day, the devotion to her tomb is kept up, and people go there in multitudes on the day of her feast. Thus it is that God glorifies His saints who, during their life, have done great things for His glory. What do we do for this same glory? Let us examine our conscience and our life. *Resolutions and spiritual nosegay as above.*

JANUARY 4Th

SUMMARY OF TOMORROW'S MEDITATION

n order to excite ourselves to lead a better life during the new year on which we have just entered, we will consider: first, the motives, second, the means whereby to pass this year holily. We will then make the resolution: first, to endeavor more ardently to perform our ordinary actions with greater perfection; second, to attach ourselves to repairing past evils by present good, and above all every day to make war to the death against our besetting sin. Our spiritual nosegay shall be the recommendation of St. Paul: "While we have time let us work good to all men." (Gal. 6:10)

MEDITATION FOR THE MORNING

Let us adore Jesus Christ, giving us, in His goodness, another year in which to work out our sanctification and to merit a place in His paradise. Let us thank Him for this grace, and endeavor to profit by it.

FIRST POINT

✝ Motives for Spending this Year Holily

First, we have a miserable past to repair. God gave us the year that has just closed in order to employ it for our sanctification. What use have we made of it? He bestowed upon us all kinds of blessings in the natural and the spiritual order. What fruit have we drawn from them? Have we become better? Alas, how much evil committed! How much good omitted or ill-done! What an abuse of graces! Great God, when Thy justice shall put in one of the scales of Thy balance all that Thou hast done for me, and in the other all that I have done against Thee, together with the small amount of good which I have performed, I tremble lest Thou shouldst say to me as Thou didst to the King of Babylon: "Thou art weighed in the balance," (Dan. 5:27) and the weight of My grace has borne down the weight of your merits. The only resource remaining to me is to amass during the present year a superabundance of good, which shall compensate the superabundance of evil. Second, we have the present to sanctify. We shall have to render to God a strict account of all the moments of the present year. Each moment ill-employed or even only uselessly, will be brought against us. Oh, if we but knew the value of the gift of God! (John 4:10) Third, we have the future to foresee. And what more uncertain to foresee! Upon the globe about seventy-six persons die every minute, 4560 every hour, 109440 every day; nearly forty million every year. Shall I not be of this number during the year which has begun? If I but knew it, how well I would live! How I would abstain from all sin! How holily I would perform even my least important actions! How I would keep my soul always pure! My death might be sudden, but it would not be a calamity, because it would not be unforeseen. Therefore St. Antony said to his disciples: "Live each day as though it were the last of your life;" and St. Bernard recommended his disciples to do everything as if they were to die immediately afterwards.

SECOND POINT
✝ Means Whereby to Spend this Year in a Holy Manner

First, we must attach ourselves to performing our ordinary actions well, even down to the most common amongst them, which appear to be nothing in the eyes of the world; that is, to do them at the proper time and in the right manner; to perform them for God, with an ardent desire to please Him. Therein holiness consists, much more than in the extraordinary actions which, for the very reason that they are extraordinary, are rare. Second, we must always be endeavoring to live better during the present moment than during the one which preceded it. If we have done well we must strive to do still better. True virtue never says: It is enough. In this matter, not to advance is to go back. Always to advance, such is the word of command; always to rise higher, such is the rule of the just. (Ps.86:5) Third, we must study our besetting sin, and when we know it well, make war to the death against it all the year long, by means of vigilance, of examination of your conscience, of good confession, and fervent prayer. "If, every year," says the author of the Imitation, "we tear out a vice from our hearts, we shall soon be perfect." (1 Imit. 11:5) Let us be deeply penetrated with these three means for passing the year holily, and let us make a strong resolution to do so. *Resolutions and spiritual nosegay as above.*

January 5th

SUMMARY OF TOMORROW'S MEDITATION

e will meditate tomorrow upon a vice which forms one of the principal obstacles to the sanctification of the new year on which we have just, entered. This vice consists in the routine or habit of doing everything hastily and without reflection. We will consider: first, the gravity of this evil; second, its remedies. We will then make the resolution: first, to perform with great exactitude and in the best possible manner our spiritual exercises; second, to reflect before acting, in order to excite ourselves to perform everything in a very holy manner, and with the aim of pleasing God in every one of our actions. Our spiritual nosegay shall be the prayer of the Macabees: My God, give me a heart to love Thee and serve Thee as I ought. (2 Mach. 1:3)

MEDITATION FOR THE MORNING

Let us adore God, the Sovereign Lord of time, the arbitrator of our life and of our death, who gives us this new year, not that we may dispose of it after our own liking, but in order to employ every moment of it in serving Him well. Let us ask of Him grace not to fall this year into the vice which paralyzed all the preceding years; the vice of routine and want of reflection, on which Jeremias pronounced this terrible lamentation: "All the land is made desolate because there is none that considereth in the heart." (Jer. 12:1)

FIRST POINT

✝ Gravity of the Evil of Routine or Want of Reflection

What greater evil can we imagine than an evil which renders the graces of God useless, faith sterile, the reform of morals impossible? Now such is the evil of routine or want of reflection. First, it renders graces useless. God gives us the grace of prayer; but prayer performed through routine and without reflection reduces itself to a mechanical movement of the lips, incapable of honoring God or obtaining anything from man. God bestows upon us the gift of a good thought; of a pious movement, of a warning precious for our salvation. But this seed, which would have brought forth fruit if it had been ripened by reflection, is nothing but seed sown upon the high read, where vain imaginations and worldly matters tread it under foot, and cause it to perish. God grants us the grace of His sacraments; but the life of routine and want of reflection paralyzes all the fruit of it. God grants us a new year wherein to work out our salvation, but routine, unless we destroy it, will only serve to accumulate upon our heads, like a fresh anathema, a year of abuse of graces added to the preceding years. Second, routine and want of reflection render faith sterile. It is a deplorable thing to see what becomes of faith under the empire of routine. It has become nothing else within the soul but a secret portion of ourselves into which we never enter, or an obscure distance whence its light no longer reaches our eyes; so that we believe as though not believing; we speak, we act, we think, as though we did not really believe. The advance of death, the judgment which follows it, followed by paradise or hell, nothing touches us any longer. The most august mysteries of religion, the sacraments, even the Eucharist, find nothing in the soul but the coldness of marble. It is an indifference, an insensibility which nothing touches. We have familiarized ourselves with these great mysteries, we have made of them a routine: it is finished, they will be sterile for us as long as we have not cured the evil. Third, routine renders the reform of morals impossible. Carried along by it as by a river which flows always in the same bed, we never think seriously of reforming ourselves, we do not even understand the need of it, and we do not feel any energy for it. We allow ourselves to be carried along by the torrent of habits and customs; it seems to us sweeter; it even seems to us the only thing possible. In this terrible state it is as though we were asleep. Let us fear the awaking. It will be terrible!

SECOND POINT
✝ Remedies for Routine and Want of Reflection

The first remedy is prayer. Let us ask God, with all the fervor of which we are capable, to cure our sick soul (Ps. 40:5), to revive our faith (Luke 17:5), in the greatness of the Divinity, in the profound devotion due to it, and to give us grace to lead a better life during the new year. The second remedy is to be faithful to all our pious exercises, that is to say, not only to perform them with exactitude, but to perform them well, by bringing to them an attitude of recollection, a great desire to profit by them in regard to the improvement of our life, and always to treat God as God, that is to say, with sovereign respect. The third remedy is often and seriously to examine ourselves in order to see whether we still allow ourselves to indulge in our old habits of routine and want of reflection, whether our acts and our words, our intentions and our thoughts are always inspired by a spirit of faith, humility, and charity, which is the love of God that characterizes a Christian soul; and when we discover that we are falling back into our old habits, to rise promptly, setting ourselves to work with zeal and a good will. *Resolutions and spiritual nosegay as above.*

January 6th

THE GOSPEL ACCORDING TO ST. MATTHEW, 2:1-12.

"When Jesus therefore was born in Bethlehem of Juda, in the days of King Herod, behold, there came Wise Men from the East to Jerusalem, saying, Where is He that is born King of the Jews? For we have seen His star in the East, and are come to adore Him. And King Herod hearing this, was troubled, and all Jerusalem, with him. And assembling together all the chief priests and the Scribes of the people, he inquired of them where Christ should be born. But they said to him: In Bethlehem of Juda. For so it is written by the prophet: And thou Bethlehem the land of Juda, art not the least among the princes of Juda: for out of thee shall come forth the Captain that shall rule My people Israel. Then Herod, privately calling the Wise Men, learned diligently of them the time of the star which appeared to them; and sending them into Bethlehem said: Go and diligently inquire after the Child, and when you have found Him, bring me word again, that I also may come and adore Him. Who having heard the king, went their way; and behold the star which they had seen in the East went before them, until it came and stood over where the Child was. And seeing the star they rejoiced with exceeding great joy. And entering into the house they found the Child with Mary His mother, and falling down they adored Him; and opening their treasures, they offered Him gifts: gold, frankincense, and myrrh. And having received an answer in sleep that they should not return to Herod, they went back another way into their country."

SUMMARY OF TOMORROW'S MEDITATION

e will meditate tomorrow upon the vocation of the Magi, and we will consider: First, the gratuity of this vocation; second, the marvelous effects of this vocation. We will then make the resolution: first, often to thank God, during the day, by frequent outbursts of love for our vocation to the faith in the person of the Magi. Second, to lead a better life worthy of our holy vocation. We will retain as our spiritual nosegay the words of Our Lord: "You have not chosen Me, but I have chosen you." (John 15:16)

MEDITATION FOR THE MORNING

Let us transport ourselves in spirit to the stable of Bethlehem, and let us there admire the Infant Jesus, impelled by His love to communicate to the

Gentiles the blessing of His coming. A little after His birth, He sends a star to the Magi to call them to Him; He sees in them the first fruits and the vanguard of the whole of the Gentiles who will come in their train and participate in the grace of redemption; each one of us is present to His thoughts and to His love. Let us thank Him for so much goodness; let us thank Him for such love.

FIRST POINT
✝ Gratuity of the Vocation of the Magi

Happy were the Magi to have been the first to be initiated into the great secret of God respecting the vocation of the Gentiles, that is to say, of every one of us. It was the belief at that time that Judea alone enjoyed the privilege of the promises made to the Messias; by means of the vocation of the Magi it was manifest that all the nations had a share in it. (Eph. 3:4-6) Then commenced to shine forth the meaning of the magnificent announcement, which promised the empire of the world to Jerusalem, that is to say, to the Church, of which this city was the type, and which invited her to look upon all her children hastening to her from Madia and Epha. Then we might say with the Church of Paris, "Bethlehem becomes today the cradle of the new-born Church " (Hymn of the Epiphany). But whence came this happiness to the Magi? It was not from their own merits; for without faith there is no merit; besides we do not know that they had done anything more than millions of other Gentiles. Their happiness, then, had its source in the gratuitous choice of God, who, in calling them, consulted only His love and not their merits. (Rom. ix. 16) And it is thus that He always conducts Himself at the present day with respect to ourselves. Why were we not born in paganism, in heresy, in schism, in a family possessing no religion or morals, of which there are so many, and where we should have been lost? It is to the gratuitous mercy of God that we are debtors. Wherefore, more than others, have we received a Christian education, more efficacious succors of grace, more light and more faith, more good counsels and good examples? O wholly gratuitous predilection of our God can we ever thank thee enough, love thee sufficiently? Blessed be God, who in Jesus Christ has predestined us to be His children by a decree of His own good pleasure, in order that the praise and the glory of it may be given entirely to His grace. (Eph. 1:3 et seq) Yes, my God, we confess it, if we are not lost we owe it to Thy mercy (Lam. 3:22)."By the grace of God I am what I am." (1 Cor. 15:10) May I be able to add with Thy Apostle: "His grace in me hath not been void, but I have labored more abundantly than all they." (Ibid)

SECOND POINT
✝ Marvelous Effects of the Vocation of the Magi

The Magi, before the appearance of the star, lived in the darkness of paganism, and probably their life left much to be desired. But as soon as they had seen the star, and had listened to the grace which called them, they were converted, they left all, in order to belong entirely to Jesus Christ, and gave themselves up to grace in order to follow it with simplicity and courage. From that moment they were no longer men belonging to this world, but men who were wholly heavenly; they lived and died as saints, so that during eighteen centuries the Church has rendered them public worship, and honors them with the title of saints. The cathedral at Cologne preserves their bodies with reverence, and the faithful love to go and pray before their venerable remains. Wherefore do we not correspond as they did to our holy vocation? Wherefore are we so attached to this world? Wherefore not leave it, at least in affection, despising what it esteems, esteeming what it despises, hating what it loves, and loving what it hates? Wherefore, after so many solicitations addressed to us by grace, do we still listen to the lukewarmness which keeps us back, to the caprice which is full of change, to idleness which will not allow itself to be disturbed, and to self-love which idolizes itself? May the beautiful example of the Magi wake us at last and make us enter upon a better life. *Resolutions and spiritual nosegay as above.*

January 7th

SUMMARY OF TOMORROW'S MEDITATION

e will meditate tomorrow upon the faith of the Magi, and we shall consider: first, what the cost of faith is; second, the use we must make of it in the conduct of life. We will then make the resolution: first, often to thank God for the gift of faith; second, often to ask ourselves: from what principle of faith do I perform this action? Our spiritual nosegay shall be the words of St. Paul: "The just man liveth by faith." (Rom. 1:17)

MEDITATION FOR THE MORNING

Let us admire Jesus Christ causing the light of faith to shine in the soul of the Magi at the same time that He caused the miraculous star to shine before their eyes. Let us admire the liveliness of their faith which made them resolve to leave their country and their throne and to brave the criticism of the world;

to undertake a distant journey, and to recognize the great God of heaven in the form of a poor little child, laid upon straw in a stable. O truly admirable faith! Let us bless Our Lord who inspired it, and let us beg Him to make us sharers in it.

FIRST POINT
✝ What the Price of Faith is

Faith is of inestimable price, first, it is the principle of all justification, of all merit, of all true greatness. Without it sin is irremissible, all good works devoid of merit, and man a being without greatness. By it, on the other hand, we recover innocence; the least actions are raised into the supernatural order, they gain for us an immense weight of glory, and man becomes a child of God, a member and co-heir of Jesus Christ, an heir of the kingdom of heaven, the temple of the Holy Spirit, the delight of the Blessed Trinity. Second, it is the charm of the intelligence; it is the torch which enlightens and hinders it from going astray. Reason alone often casts only uncertain light; faith, the true sun of reason, reveals to us the secrets of heaven, teaches us what is most necessary for us to know, God and His unity, His nature, His infinite perfections, man and his origin, his destinies, his end, with the means of attaining to it, the falsity of wealth, which passes away, the immortal riches of a future life, the importance of salvation, the emptiness of pleasures, the futility of self-love, of its exigencies and its susceptibilities. Oh, how sad is the condition of men without faith! They are carried away by every wind of doctrine, and they know not in what to trust as regards what is the most important for them to know. Third, faith does still more than enlighten the intelligence: it confirms it in what it knows, in confirming by divine authority our own conceptions; it aggrandizes and enriches it by adding to the circle of natural sciences the lofty truths which we should never have been able to attain to by means of our own strength. Fourth, it is the joy of our heart. By it man unites himself to eternal truth, lunges with delight into this ocean of light, and enjoys the happiness of honoring God by believing on divine authority what he already knew, and by believing on the same authority what he does not comprehend, because there where God affirms we have no need to understand, and because, on the contrary, the less we comprehend, the more beautiful homage we render to divine veracity, which is of itself the sole sufficient foundation of all belief. Fifth, it consoles and sustains man in the trials of this life, which are so severe. A glance cast upon the cross, another raised to heaven, console, encourage, and fortify to such an extent as to make us find happiness in suffering, to sustain the heart in its weaknesses, to raise it up in its depression, and to hold the place of all that is wanting to us. Oh, how much to be pitied is the man who has not faith, amidst the many trials of which this life is full!

SECOND POINT

✝ Of the Use to be made of Faith in the Conduct of Life, or of the Spirit of Faith

Without a spirit of faith we are not Christians; to act without reflection and without a motive is to move like a machine; to act for the satisfaction of our senses is to live like a brute; to act from reason is to live like a pagan or a philosopher; to act from faith or from the motive of pleasing God it is in that alone that Christian life consists, the life which pleases God and which counts for heaven. We may do all we can in giving alms through human compassion, serve our neighbor in order to be served by him, be modest in order to be esteemed, restrain our passions in order not to give others a bad opinion of us; we only lose our time and our trouble, and after a life which has, perhaps, been laborious and painful, we arrive before the tribunal of God with our hands empty. With the spirit of faith, on the contrary, the soul rises and grows. Our whole life is noble and supernatural, all our actions are meritorious. When engaged in prayer, the spirit of faith renders us attentive, reverential, fervent; in our conduct it renders us punctual, exact, careful to do all things well. In our relations with our neighbor, it inspires charity, gentleness, condescension, the endurance of defects. In reverses, suffering, and infirmity, it renders us patient, resigned, and abandoned to the will of God. In the use of riches, it renders us disinterested and generous. Finally, in all our thoughts and designs, there is a great loftiness of ideas, a perfect nobility of sentiment, in all and everywhere it is holiness in action. Happy the souls, then, who have the spirit of faith, miserable those who do not possess it! *Resolutions and spiritual nosegay as above.*

JANUARY 8th

SUMMARY OF TOMORROW'S MEDITATION

e will meditate tomorrow on the fidelity of the Magi to the grace which called them, and we shall see that their fidelity is: first, prompt; second, generous; third, fervent. We will then make the resolution: first, to obey with promptitude, with generosity and fervor, all the inspirations of grace; second, we will remain often in spirit before the crib, uniting our praise with their homage, our adoration and our love with

their adoration and their love. Our spiritual nosegay shall be the very words of the pious kings: "We have seen His star in the East, and are come to adore Him." (Matt. 2:2)

MEDITATION FOR THE MORNING

Let us adore Jesus Christ sending from within His crib His star and His grace to the Magi; the one to speak to their eyes, and the other to their hearts. Let us admire their fidelity in answering the appeal of grace, and let us propose to ourselves to imitate them.

FIRST POINT
✝ The Fidelity of the Magi was Prompt

As soon as they had seen the miraculous star, they left without hesitating, without putting off until the next day, without saying, we will go. We saw, they said, and we have come. Once on their way, they did not go astray either to the left or to the right; they went straight to where grace called them. Are we equally prompt in obeying the inspirations of grace, the good advice or the good examples which are given us? Do we not put off until another time the reformation of our faults, forming projects for the future, and executing none of them? Do we not halt on the road through a continual alternative of good and evil, of amendment and backsliding?

SECOND POINT
✝ The Fidelity of the Magi was Generous

Their departure was attended with the greatest obstacles. They were kings, if tradition may be believed; how could they abandon their kingdom? They were wise men of the East, some say; how could they compromise their reputation by a step which public opinion would tax with folly? Then, the star was going to conduct them into a distant and unknown country. What fatigue to surmount! What risks to run! What dangers to traverse! But nothing stops these generous travelers. When we love, and when we have given up ourselves wholly to God, we go forward without reasoning. They, therefore, set off on their road, and, after a long journey, they arrived at Jerusalem. There they encounter another obstacle, the star disappears. It is not in the midst of the world that we find the grace which guides us. They did not then any longer know where to find the Messias they were seeking. At the same time, they were not discouraged. When we do not know, we ask advice. They inquired, therefore, publicly, and even at the court of Herod, where was the Messias, King of the Jews, who had just been born. (Matt. 2:2) How superior was their courage to all human respect, and even to fear of the suspicious and cruel king who reigned in Jerusalem! The synagogue, interrogated by Herod on this question, answered that Bethlehem was the place of His birth. Immediately the Magi resume their travels to the little town which has been indicated to them, and continue their journey until they have found Jesus. Thus acts the generous soul; it goes to God in spite of all obstacles; it knows how to bear privation, discomfort, and suffering in the performance of duty, and does not care for what is said; it wills God alone and its own perfection and counts all the rest as nothing.

THIRD POINT
✝ The Fidelity of the Magi was Fervent

Who can say with how much delight they made this holy journey, how they spoke to each other of the happiness which awaited them at the end of it, how they animated each other, how they anticipated, by holy desires, the moment of prostrating themselves before the new-born God; how, during the disappearance of the star, they kept up their courage, a beautiful example of fervent souls, who do not allow themselves to be cast down by trials, who remain firm in the midst of darkness and the privation of sensible enjoyments? Who can imagine, how, on seeing the star again, their hearts revived and were in flamed. (Matt. 2:10) Is it thus that we welcome grace, when its light offers itself to us? Oh, if we but knew how to appreciate it! (John 4:10.) Lastly, our thrice-happy travelers arrive at the crib; and there, far from their fervor being disconcerted or cooled at the sight of so poor a place, of so poor a woman, of such poor swaddling clothes, they are overcome with stupor before such greatness brought low, so much splendor hidden, so much majesty diminished; they prostrate themselves with their faces on the ground, and they adore. (Matt. 2:2) What pious homage is contained in this adoration, what respect, what love, what joy, what astonishment, what praise, and what offerings! Oh, what beautiful models for us in our prayers, or before the Blessed Sacrament! *Resolutions and spiritual nosegay as above.*

January 9th

SUMMARY OF TOMORROW'S MEDITATION

We will meditate tomorrow: first, upon the presents offered by the Magi to the Infant Jesus; second, upon the presents which, following their example, we ought to offer to Him. We will then make the resolution: first, frequently to offer, during the day, our adoration and our love to the God of the crib, in union with the Magi; second, in our prayers to imitate the fervor of these pious kings. Our spiritual nosegay shall be the ancient prayer of the Church of Paris: "To the Child Jesus the gold of charity, the myrrh of mortification, and the incense of prayer." (Prose de Paris)

MEDITATION FOR THE MORNING

Let us transport ourselves in spirit before the crib, in the society of the Magi, so profoundly imbued with respect, so burning with love; and let us unite ourselves with all these pious sentiments. If we do not imitate them, let us be afraid that the Infant Jesus, in His crib, will complain (Jerome, Ep. ad Sabin. diac.)

FIRST POINT
✝ The Presents Offered by the Magi to the Child Jesus

The Magi, says the Gospel, having opened their treasures, offered Him gold, incense, and myrrh, mysterious gifts which, in regard to their faith, had a signification and a language of their own. Gold signified the tribute of homage which they paid to Him as the great King, the Sovereign of the universe, the Master of all the treasures of heaven and earth. The incense signified the tribute of praise and of prayer which they presented to Him as to the Living God, towards whom the incense of their prayers ought to ascend from all creatures. The myrrh, which is employed in the embalming of the dead, was a profession of faith on their part in the holy humanity which was united in the crib to the Divinity, and which, as our Pontiff and our Victim, He would immolate for us one day on the cross (Prose de Paris). It would be impossible to conceive with what sentiments of humility and devotion, of gratitude and of love, the pious Magi offered these presents; what tears of joy and tenderness flowed from their eyes, and what ardent desires they experienced in making a God so amiable to be known and loved. Therefore Jesus, not content to show them, by looks full of love, how greatly these presents pleased Him, showed it to them still more by a reciprocity of presents. In exchange for the gold, He gave them the gift of wisdom, to understand the most lofty mysteries and to teach them to others; in exchange for the incense, He imparted to them the gift of piety, enabling them to love God alone, and to despise all else; in exchange for the myrrh, He enriches them with the spirit of mortification and of sacrifice, which made of them apostles and martyrs. O my God, how good it is to serve Thee thus, and to give ourselves wholly to Thee! Thou renders a hundred-fold what is given to

Thee. Grant to me, as Thou didst to the Magi; the spirit of wisdom, of prayer, and of sacrifice. I have no other title for being heard but my profound misery; may this title suffice me in presence of Thy mercy.

SECOND POINT
✝ Presents which, in Accordance with the Example of the Magi, we ought to Offer to Jesus Christ

It is not here gold, or myrrh, or incense which Jesus asks of us, but much rather the interior dispositions symbolized by these three presents, and which a beautiful prose of the Church of Paris sums up in these three words: "Gold symbolizes charity; myrrh, mortification; incense, holy desires." First, charity, of which gold is the symbol, and which is so agreeable to the Infant Jesus, is that interior disposition which makes us love God with our whole soul, with our whole heart, and with our whole strength. We love Him not only in Himself, but in our neighbor; we succor Him in the person of the poor; we solace Him in the unhappy; we console Him in the afflicted; we assist Him In all those to whom we can be useful, in those even of whom we have to complain, and that on account of His words: I look upon as done to Myself all that is done to the least of Mine (Matt. 25:40). Second, mortification, of which myrrh is the symbol, is the virtue which preserves the soul in purity and the body in integrity, to the extent of making of them a living sacrifice, holy and agree able to God, such as the Apostle requires. (Rom. 12:1) Third, by the holy desires, represented by the incense, is to be understood the prayer of the humble man presenting himself before God as a poor creature who has nothing except miseries to be solaced, as a sinner who has nothing to offer but faults to be expiated, a will to be straightened, a heart to be warmed, a memory to be purified, an understanding to be enlightened. Lastly, there is to be understood thereby not only obligatory prayers, or those habitually said in the morning and the evening, but also mental prayer, and that deepest kind of prayer which is uttered before the tabernacle or the crucifix; habitual prayer, which is expressed in pious aspirations and ejaculations, and which may be mingled with all the acts of life, in all places and at all seasons. Are we faithful in offering these presents to Jesus? *Resolutions and spiritual nosegay as above.*

January 10th

SUMMARY OF TOMORROW'S MEDITATION

e will meditate tomorrow upon the sojourn of the Magi at Bethlehem, and we shall consider: first, how holily they lived there; second, how we may imitate them. We will then make the resolution: first, to make a visit to the Blessed Sacrament during the day, after the example of the Magi visiting the Child Jesus in His crib; second, to keep ourselves as much as possible in a spirit of recollection and of union with God. Our spiritual nosegay shall be the words of the Imitation: "To be with Jesus is a delightful paradise." (2 Imit. 8:2)

MEDITATION FOR THE MORNING

Let us adore the Infant Jesus kindly receiving the Magi each time that they went to visit Him during their sojourn at Bethlehem. O precious visits! O moments of Paradise! Let us congratulate the Magi on them. Let us thank Jesus Christ for them.

FIRST POINT

✝ How Holily the Magi Lived during their Sojourn at Bethlehem

The thrice-blessed Magi took care not to quit Bethlehem after their first visit; it is impossible to enjoy so much happiness without wishing to prolong it; people do not come from so great a distance to enjoy so pure a joy without giving themselves the pleasure of multiplying it; more over they must rest after enduring so much fatigue. And therefore, there is no doubt but that the Magi remained several days at Bethlehem; and during that time they often went to visit the Child-God: they took Him in their arms, contemplated His divine features, pressed Him to their bosom, covered Him with their kisses, watered Him with their tears; and who can say with what sentiments of admiration, of love, of thanksgiving, and of devotion they gave up their whole persons to the service of the Divine Child? Who, on the other hand, can say what enlightenment, what benedictions, what flames of love the Infant Jesus shed upon their souls, and how short each one of their visits seemed to them? It was with regret that they withdrew, and as soon as they could they hastened to return, saying with David: "As the heart pants after the fountains of waters, so my soul pants after Thee, O God!" (Ps. 41:2) And they were always kindly received, and new graces followed upon the preceding ones; then, after having rendered their homage to the Child, they spoke to Mary and to Joseph, begging them to explain the marvels of the mystery they had come to contemplate. And Mary and Joseph, always ready to give them pleasure, told them all they knew. O holy intercourse! How it ravished the hearts of the Magi, how it was impressed upon their memories! They spoke in their turn; and from the depths of their hearts issued words which Mary deemed worthy to be kept in her heart. (Luke 2:19) In the interval of these holy interviews, of what did they think except of Jesus? Jesus was everything to them (Coloss. 3:2). So holy was the life of these happy Magi during their sojourn at Bethlehem! What a lesson for us! How well it teaches us the profit we may derive from the real presence of Christ in our tabernacles!

SECOND POINT
✝ **How we ought to Imitate the Magi in their Sojourn at Bethlehem**

We can imitate them, first, when we visit the Blessed Sacrament; for in the tabernacles we have the same Man-God who was in the crib, with this difference, and it is one which overflows with love, that the Magi arrived at the crib only after having taken a long journey, whilst tabernacles, numerous as they are, are never at any great distance from us. Oh, if we could but take to these tabernacles the faith and the piety of the Magi, how many graces should we not bring away! We can, second, imitate the Magi when we communicate; for then we not only press Our Lord in our arms, as these happy travelers did, but we receive Him in our hearts; we are one with Him, so to speak; and this is a happiness the Magi did not possess. After having thus incorporated Him, we can during our act of thanksgiving converse with Him, speak to Him and listen to Him, taking the Magi at the crib as our model of acts of thanksgiving after each communion. We can, third, during the course of the day, imitate the holy life of the Magi outside the stable of Bethlehem, by means of the spirit of recollection which makes of our hearts a sanctuary, where we converse with God, an amiable solitude, where nothing enters except God and the soul. There, like the Magi in the stable of Bethlehem, we enjoy God, we can see Him, speak to Him, listen to Him, take advice from Him in our doubts, call Him to our aid in difficulties or dangers, tell Him that we love Him, and ask that we may love Him ever more and more; offer Him our actions, our life, consecrate ourselves to Him without reserve, thank Him for His benefits, burst forth into adoration, praise, thanksgiving, entreaties, and supplications, There, with gratitude and love, we gather together the good thoughts which He sends us, the pious sentiments which He suggests to us, the holy resolutions He puts into our hearts, and we thus make our whole life holy, as was that of the Magi. Happy the soul which understands these things! More happy still he who puts them in practice! (3 Imit. 1) *Resolutions and spiritual nosegay as above.*

JANUARY 11ᵀʰ

SUMMARY OF TOMORROW'S MEDITATION

e will finish tomorrow our meditations on the Magi by considering: first, their farewell to Jesus, Mary, and Joseph; second, their return home; third, their conduct after their return. We will then make the resolution; first, often to assure Our Lord during the day that we desire to live for Him alone; second, to excise ourselves to perform every one of our actions in the most perfect manner possible. Our spiritual nosegay shall be the words which the Gospel says of the Magi: "They went back another way to their country." (Matt. 2:12)

MEDITATION FOR THE MORNING

Let us adore the Infant Jesus receiving the farewells of the Magi, and addressing to them His own, not by means of external words, since the law of silence is imposed upon Him, but by the sweetness of His expression, which speaks to their eyes, and by the sanctity of His inspirations, which speak to their hearts. Oh, how many graces did not the Magi carry away with them from this last visit; and how preciously they kept them in their hearts, down to their last sigh! Let us bless Our Lord for it; let us congratulate our holy travelers.

FIRST POINT

✝ The Farewells Addressed by the Magi to Jesus, Mary, and Joseph

If the Magi had consulted their own hearts only, they would have remained longer, or rather always, at Bethlehem: it was to them paradise upon earth; but duty called them elsewhere, and they comprehended that they must sacrifice even the pleasures of piety, even the delights enjoyed in spiritual exercises, in order to go where the duties incumbent upon us call us. Whatever it might cost them they decided to take their departure, and went to make their last farewells to Jesus, Mary, and Joseph. Who can say how touching were these farewells, with what tenderness they kissed and watered with their tears the feet of the Divine Infant; how they thanked Him afresh for having called them by means of the miraculous star, swore to Him everlasting fidelity, esteeming themselves more honored to be His vassals than to command the universe? Mary, in the place of her Son, replied to their fervent farewells, and confirmed the Magi in their faith in the greatness of the Child-God, and in the practice of the perfect life they were henceforth to lead. The humble Joseph encouraged them on his side to engrave these good words in their heart, and they went away happy after such an interview. Oh, how good it is to converse with Jesus, Mary, and Joseph, whether it is in prayer or before the tabernacle, and to remain united with them in heart, through prayer and recollection!

SECOND POINT
✝ Return of the Magi to their own Land

The Magi, after having bidden farewell to the crib, went to take a little repose before leaving very early the next morning. But behold, during the night an angel from heaven comes to tell them that Herod, finding he has been deceived by them, has been plotting to take away their life, and that therefore they must return by another road. Herein are contained three precious lessons. The first is that Jesus watches over, continually, even during our sleep, and that He often keeps us from dangers which threaten us and which we could not foresee. The second, that it is after having found and enjoyed God as the Magi did, we must no longer walk in the same way as before, but in a new and more perfect way, different from that which is followed by the multitude. God grants His special graces only with this object in view, and it is abusing them to walk always in the same old tracks. The third reason is that after having quitted the: path to heaven through sin, we can only return to it by the way of innocence; after having left it to enjoy the pleasures of the world, we can return to it only by means of sorrow and penitence, beyond this there is no salvation. Let us think deeply on this.

THIRD POINT
✝ Conduct of the Magi after their Return to their Country

Hardly had the Magi returned home than they made themselves apostles of the new-born God; everywhere they published the birth of the King of the universe, they preached the new spirit which He had come to bring to this world, the spirit of humility, of poverty, of mortification, of gentleness, and of devotedness; and they confirmed these beautiful teachings by the holiness of their life, by the power of the grace with which they were filled, by a fervent apostolate, which showed them to be heavenly men and profoundly convinced; lastly by their blood, which they had the happiness to shed for the Gospel, and thus they were at once evangelists and martyrs. Such was the marvelous change wrought in the Magi by a few days passed at the crib. Why, enjoying every day the same God at the holy altar, do we not become better? What are we waiting for before giving ourselves entirely to Him? Will it be time enough to begin to live well when we must have done with life? *Resolutions and spiritual nosegay as above.*

First Sunday after Epiphany

SUMMARY OF TOMORROW'S MEDITATION

After having studied the happiness of the Magi, we will meditate tomorrow on the conduct of Herod in these circumstances; it is signalized by three characteristics: first, his disquiet at the tidings of the birth of the Messias; second, his hypocrisy; third, the deception he well deserved. We will then make the resolution: first, to attach our hearts to God alone, and always to go straight to Him without turning aside and without dissimulation; second, to confide in His providence in all events. Our spiritual nosegay shall be the maxim of the Holy Spirit: "A perverse heart is abominable to the Lord: and His will is in them that walk sincerely." (Prov. 11:20)

MEDITATION FOR THE MORNING

Let us adore Jesus Christ bringing peace and happiness to men of good will, (Luke 2:14) and leaving to His enemies trouble and wretchedness. (Is. 57:21) Let us thank Him for His goodness towards His own, and let us admire His justice towards those who disown Him.

FIRST POINT

✝ The Disquiet of Herod on Hearing of the Birth of the Messias

This birth was doubtless the happiest of events for the earth; and the tidings of it had rejoiced the hearts of the Magi. Herod appreciated it in a very different manner. When, with the simplicity and candor of an upright soul, the Magi came to announce to him this great event, and to ask him where the Saviour, so long expected, had been born, the monarch was troubled, he was disquieted for his crown, and all Jerusalem was troubled with him. Thus all hearts which are under the influence of a passion are troubled. If we are but blamed, if we are humiliated, if our desires meet with opposition, or if we only fear something similar, if we but imagine ourselves not to be sufficiently esteemed, it is enough; we are troubled and sad; we cannot bear our pride, our vanity, the love of our own ease ever to be interfered with, nor even that they should be touched with the fingers end. There is no peace or happiness except for him who, freed from all attachment, has no ties here below. (3 Imit. 31:1) Let us beg of God to enable us well to understand this important truth.

SECOND POINT
✝ Hypocrisy of Herod

"Herod" says Holy Writ, "privately calling the Wise Men, learned diligently of them the time of the star which appeared to them, and sending them into Bethlehem said, Go and diligently inquire after the Child, and when you have found Him, bring me word again, that I also may come and adore Him." (Matt. 2:7-8) It was thus that under the false guise of respect and piety this hypocritical prince hid his design of putting to death the Divine Child. Such hypocrisy as this revolts us; it is in fact abominable both to God and man. Hypocrisy is a lie in action, blasting human dignity, and worthy of all contempt. However, shameful as is this vice, it is more common than we think; for those are hypocrites who assume the semblance of virtue without caring to posses the reality, who behave themselves in secret quite differently from what they do in public, who think more about hiding their faults than of eradicating them. Now, is not this the history of many persons, and perhaps of ourselves? Those are hypocrites who speak in one way and act in another; who sacrifice sincerity to self-love, who speak evil of themselves in order to incite others to speak well of them and to affirm the contrary of what they assert. Now, do we not recognize ourselves under these characteristics also? Lastly, those are hypocrites who are wanting in integrity in their conduct and their language, who make use of dissimulation and duplicity, and even easily allow themselves to utter falsehoods. Now, does not all this often happen to ourselves? Oh, how great is the number of hypocrites and how few souls there are who are really upright and sincere, who love frankness above all things, even when it is purchased at the expense of their self-love. How few there are of whom we can say, as of Nathaniel, "Behold an Israelite, indeed, in whom there is no guile." (John 1:47) no equivocation, who is always simple and upright, always a friend of truth!

THIRD POINT
✝ The Deception of Herod Well Deserved

The wicked can do nothing against God; the omnipotent Master knows well how to turn their plots to their own confusion, and to the greatest possible good to His elect. Thus He turned to naught the impious plans of Herod, by commanding the Maji to return to their own country by another way and Joseph to fly into Egypt with the Child. If Herod caused the children of Bethlehem to be massacred, the massacre only gave new saints to heaven, and delivered up the tyrant to the execration of all future ages. Thus will it be always with those who persecute Jesus Christ in His Church or in His members. Let us trust in God, without ever allowing ourselves to be cast down by the temporary triumph of our enemies. In the strife of Satan against the saints God will always have the last word and will finish by gaining the upper hand. He permits us to be attacked, only to give us opportunity for the exhibition of the most splendid virtues. *Resolutions and spiritual nosegay as above.*

Monday in the First Week after Epiphany

SUMMARY OF TOMORROW'S MEDITATION

efore entering into the details of the actions of the Incarnate Word, we will meditate upon certain general features of His life of which each particular act is, as it were, the application. The first feature on which we will meditate tomorrow is His title of Redeemer. We shall see: first, how well Jesus merits this title; second, what obligation this title imposes upon us. We will then make the resolution: first, often and lovingly to kiss the crucifix, to salute it with a heart full of gratitude wherever it presents itself to our eyes; second, to place, above every other kind of interest, the interest of our own salvation. Our spiritual nosegay shall be the words of St. Paul: "Christ died for all, that they also who live may not now live to themselves, but unto Him, who died for them and rose again." (2 Cor. 5:15)

MEDITATION FOR THE MORNING

Let us kneel down in spirit before the crib, between Mary and Joseph; let us adore Jesus Christ under the amiable title of our Redeemer, suffering, as man, in our place, giving, as God, an infinite value to His sufferings. Oh, how well He merits through this title our thanksgivings, our praise, and our love!

FIRST POINT

✝ Jesus our Redeemer

Let us here admire the magnificence of our redemption. Three considerations show us the excellence of it: first, Jesus Christ has withdrawn us from the abyss of sin by meriting the pardon of it for us. The sin of Adam had closed heaven and opened hell. Jesus has given us back our rights to heaven, and those alone fall into hell who will not be saved. To the sin of Adam we have added our own personal faults, another much more serious abyss, for Adam sinned but once, while we have often sinned. Every day we still sin, and as long as we live we shall always be capable of sinning. Now, oh, how wonderful, although we sin, the blood of Jesus Christ is always there, ready to flow upon us to purify us; so that in Jesus Christ, our Redeemer, we find more than we had lost in guilty Adam; grace brings us more blessings than sin had caused us evil. (Rom. 5:20) And the Church has reason to exclaim, when speaking of the sin of Adam: Happy fault which gained us a Redeemer who obtains grace for all our faults; sin, in a certain sense necessary, consequent on which was given to us this Redeemer whom we required for our thousand personal prevarications. (Bened. cer. pasch) Second, Jesus Christ, by His redemption, does not merit only the pardon of our faults, He merits also all the graces which make saints, all the sacraments, all the means of salvation which exist in the Church, all the instructions, all the good thoughts, all the holy desires. "With the Lord there is mercy, and with Him plentiful redemption." (Ps. 129:7) and Thou art infinite in Thy largess. Third, though our Redeemer might have redeemed us and procured for us all these blessings by one single sigh, He willed, in order to show us more love, and to take away all pretext from cowardice, to give the whole of His blood, and all His sufferings to die upon the cross and renew His sacrifice every day on all the altars throughout the world. O Divine Redeemer, how good Thou art! How much better dost Thou treat us than Thou didst the prophets, who desired to see what we see and did not see it, better than so many nations who have not yet received the Gospel! Alas! what would it have served us to be born, if we had not been redeemed?

SECOND POINT
✝ Our Obligations towards Jesus our Redeemer

They may be reduced to two: love and the zeal for salvation, first, love. We ought to love Thee, O heavenly Father, who didst first so love the world as to give it Thy only Son. (Bened. cer. pasch.) O wonderful condescension of Thy love for us; O ineffable charity! In order to purchase a slave, Thou dost deliver up Thy Son. Can I, after that, hesitate to sacrifice to Thee all I have, my body, my soul, my heart, the whole of my being! We ought to love Thee, O eternal Son of God, who wert well pleased to deliver Thyself up to death, and to such a death, in order to save us, Thy enemies, Thy ungrateful children! If we owe ourselves entirely to Thee, as being created by Thee, what do we not owe Thee as being redeemed by Thee, and redeemed in such a manner! (St. Bernard.) It cost Thee only one word to create the universe, but in order to redeem me, what labors, what fatigue, what torments and ignominy! In creating me Thou didst give me to myself; in redeeming me Thou didst give Thyself to me. What shall I render to Thee, O my God, in compensation for Thyself? (St. Bernard) I ought to be entirely Thine, wholly Thine alone, always Thine! There is justice in living only for a God without whose death I should not live, and there is even profit in serving a God who promises me Paradise in return. Second, we owe it to Jesus, our redeemer, to have, before all else, great zeal for the salvation of our soul, for it would be unworthy of us to neglect a soul for which a God has done so much, a soul for which a God has died, and to commit sin, the reparation of which cost Him so dear. To zeal for the salvation of our soul we ought to unite zeal for the salvation of our brethren. Jesus Christ asks us to help Him in this great work (1 Cor. 3:19). His blood cries aloud to us: Be zealous, help Me to save the world, for it would be in vain for Me to have shed My blood for a soul over which you have an influence, if you did not help Me to save it. His wounds cry out to us: Be zealous, it would be in vain for us to have been opened for it, if you do not help us to withdraw it from its blindness. Who would shut his ears to these supplications of a God? *Resolutions and spiritual nosegay as above.*

Tuesday in the First Week after Epiphany

SUMMARY OF TOMORROW'S MEDITATION

We will meditate tomorrow on the second general characteristic of the life of Christ, and we shall see: first, that this Divine Saviour is our Head; second, that this title imposes serious obligations upon us. We will then make the resolution, first to maintain union with Jesus Christ within us by frequent and loving aspirations; second, to respect in ourselves and in our neighbor the character of members of Jesus Christ. Our spiritual nosegay shall be the words of the Apostle: "Yet are the body of Jesus Christ and members of one member."(1 Cor. 12:27)

MEDITATION FOR THE MORNING

Let us adore Jesus Christ, who, after having bought us as our Redeemer, communicates to us, as our Head, the fruits of the redemption. Let us thank

Him for this goodness, and let us beg of Him to enable us to understand the excellence of the title of Head which he has been pleased to take in relation to us, and the obligations which this title imposes upon us.

FIRST POINT
✝ Jesus Christ is our Head

Jesus Christ, says St. Paul, is the Chief or the Head of a body of which we are the members. He is, says St. Paul, a Vine, of which we are the branches; whence it follows that, as the head and the members form but one sole body, as the trunk and its branches, the stock and the shoots, form but one and the same vine, so Jesus Christ and Christians form but one whole; that, as the members derive all their life from one head, as the branches live only by union with the vine, so the Christian derives the whole of his supernatural life from his union with Jesus Christ. This union begins at baptism, which grafts us upon Jesus Christ; (Rom. 6:5) it is sealed by confirmation, and is maintained by the Eucharist; (John 6:57) and when sin has broken it, it is renewed by penitence and extreme unction. Lastly, in the ordinary course of life, it is nourished in us by faith, (Eph. 3: 16-17) grace, and love; and the more faith, grace, and love render this union intimate, the more the Christian spirit lives in us. This spirit languishes if the union is weakened, and it dies all at once if it be broken. It is a misfortune all the more to be dreaded, because this union is the principle of all our merits; without Jesus Christ our works are nothing (John 15:5); all is dead in us, as the body is dead when it is separated from the head. On the contrary, when we are united to Jesus Christ, our prayers, our sufferings, our least works become infinitely meritorious; they procure heaven and its eternity. It is from Jesus Christ, as our Head, that all our good thoughts proceed, all the pious movements, all the interior graces which make saints. Hence those grand words of St. Paul: "I can do all things in Him who strengthened me." (Philipp. 4:13) Hence Christian confidence: "There is now, therefore, no condemnation to them that are in Christ Jesus." (Rom. 8:1) Jesus Christ communicates to them, as to His members, all His rights upon grace here below, all on glory in eternity. How happy is life in this union, even amidst labor and fatigue! How sweet and full of hope is death! God, before whom I am to appear, is the adorable Head of which I am a member. He lives with me, He lives in me; how shall I not hope in Him?

SECOND POINT

✝ What are the Obligations Laid upon us through this Title of Members of Jesus Christ, our Head

We ought, first, to keep our heart and body in a state of perfect purity. It would be indecent to be an impure and fastidious member under a Head which is holy and crowned with thorns; to ally together ambition, vanity, and effeminacy with the humility, modesty, and innocence of the Savior: the vices and the baseness of man with the perfections of God. We ought second, to have tender charity for all Christians. As soon as they are members of Jesus Christ and form with us but one body, of which this adorable Saviour is the head, it is as though we wounded Jesus Christ in the apple of His eye when we offend them. (Zach. 2:8) Even if they are imperfect or vicious; even if they are our enemies, we ought to love them as we love our defective members, as Jesus Christ loves them. We ought, third, to love Jesus Christ tenderly, strongly, and without variation. As soon as we are made one with Him, we ought to lose our heart in His; we ought to interest ourselves in all that touches Him, weep and make reparation for the outrages inflicted on Him, sigh over the trials of His Church and rejoice over its glories. The head cannot be struck or even threatened but the whole body is moved, and the hand stretched out to protect it. Hence it is that the saints were so sensitive to the interests of Jesus Christ; shed tears on seeing Him offended, whilst meditating upon His Passion and uniting themselves with Him by communion. Is it thus we fulfill our duties of members of Jesus Christ? Do we lead a life worthy of such a Head? Do we love our brethren, and do we treat them as the very members of Jesus Christ? Lastly, are the interests of Jesus Christ, of His glory and of His Church, dear to our hearts, and do we protect them as the members protect the head when it is in peril? *Resolutions and spiritual nosegay as above.*

Wednesday in the First Week after Epiphany

SUMMARY OF TOMORROW'S MEDITATION

We will meditate tomorrow on the kingship of Jesus Christ, the third title which constrains us to serve Him, and we shall see: first, that He is our King; second, what we owe Him under this title. We will then make the resolution: first, often during the day to salute Jesus Christ as our King, and to consecrate to Him, by this title, every moment of our life; second, to obey all His orders, even His desires that is to say, the evangelical counsels and the inspiration of His grace. Our spiritual nosegay shall be the cry of love: "To the King of ages, immortal, invisible, the only God, be honor and glory." (1 Tim. 1:17)

MEDITATION FOR THE MORNING

Let us adore Jesus Christ as our well-beloved King, who came here below to conquer heaven for us; who places Himself at our head in order to lead us thither, and shows Himself first to all. Let us attach ourselves to Him as subjects to the best of kings; let us pity the blind Jews, who said: "We will not have this man to reign over us." (Luke 19:14) We, on the contrary, will repeat our baptismal act: "I attach myself to Thee, O my Christ and my King!"

FIRST POINT
✝ Jesus Christ is our King

He is so by right of nature, since, as Creator, He has made us what we are. (Ps. 99:3) He is so by right of conquest, since He has bought us at the price of His own blood (Acts 22:28), and knew if He were not our King by this double title He ought still to be through the free desire of our hearts. For He is infinitely worthy of it; He is an almighty and beneficent King, who lives only for the happiness of His subjects; who makes it His glory to render them eternally happy; who commands nothing but what is just, nothing but what is good and useful; who Himself is the first to do all that He orders or counsels, without willing to be better treated than His subjects; who is the first in labors, fatigue, and privation; the first in humiliation and suffering; the first in all things; bearing His cross at our head and saying: follow Me. He is a King who promises to those who serve Him the most magnificent recompenses, and performs all that He promises; He is a King who is perfectly acquainted with the merits of each person, and recompenses each according to his deserts; He is an immortal King who can never fail us; we may lose our lives in His service, but far from losing with our lives the fruits of our services, it is, on the contrary, then that our enjoyment be gins. Lastly, He is a King in whose service victory is never doubtful, because at the same time that He gives the grace of conquering He gives up to His own all the fruits of victory, and reserves for Himself only the pleasure of enriching us. O Jesus, O my King! How good it is to be Thy subject. Reign over me, over my body and my soul, over my will and all my desires, over all my thoughts and the employment of all my moments. (Ps. 44:5)

SECOND POINT
✝ What we owe to Jesus Christ in His Quality of King

We owe Him, first, to attach ourselves to Him with our whole soul. We promised Him to do so at our baptism; we ratified this engagement at our confirmation, wherein we enrolled ourselves under His banner as His soldiers; we have sworn it every time we have received the sacraments, and if we had not made this oath we ought still to make it. For besides that Jesus Christ has every possible title to be the King of our hearts, is it not an honor for us to belong to so great a King? Is it not our interest to be the subjects of a monarch so lavish of His graces and His love? Is it not a happiness for us to be already engaged in this present life in His service, and enrolled under His banner, since without that there is only discomfort, bitterness, sadness, and deception? We owe it to Him, second, to follow Him wherever it seems good to Him to lead us, and never to desire to be treated better than the brave Urias, who said: "The ark of God and Israel and Juda dwell in tents, and my lord Joab and the servants of my Lord abide upon the face of the earth; and shall I go into my house to eat, and to drink and to sleep with my wife? By thy welfare and by the welfare of thy soul I will not do this thing." (2 Kings 11:2) It is our duty in every circumstance to walk in the footsteps of Jesus our King, to be humble, mortified, obedient, patient, and poor, as He was in the crib and on the cross; to pray like Him and in union with Him; to speak like Him; to act like Him; and always to be animated with the sentiments of the generous captain of David, Ethai, who said, "As the Lord liveth, and as my lord the king liveth, in whatsoever place thou shall be, my lord king, either in death or in life, there will thy servant be." (2 Kings 15:21) We owe it to Him, third, to obey Him in everything. "If He shall say to me, Thou pleases me not, I am ready; Let Him do that which is good before Him." (2 Kings 15:26) "Lord, what wilt Thou have me to do?" (Acts 9:6) "Speak, Lord, for Thy servant heareth." (1 Kings 3:9) My heart is ready. I offer myself to Thee to do all that Thou wouldst have me do. Heaven preserve me from resisting even the very least of Thy desires; I know that disobedience to a word of counsel often leads to the violation of a precept. I desire to be all Thine; all for Thee, all like Thee. It would ill become me to desire to be better treated than Thou. *Resolutions and spiritual nosegay as above.*

Thursday in the First Week after Epiphany

SUMMARY OF TOMORROW'S MEDITATION

We will meditate tomorrow on a fourth title of Jesus Christ, which is well adapted to make us attach ourselves to Him. We shall see, first, that He is our Master through His teachings; second, what we owe to Him because of this title. We will then make the resolution: first, to venerate in Him the Master who is entitled to direct us in every detail of our conduct; second, to follow His divine teachings without paying any attention to what the world may say or think of us. Our spiritual nosegay shall be the words of the Gospel: "Neither be ye called masters, for one is your master, Christ." (Matt. 23:10)

MEDITATION FOR THE MORNING

Let us adore Jesus Christ as the great Master come down from heaven to each us the science of salvation. (Ps. 93:10) Man speaks only to the ears of the body; Jesus Christ speaks to those of the heart. (St. Augustine, Tract 3 in Ep. Joan) Let us prostrate ourselves at the feet of this best of masters; let us attach ourselves to His divine lessons, and let us say with St. Vincent de Paul: "Lord! What happiness to be Thy scholars!"

FIRST POINT
✝ **Jesus Christ is our Master through His Teachings**

The heavenly Father declared it from on high up on the banks of the Jordan: "This is My beloved Son, hear ye Him." (Luke 9:35) The Saviour Himself proclaimed that He was our sole Master and St. Paul teaches us thus: "God who at sundry times and in diverse manners spoke in times past to the fathers by the prophets, last of all in these days hath spoken to us by His Son, whom. He hath appointed heir of all things, by whom also He made the world." (Heb. 1:1-2) How happy we are to have such a Master! First, He is an infallible Master; heaven and earth may pass away, but His words will not pass away; He knows everything with certainty, and His science is taken from the very source itself of eternal truth. "The only begotten Son who is in the bosom of the Father, He hath declared Him." (John 1:18) Every time then that we can say with regard to anything whatever "Jesus Christ has said it," it is true, for He is truth itself (John 14:6); the thing is good, for He is the way which leads surely to heaven. (Ibid) He is the theologian who forms the faith; the casuist who directs the conscience; the counselor who rules the conduct, and the Church with all her doctors does not merit our belief except for the reason that she is His organ. Second, He is a Master of incomparable ability; who makes us learn quickly all that He teaches, who enlightens the understanding to comprehend His doctrine and also disposes the will to appreciate it. When we have God for our Master, says St. Ambrose, how quickly we learn the lessons that are taught us! Third, He is a Master who knows how to put His teaching within the reach of the most simple, who speaks to the heart rather than to the mind, and in one instant raises the humble soul to the knowledge of more truth than he would have learnt in ten years in a school which had men at the head of it. O Saviour, what an excellent Master Thou art! And how happy we are to receive Thy lessons!

SECOND POINT
✝ What we owe to Jesus Christ in His Quality of Master

We owe it to Him to take Him as the Supreme Regulator of our determinations, of our sentiments, and of the whole of our conduct. "Lord, to whom should we go? Thou hast the words of eternal life." (John 6:69) On the one side the world deceives us; on the other our reason is short-sighted and does not change the heart, of which the ancient philosophers who moralized so much, and who led such evil, lives, are a proof; it is powerless to sustain the soul in temptation, to console it in troubles; a glance of the eye, a sigh directed towards Thee, O my God, says more to me and consoles me better than any words of man. "Jesus Christ has said it;" this one word is of greater value in enabling me to believe, and is more decisive in making me act than all the reasons adduced by the human understanding. Jesus Christ h as said: "He that contemneth small things shall fall by little and little." (Ecclus. 29:1) I believe it. He has said: Woe to you here below who live in pleasure and in the midst of honors and riches; blessed are the poor; blessed those who weep; blessed those who suffer (Luke 6:24 et seq). I believe it. He has said: "Every one of you that doth not renounce all that he possesseth cannot be My disciple." (Luke 14:33) I believe it. I do not understand how happiness can be found in the cross, glory in contempt, peace in war, but the Master has said so. He would not have said it if it had not been true; I believe it; I refer myself to Him, and I regulate my conduct in accordance with it. We owe it to Him, second, to study the Bible, the writings of the apostles, and books of piety in which His divine lessons are developed, to take pleasure in pious books, to listen with the docility of a pupil seated at the feet of his master, and by the help of these books to be filled with the Christian spirit in order that we may conform the whole of our conduct to it in all things. We owe it to Him, third, to despise the spirit and maxims of the world, as being in direct opposition to His spirit and His maxims. The world may censure us let it do so; it is a bad judge, it is an ignorant and deceiving master, against whom Jesus Christ has cast His anathemas. Let us examine ourselves as to whether we are docile disciples of Jesus Christ, and whether our sentiments and our conduct are always in harmony with His maxims. *Resolutions and spiritual nosegay as above.*

Friday in the First Week after Epiphany

SUMMARY OF TOMORROW'S MEDITATION

We will continue to study Jesus Christ as our Master, and we shall see: first, that each one of His actions is a lesson; second, that this lesson in action is the best of all teachings. We will then make the resolution: first, to ask of ourselves with regard to each one of our actions how Jesus Christ would perform it, so that we may act in the same manner; for example, in prayer, what would be His devotion, His piety; in our relations with our neighbor, what would be His gentleness, His complaisance, His endurance; in our private life, what would be His humility, His abnegation, His recollection; second, to resolve on some particular action, in which we will carry it into practice. Our spiritual nosegay shall be the words of the Imitation: "May our principal study be to meditate on the life of Jesus Christ."(1 Imit. 1:1)

MEDITATION FOR THE MORNING

Let us prostrate ourselves before Jesus Christ like humble pupils at the feet of their master. Let us adore Him as the supreme Master, who began by performing before teaching (Acts 1:1) and who has instructed us by His example still more than by His words. Oh, how different He is from the Pharisees who taught in one way and acted in another. (Matt. 23:3) Let us rejoice that we have so excellent a Master, and let us render to Him all our homage.

FIRST POINT

✝ Each Action of Jesus Christ is a Lesson

Jesus Christ places Himself before us as a master before his apprentice, saying to us: Look at what I do, and do likewise. (Ex. 25:40) Study Me in detail, whether it be in the recital which the Gospel gives of My life, or in the idea that you yourselves can easily form of it. I have done nothing but what was to show you by My example how you ought to do it yourselves. (John 13:15) I labored, I rested, prayed, conversed, I appeared at church and in public places, in society and in solitude, to teach you how to conduct yourselves in all these things. I subjected myself to even the commonest actions, such as sleeping, eating, serving My disciples, in order to show you how, in everything and everywhere, you can be holy. You cannot, it is true, imitate Me in My miracles; but in the manner in which I worked these miracles, and in the circumstances which accompanied them, you will still find something to imitate. This language of our good Master has been understood by all the saints. All have looked upon and recommended the imitation of Jesus Christ as the purest mirror of holiness: as the perfect rule of Christian life, says St. Bonaventure. St. Vincent de Paul, before acting, always asked himself: How would Jesus Christ have acted in my place? Before speaking or giving advice, he said to himself: What would Jesus Christ say in these circumstances? Always and everywhere, moderating the hasty impulses of nature, he would pause to consult Jesus Christ. Oh, what a beautiful example! What a divine lesson!

SECOND POINT

✝ The Teaching in Action which Jesus Christ has given us is the most excellent of all Lessons

First, this teaching is perfectly convincing and leaves no room for any objection or protest. Which of us could murmur and complain beneath the weight of the cross when we see a God bear upon His shoulders a cross infinitely heavier than ours, when we hear Him say to us: "If thorns tear your feet in the path of life, they did not spare Mine. If you have had afflictions, I have had more than yours to bear; My soul has been sorrowful even unto death. If you have to bear suffering, I have endured more than you; your flesh has not been torn into strips by lashes, and your head has not had upon it a crown of thorns." Now, in presence of such an example, who would not have patience and courage? Who would not be gentle, obedient, humble, resigned? Who would not cheerfully wear the livery of the holy passion of our Good Master? Second, this teaching is infinitely consoling. By following it we are sure of our salvation and we have impressed upon us the character of the predestinate (Rom. 8:29). What consolation at the hour of death when kissing the crucifix, which will then be our sole hope, that we have constantly endeavored to become a living copy of the Saviour, and to live His life (Gal. 2:20). And when we leave this world, with what confidence shall we present ourselves before the tribunal of Jesus Christ if we can say to Him: Lord, I have applied myself always to do what I have seen Thee do; what I have presumed Thou wouldst have done in my place.

I have endeavored to resemble Thee in all things, certain of the excellence of my model, (2 Tim. 1:12) assured that in leaning upon Thee I should not be confounded. (Ps. 30:2) *Resolutions and spiritual nosegay as above.*

Saturday in the First Week after Epiphany

SUMMARY OF TOMORROW'S MEDITATION

e will consider tomorrow our adorable Master, Jesus Christ, teaching us by His example the use we must make of our intelligence. This faculty of our soul has two operations: it thinks and it judges. Now, Jesus Christ teaches us by His example, first to have only holy thoughts; second to pronounce only wise judgments. After these two reflections we will make resolutions: first, to keep ourselves on guard against useless thoughts, vain imaginations, the dissipation of our senses, and to maintain ourselves in a spirit of inward recollection. Secondly, to judge of all things as God judges, and as the Gospel teaches us to judge them. Our spiritual nosegay shall be the words of the Imitation: "Happy the eyes which, closed to outward things, are entirely given up to interior things." (3 Imit. 1:1)

MEDITATION FOR THE MORNING

Let us adore Jesus Christ for the marvelous and divine use He makes of His intelligence. Oh, how holy, elevated, and heavenly were all His thoughts! How upright, wise, and conformable to the judgments of the Divinity, which dwelt in Him substantially, were all His judgments! Let us praise Him for having made so noble a use of His intelligence.

FIRST POINT

✝ The Holiness of the Thoughts of Jesus Christ

The holy soul of the Savior opened itself only to pious thoughts, which were wholly for God, wholly to God or in God. Exterior things, far from dissipating it, raised it to the adoration of the power, the wisdom, the greatness, and the goodness of God which it saw impressed upon them. In all the events of this lower world, it appreciated only the side which had relation to the greater glory of God. So that during whole days it was a recollection in God from which nothing could distract it, and even the nights were for it as it were one continual prayer (Luke 6:12). In this holy soul there were no idle thoughts, no flights of the imagination, none of those preoccupations which absorb or trouble the imagination. Alas! If I compare myself with this beautiful example, what a difference there is! I abandon myself to a thousand idle thoughts, to a thousand frivolous imaginations. I occupy myself with everything else, rather than with God. Imprudent as I am, I forget that I am thereby not loving God with my whole heart (Mark 12:30), that the account I shall have to render of the vain thoughts, of the time lost in reveries, is not less to be feared than the account of idle words and of hours spent uselessly. I carry my blindness so far as not to see that the habit of indulging useless thoughts destroys all disposition to prayer and to meditation, dissipates the mind, weakens the heart. That evil thoughts are separated from useless thoughts by only a single step, a step easy to make, and that the passions are hardly less strengthened by the representation of absent objects than by the enjoyment of present ones. Oh, my God, I recognize and confess before Thee, the strange abuse which I have made of my intelligence and the necessity of putting an end to it by means of interior and exterior recollection, by fidelity to my spiritual exercises, by flying from the world, which makes me dissipate my thoughts, and by promptitude in chasing away useless thoughts, the very moment they present themselves to me. Such was the practice of the saints, and they found therein not only their holiness but their happiness, because, after the first efforts, which alone are difficult, the habit of union with God, the fruit of war waged against useless thoughts, is a foretaste of Paradise. Oh, what reproaches have I not here to address to myself! What dissipation of mind! What flights of imagination! How much time lost in reveries or useless thoughts, or thoughts that are foreign to what ought then to be occupying my mind!

SECOND POINT
✝ The Wisdom of the Judgments of Our Lord

They were judgments which were always equitable in their principle and their application. "As I hear," says Jesus Christ "so I judge." (John 5:30) That is to say, that He consulted the judgment of God with regard to everything, in order to make it afterwards the rule of His own judgments. Is it thus that we act? Do we not judge in accordance with the suggestions of the senses and the imagination, according to the interests of our passions, according to the judgments of the world, which are often as deceiving as are our own and sometimes even more so? Let us learn from the example of Jesus Christ never anymore to judge anything until we have taken counsel of God and read, in a manner, upon His face and in His eyes how we ought to judge, approve or disapprove. (Ps. 16:2) Then we shall consider all things as nothing in comparison with our salvation and with eternity; and we shall readily console ourselves for losses and misfortunes, as long as our salvation does not suffer thereby; then the world will be nothing more for us than a prospect which causes an illusion to the eye, a dream which disappears at our waking, a charm which troubles our senses; and we shall no longer say that he is happy and worthy of envy who is rich, powerful and honored. We shall say, on the contrary, that desirable is the fate of him who suffers, who is forgotten and who is counted as nothing, but who loves the position in which God has placed him. Then we shall judge of all things during life as we shall judge of them at the hour of death and throughout eternity, and as those now judge of them who, having preceded us into the tomb, had allowed themselves to be seduced by the world. May we then, after considering these things, reform all our judgments, change the ideas which we form of things, no longer call evil that which is good, nor good that which is evil, despise what the world esteems, and esteem what it despises. *Resolutions and spiritual nosegay as above.*

Second Sunday after Epiphany

If any one desires to meditate upon the Holy Name of Jesus, which the Church honors to-day, he will find the meditation for it on January 2

THE GOSPEL ACCORDING TO ST. JOHN (2:1-11)

"And the third day there was a marriage in Cana of Galilee: and the Mother of Jesus was there. And Jesus also was invited, and His disciples, to the marriage. And the wine failing, the Mother of Jesus saith to Him : They have no wine. And Jesus saith to her: Woman, what is it to Me and to thee? My hour is not yet come. His Mother saith to the waiters: Whatsoever He shall say to you, do ye. Now there were set there six water-pots of stone, according to the manner of the purifying of the Jews, containing two or three measures a piece. Jesus saith to them: Fill the water-pots with water. And they filled them up to the brim. And Jesus saith to them: Draw out now, and carry to the chief steward of the feast. And they carried it. And when the chief steward had tasted the water made wine, and knew not whence it was, but the waiters knew who had drawn the water, the chief steward called the bridegroom, and saith to him: Every man at first sets forth good wine, and when men have well drunk, then that which is worse. But thou hast kept the good wine until now. This beginning of miracles did Jesus in Cana of Galilee, and manifested His glory, and His disciples believed in Him."

SUMMARY OF THE TOMORROW'S MEDITATION

e will interrupt tomorrow the order of our meditations that we may reflect on the presence of Jesus and Mary at the wedding of Cana, as it is related in the Gospel. We shall, first, learn from it the happiness of living in union with Jesus and Mary; second, we will study the manner of practicing this union. We will then make the resolution: first, often to think of Jesus and Mary and to invoke them with confidence; second, to propose them to ourselves as models in all our actions. Our spiritual nosegay shall be the words of the Imitation :"To be with Jesus is paradise, to be without Him is hell." (2 Imit. 8:2)

MEDITATION FOR THE MORNING

Let us transport ourselves in spirit to the feast of the wedding of Cana; let us there consider Jesus and Mary honoring this feast by their presence, edifying all the guests by their modest deportment, their gentle and affable manners. Let us particularly adore Jesus working the first of His miracles there, a miracle of kindness and obligingness.

FIRST POINT
✝ The Happiness of Living in Union with Jesus and Mary

How happy were the bride and bridegroom to have invited Jesus and Mary to their feast! Thanks to so august a presence, all was holy and edifying there, all was happiness. When the wine failed, Mary, who has always her eyes open to the needs of those who love her, perceived the embarrassment into which the good people were about to be plunged, and without waiting for them to claim her intercession, she makes an appeal to the omnipotence of her Son. After exhibiting an apparent hardness, which teaches us that in the divine order natural and purely human sentiments have no right to intervene, Jesus changes the water into a delicious wine, which causes the chief steward to exclaim: How is it that you kept the best wine till the end? Oh, what does not one gain by living in union with Jesus and Mary, and performing all one's actions in this union! Then all the bitterness of this life is softened, and all graces are given to us; Jesus and Mary assist us and enable us to find sweetness even in death itself, which they change into a joy, according to the words of the holy religious who said: "I did not think it was so sweet to die." But, on the other hand, how sad life is, separated from Jesus and Mary. It is the life of the world, where something is always wanting, (John 2:3) and the divine consolations are no longer there. In the world there is no enjoyment without trouble, and often sorrow only is found where it is hoped that pleasure will be met with. If we had all the good things which the world can give, we should still be unhappy, because these good things, insufficient to satisfy a heart made for the infinite, engender only satiety and disgust; so true it is that the world deceives its disciples in promising them happiness. The world is a reed; if you lean upon it, it bends and allows you to fall, or else it breaks and pierces your hand; sometimes even it kills you. Yes, my God, outside Thee there is nothing but deception, sorrow, and weariness; in Thee alone happiness. Are these the sentiments I entertain of the world and of Jesus Christ?

SECOND POINT
✝ Manner of Living in Union with Jesus and Mary

There is another union than that of the body; it is the union of souls, which is possible even amongst those who are absent from one another; even among those whom death has separated from us, even should they have lived centuries ago. Spirits unite themselves with each other by thinking of one another, hearts by loving one another, wills by being blended together. If, then, we wish to live united with Jesus and Mary, we must, first, think often of them, who never forget us; think of their virtues, of their holy examples, in order to imitate them, often asking ourselves what would Jesus and Mary do, what would they think, what would they say in these circumstances? Then applying ourselves to act, think, and speak in the same manner. We must, second, love them tenderly, be one heart and one soul with them, often assure them of our devotion, do everything to please them, and as they love those who love them (Prov. 18:17), they will unite themselves to us; they will make us live their life, and will fill us with their grace. We must, third, unite our will with that of God, whatever may happen, in happy events or those which are the reverse, in all we have to do or say; and as Jesus and Mary never willed anything but the will of God, and willed it with all their hearts, we shall thereby find ourselves to be necessarily united to them. The will of God will be the rallying point, the link between us and them; and happy to find ourselves at this delightful meeting place, we shall there enjoy the delights of internal peace, together with that unutterable tranquility of soul which, is the true beatitude of this present life. (Matt. 5:9) How, up to this day, have we practiced this triple union? First, do we often think of Jesus and Mary, sometimes to invoke them, and sometimes to imitate them? Second, do we tenderly love Jesus and Mary, and do we often assure them of our love and of our devotion? Third, do we love to have but one sole and same will with them, which is the most holy and most amiable will of God in all things? *Resolutions and spiritual nosegay as above.*

MONDAY IN THE SECOND WEEK AFTER EPIPHANY

SUMMARY OF TOMORROW'S MEDIATION

After having learnt from Jesus our Master the use we ought to make of our intelligence, we shall see tomorrow what is the use we ought to make of our heart. We shall learn from Him that our heart ought to be: first, all for God; second, all for God alone. We will then make the resolution; first, to perform all our actions, small and great, from love to God, that is to say from the sole motive of pleasing Him; second, to multiply as much as possible, night and day, acts of love, saying with the Psalmist: "I will love Thee, O Lord," (Ps. 17:1) or with St. Ignatius: "Give me Thy love; it is enough. I desire nothing else." These two aspirations shall be our spiritual nosegay.

MEDITATION FOR THE MORNING

Let us adore the Heart of Jesus as the divine pattern after which ours ought to be formed. Let us penetrate into this sanctuary; let us admire the ineffable beauty of it and its adorable perfections. Oh, if but once we really enter into it, (2 Imit. 1:6) what light and what virtues should we not carry away with us!

FIRST POINT

✝ The Heart of Jesus Teaches us to Give our Heart entirely to God

What was it, in reality, which touched this Divine Heart? What did it love, what did it desire, what did it breathe for, unless it were the greater glory of its Heavenly Father? To behold Him known, loved, adored, and served by all creatures, Himself to accomplish all the divine will, to repair the injuries caused by man to His eternal grandeur: this was that to which all the movements of His great Heart tended; this was the motive of its fears and its hopes, its joys and its sorrows; this was what set it in action or kept it in repose. It was its nourishment, its life. (John 4:34) He said :A man devoured by hunger and thirst is less delighted when he is able to obtain nourishment or drink from a fountain of living water than this Divine Heart when it could do something for the glory and love of God, its Father. To perform that, nothing else was of any account, neither to live in poverty or by labor, nor to die on the cross; and it did not think it was paying too dearly for a benefit so great in buying it at the cost of all kinds of torments, of all kinds of ignominies, even by death itself. 0 Jesus, who will give me a heart like to Thine, a heart whose whole ambition and whose whole joy will be to love God and to make Him loved, to act and to suffer for Him! 0 Eternal God, I have loved Thee too little and too late. Alas! I have hardly begun even yet to love Thee well. Take from me my heart of stone and give me a feeling heart; or, rather, give me a heart which is of stone for everything which is not Thee, and for Thee, a heart which is tender, great, and generous! Transform my heart into the Heart of Thy Son. May all my impetuosities be allayed, my cares, my sorrows, my imperfect desires consumed upon the furnace of holy love, and may I bring back from it a greater charity towards God and towards souls.

SECOND POINT
✝ The Heart of Jesus Teaches us to Give all to God alone

The Sacred Heart, believing that it is not too much for the heart of so small a creature to love a God so great, was careful not to share it, that is to say, not to give the least affection to the creature for itself, or to allow it to be afflicted or to rejoice, to be cast down or lifted up by any foreign object. It was not sufficient for it that God should occupy the first place within it, as if the remaining portions could without injustice be given to others than God; as if the creature, once permitted to share it, would not seize hold of the greater part. With Thee, 0 my God, it is all or nothing. The creature, if it be given ever so small a place in the heart, always arrogates to itself the first. This is what experience teaches me. Whole days and months are necessary to console me for an insignificant misfortune, for the loss, the absence, or even the indifference only, of a friend, whilst, 0 my God, I console myself so easily for having displeased Thee! An undertaking which interests my vanity or my cupidity preoccupies me to such an extent as to rob me of my repose and take my attention from my other duties, a fortunate success transports me: whilst I am so cold in regard to Thy interests, so little touched by what concerns Thy glory. I so little regret to see others offend Thee or to offend Thee myself. Oh, how ashamed I am of this false love, which does not know how to be touched, or moved, or feel compassion, or be uneasy about the object which is loved. Therefore, let there be no sharing ; let my heart be wholly given to God alone.

O Heart of Jesus, obtain for me the grace of reaching this height; I am so far distant from it I purify my heart from all that is not Thee, and may I no longer live for anything but Thee alone. *Resolutions and spiritual nosegay as above.*

Tuesday in the Second Week after Epiphany

SUMMARY OF TOMORROW'S MEDITATION

We will again consult Jesus Christ, tomorrow as our Master from a fresh point of view. We will study: first, the divine principle from which all His acts proceed; second, the vicious principle from which ours too often proceed. We will then make the resolution: first, to do and say nothing from natural motives, but from dependence on the spirit of God, from love to God alone, and the simple desire of serving Him without seeking our own personal satisfaction; second, to examine ourselves before, during, and after our principal actions; before, to disengage ourselves from nature and unite us to the spirit of God; during, in order to maintain ourselves in this disposition; afterwards, to see whether there has not been a mixture of nature in them. Our spiritual nosegay shall be the words of St. Paul: "Whosoever are led by the Spirit of God, they are the sons of God." (Rom. 8:14)

MEDITATION FOR THE MORNING

Let us adore Jesus Christ, performing so divinely all His actions, small or great, that nature had no part, whatever in them. The Spirit of God was the sole principle, the inspirer and the motive power of them all; He was the soul of them, so to say. Let us admire, praise, and bless the pleasure which the heavenly Father takes in actions such as these; and let us entreat Jesus Christ to enable us to understand this mode of action and give us courage to carry it out.

FIRST POINT

✝ The Divine Principle whence Proceed all the Acts of Jesus Christ

In all that Jesus Christ did, said, or thought, He was always animated by a divine principle; the Spirit of God was, as it were, the soul of His soul. "Of Myself," He said, "I do nothing." (John 8:28) "I cannot, of Myself, do anything." (John 5:30) "I am not come of Myself." (John 7:28) "I speak not of Myself. But the Father Who abideth in Me doth the work." (John 14:10) If

He goes into the desert, it is the Spirit of God which leads Him there; if He evangelizes, it is the Spirit of God which guides Him and inspires His words. (Luke 4:18) Whatever He does, it is always through the movement of the Spirit of God, which acts. Herein is the true pattern of a really Christian life. It is not enough to act by the spirit of grace, as did those mysterious animals of whom Ezechiel says that the sole impulse of the spirit directed them on their course. (Ezec. 1:12) We must not be beforehand with, but wait and instantly follow the impulse of the Spirit of God, as regards things to be done or said and as regards the time and manner of doing or saying them. In duties which are in harmony with our likings we ought only to dwell upon the will of God, which orders them. In everything we ought only to be as instruments with which God works, remaining always indifferent beneath His hand, in order that He may use us as it pleases Him. Then our most ordinary actions will be as so many divine actions, since more of the action of God will enter into them than of ours. They will be more meritorious than any, however great, which fervor, mingled with self-will, might inspire; and if we are apostolic men, the Spirit of God, speaking by our mouth, will work miracles of conversion. (Matt. 10:20) Let us examine if it is thus that we act.

SECOND POINT
✝ The Vicious Principle whence our Actions often Proceed

First, we act without reflection. It costs us too much, to pay attention to the principle which makes us act. We proceed often without first reflecting and offering our action to God, but in a disposition of heart which often gives theme to the words which come out of the mouth; and we do not reproach ourselves, because, we only think of the external act, without taking any heed of the internal, in which lies all the merit. Second, we act from natural activity. We allow ourselves to be carried away by this activity when we ought to restrain and mortify it, in order to allow grace time to act and inspire us, so that we may do everything with calmness and moderation, without either haste or slowness. Third, we act from liking or pleasure. We cast ourselves with ardor into what pleases us, and we are like ice in regard to everything which displeases us, as if we ought to care about anything in our actions but the will of God, which ordains them; as if we ought not to be ready to interrupt or to quit any of our occupations as soon as ever the will of God calls us elsewhere. Fourth, we act from self-will. It is that which spoils our best actions and takes from us the greater part of our merits. Let us examine if our actions do not often proceed from someone or other of these bad principles. How many times, whilst saying that we desire to please God, do we not wish to please Him only according to our own tastes or, at any rate, without renouncing all other pleasures except that of pleasing Him. God alone is not sufficient for us, and it is not His good pleasure alone which makes us act. *Resolutions and spiritual nosegay as above.*

WEDNESDAY IN THE SECOND WEEK AFTER EPIPHANY

SUMMARY OF TOMORROW'S MEDITATION

We will meditate tomorrow on a saying of St. Paul, which is the conclusion, and, as it were, the sum total of all the titles which we have admired in Jesus Christ: "Christ is all," (Coloss. 3:2) that is to say, first, that Jesus Christ is everything for us; second, that, without Jesus, all the rest is as nothing to us. We will then make the resolution: first, often during the day to pour forth aspirations of love towards Jesus Christ; for example: Jesus Christ is all. All which is not God is nothing to me; I ought to count it as nothing. God alone suffices me; second, to break off all attachment to what is not God, or according to God. Our spiritual nosegay shall be the saying which is the subject of our meditation: Jesus Christ is everything to us.

MEDITATION FOR THE MORNING

Let us adore Jesus Christ as the treasure of heaven and earth; with Him we are rich, without Him we are poor. (St. Ambrose) Let us rejoice in Him as did the Blessed Virgin, who sings in her canticle: "My spirit hath rejoiced in God my Saviour." (Luke 1:47).

FIRST POINT
✝ Jesus Christ is Everything for us

He does of a truth unite in His Person all the titles which are the most suitable for interesting, touching, and gaining the heart. He is our father in the order of nature, since He created everything. (John 1:3) He is our father in the order of grace, seeing (John 14:6) that He calls Himself the life of our soul, and because without Him our works are dead, they have life only through Him (Coloss. 3:4). He is our brother Son of man, like us; after His resurrection He calls the apostles His brethren. (Matt. 28:10) He is our lord and master, for He redeemed us at the price of His blood. He is our friend, our familiar friend, the friend of our heart. (John 15:15) He is our benefactor; from Him we have all that we possess and all that we are. (John 1:16) He is our head who infuses His divine life into our members; He is our good shepherd who feeds us with His own flesh; our physician who heals all our wounds; our advocate who pleads our cause before His Father; He is the truth which enlightens us, the light which guides us, the wisdom which directs us, the justice which sanctifies us (1 Cor. 1:30); He is the gentleness, the goodness, the humility, the charity, the holiness which ought to live and shine in us; the way which leads to heaven and the gate by which we enter therein. Oh, what good reason, then, have the saints to say: He who has Jesus has everything. "Since I had the happiness of knowing Jesus Christ, and to see some of the lineaments of His beauty," said St. Teresa, "all which is upon earth fills me with disgust, because in Him, in an infinitely superior degree, is all that the heart can wish for. He is too avaricious, or misunderstands the value of so great a treasure, who, possessing it, wishes to add anything else to it." Hence the ejaculation which St. Francis of Assisi delighted to repeat during whole hours: "My God and my all." And truly to desire anything outside Jesus would be to commit an insult against Him, and to say to Him that He is not sufficient to fill our souls; it would be to chase Him out of our heart, since we know that He will not have a divided heart; it would be to lose our senses, says the author of the Imitation. (2 Imit. 8:1) Let us examine ourselves and see whether Jesus Christ is really everything for us, and whether we do not indulge in some attachment which disputes His place in our heart.

SECOND POINT
✟ Without Jesus all the Rest is as Nothing to us

Let us ask all those who enjoy riches, pleasures, or honors, whether they are happy, and we shall receive from them nothing but answers expressing unhappiness, weariness, and disgust. We shall be told of mortal displeasure, of overwhelming contrarieties, of excruciating remorse. It is because without Jesus all is nothing, everything leaves a frightful void in the heart. "Thou hast made us for Thee, O God, and outside Thee there is no repose for the heart," said St. Augustine. "What can the world give you without Jesus," says the author of the Imitation. "To be without Jesus is hell. He is poor who lives without Jesus; he who loses Jesus loses more than the whole world. If Jesus is not your best friend you will be profoundly sad and desolate." (2 Imit. 8:2) On the other hand, he who possesses Jesus has everything, so that the possession of the whole universe added to the possession of Jesus would be a burden rather than an enjoyment. For him who knows how to find all in Jesus everything else is insipid and disgusts. Let us ask pardon of Jesus Christ for having up to the present time so little enjoyed Him, so little appreciated

Him, and let us propose to ourselves to repair the past, by living no longer except for Jesus, and desiring nothing else in time and throughout eternity. *Resolutions and spiritual nosegay as above.*

Thursday in the Second Week after Epiphany

SUMMARY OF TOMORROW'S MEDITATION

We will meditate tomorrow upon another saying of St. Paul. After having said that Jesus Christ is all, he adds that He is in all, (Coloss. 3:11) and from these words we shall learn to see Jesus Christ: first, in every person; second, in all things; third, in all our actions. We will then make the resolution: first, to greet our neighbor with the same charity as though it were Jesus Christ Himself; second, to see and honor Jesus Christ in all things and in all our acts. Our spiritual nosegay shall be the words of our meditation: "Jesus Christ in all."

MEDITATION FOR THE MORNING

Let us adore the Holy Spirit showing us Jesus Christ in everything. One of God's words, it has often been said, is worth more than all the speeches of men. It is particularly true in the present case; it shows us Jesus Christ living and acting in everything, governing and ruling all events, presiding over all our actions, and presenting Himself to us in them as our Model. Oh, how adorable is Jesus! How amiable He is in all things! Let us render to Him homage in union with the twenty-four elders of the Apocalypse: "We give Thee thanks, O Lord God Almighty, who art, and who was, and who art to come, because Thou hast taken to Thee Thy great power, and Thou hast reigned." (Apoc. 11:17)

FIRST POINT
✝ Faith Teaches us to See Jesus Christ in all Men

It shows us Jesus in our superiors: "He that heareth you, heareth Me, and he that despiseth you, despiseth Me" (Luke 10:16), says our divine Saviour. And St. Paul says: "He that resisteth the power, resisteth the ordinance of God." (Rom. 13:2) It shows Him to us in the persons of those whose duty it is to instruct, us: "For Christ, therefore we are ambassadors, God as it were exhorting by us," as the same apostle says. (2 Cor. 5:20) It points Him out to us in the ministers of the sacraments. It is He who baptizes by their hands, who absolves by their mouth, who consecrates by their ministry. It teaches us to see Him in the poor and the lowly: "As long as you did it to one of these My least brethren, you did it to Me;" (Matt. 25:40) in the sick, in strangers, in prisoners, in all those who are in affliction: "I was hungry, and you gave Me to eat; I was thirsty, and you gave Me to drink; I was a stranger, and you took Me in; naked, and you covered Me; sick, and you visited Me; I was in prison, and you came to Me." (Matt. 15:35,36) Finally, it shows us all men without exception as members of Christ; He abides in them and they are His temples: "You are the temples of the living God, I will dwell in them." (2 Cor. 6:16) If this doctrine were better understood, how much we would all love one another, how much we would all respect one another! There would be an end to all quarrels and bickerings, to all cruel words, to all backbiting. In all things and at all times we would observe charity; charity with its forbearance, its kind attentions, its amiable and graceful manners. Let us examine our conscience; let us ask pardon for the past and make good resolutions for the future.

SECOND POINT
✝ **Faith Teaches us to See Jesus Christ in Everything**

It shows Him to us in our body: it is He who moves it at our pleasure; in the air we breathe: it is He who prepares it in a suitable manner; in the sun: it is He who sends us the sweet light of it; in the flowers of the fields, the beauties of nature, the magnificence of the skies: it is He who has created all these marvels to embellish our exile; in the earth: it is He who renders it fruitful; in the water: it is lie who refreshes us by its means; in the fire: it is He who by its flame warms us; in the animals: it is He who nourishes us through them, gives us clothing, contributes to our pleasure, and renders us a thousand services; in rain: it is He who sheds it according to the needs of the earth; in the succession of days and of seasons: it is He who disposes them with such perfect regularity; in food: it is He who furnishes it to every creature that breathes, prepares it for us, and serves it to us through His members, the other men employed in our service; lastly, in all events: it is He who disposes them for our good with so much care that nothing happens except through Him, not even the fall of one of our hairs; with so much assiduity, that even when we sleep He watches by our bedside; with so much kindness, that it is as though He were full of care for us. (Ps. 39:18) If events are favorable, it is His goodness which humors our weakness; if they are contrary to us, it is still His love, which for the sake of our salvation makes us bear the cross with Him. Lastly, whatever happens, men are only His instruments; He is the Sovereign Master who directs all for our greater good. In a more elevated order of things, He gives us His angels to guard us, His apostles to instruct us, His martyrs to protect us, His saints to edify us, His sacraments to unite us to Him, His spirit to animate us, His Church to direct us, and His graces to go everywhere seeking for sinners to convert, the lukewarm to heat, the just to sanctify (Coloss. 3:2). Oh, how amiable Jesus is, and how ungrateful we are!

THIRD POINT
✝ Faith Teaches us to See Jesus Christ in all our Acts

When we rise in the morning, He is the Sun of Justice whom we ought to salute at our awakening; when we dress, He is the robe with which we ought to cover ourselves. (Rom. 8:14) When we pray it ought to be in Him and by Him; when we read, He is the truth we ought to adore, hidden beneath the bark of letters; when we take our recreation, it was He who bought for us, at the price of His blood, the recreation of which our sins had rendered us unworthy; when we walk, it is in His company, because as God He is everywhere present; when we take our repose it is on His heart, and as it were in His arms. (Ps. 4:9) Lastly, all we do or say, we ought to do and say it in His name, for His love and with the aim of giving Him pleasure. (Coloss. 3:17) *Resolutions and spiritual nosegay as above.*

Friday in the Second Week after Epiphany

SUMMARY OF TOMORROW'S MEDITATION

Following upon the general considerations which have occupied us in the preceding meditations, we will now meditate upon the first years of the Word Incarnate upon earth, and we will consider how much His holy infancy merits, first, our admiration; second, our love. We will then make the resolution: first, to perform all our actions from love for the Infant Jesus and with the object of pleasing Him; second, to multiply as much as possible aspirations of admiration and of love toward Him, and to preserve the memory of Him continually in our hearts. Our spiritual nosegay shall be the words of St. Bernard. "The more Jesus makes himself little for us the more we love Him."

MEDITATION FOR THE MORNING

Let us adore Jesus Christ reduced, for love of us, to the form of a little child in a cradle. Let us offer Him all the homage offered by Mary and Joseph, as well as that of the angels who form an invisible guard around Him, and let us ask of Him the grace to be deeply penetrated in our prayers with the sentiments of admiration and love which are due to Him.

FIRST POINT
✝ The Homage of Adoration due to Jesus Christ in the Cradle

To the human eye, there is nothing more simple or less likely to attract admiration than the Divine Infant in the cradle; but to the eye of faith, what marvels, what causes for astonishment reveal themselves! This little child who appears so poor is the eternal God, whose power has created everything, whose strength moves all things, whose wisdom governs all; this orphan, who sucks the breast of a woman, who is wrapped in swaddling-clothes, is the God who reigns on high in heaven, and on whom all empires depend. He is the Eternal Word, and yet His embarrassed tongue cannot articulate sounds, and can only utter wailings! He is whom the prophet has said that "the hills of the world were bowed down by the journeys of His eternity," (Habac. 3:6) and yet His weak and tottering feet cannot sustain Him: if you withdraw your hand He falls to the ground; He is the uncreated wisdom and He seems to be nothing but ignorance. He is supreme power, and you see in Him nothing but weakness; He is the first in sovereignty, and He seems to be in the most extreme dependence! O God, what a mountain of mysteries! Who would not prostrate himself and be annihilated in the presence of such lofty marvels! Oh, why have I not a spirit sufficiently humiliated to adore, as I ought, so much littleness which conceals so much grandeur, so much weakness which conceals so much strength; so much powerlessness which conceals so much power; so much abasement which conceals so much elevation! After having passed two or three years in this state, Jesus, having reached the age at which ordinary children stammer their first words and make their first steps, begins to speak and to walk. Oh, how delightful it was to hear Him uttering the first words, by which He called God His Father, Mary His mother, Joseph His second father, and uttered His first prayer! How beautiful it was to see Him taking His first steps, rendering His first services to Mary and Joseph with all the charm attendant upon childhood; later on going and coming about the house, speaking with so much kindness, leading a life so pure, so innocent, and so sweet! Let us represent to ourselves by faith what it has pleased God to hide from us; and falling on our knees before this blessed Child, pour forth in His presence all the admiration, the complaisance, and the adoration of which our hearts are capable.

SECOND POINT
✝ Homage of Love due to Jesus in His Cradle

If Jesus Christ had appeared all at once in the guise of manhood, in the splendor of His majesty, in the apparel of His greatness, we should have trembled before Him to such an extent as to be afraid of approaching Him; but as He descended upon earth to make Himself loved and not to make Himself feared, He takes the form of a little Child, because there is nothing more amiable than a little child with its candor, its simplicity, its gentleness, all its innocent qualities which gain even the most barbarous heart. We naturally love children; but how much more ought we to love the holy Infant Jesus, the most beautiful, the sweetest of the children of men, reflecting on all the features of His face the love which He bears us. Oh, who will give us a heart loving enough in order to love as we ought the adorable littleness of this little child? Who will give us to be melted to tears in His presence, that so we may repair our misfortune in loving Him too little until now? Ah, Divine Infant! I give Thee my heart, I consecrate it forever to Thee, and will no longer live except in Thy holy love. *Resolutions and spiritual nosegay as above.*

Saturday in the Second Week after Epiphany

SUMMARY OF TOMORROW'S MEDITATION

e will consider tomorrow: first, the gratitude, second, the confidence we owe to Jesus Christ in His cradle. We will then make the resolution: first, often to utter aspirations of gratitude towards the Divine Child; second, never to allow ourselves to be cast down and discouraged by our weakness, but to encourage ourselves constantly to lead a better life, and to have confidence in the help of Jesus. Our spiritual nosegay shall be the canticle of the Church: "Who would not render love for love to so loving a God?"

MEDITATION FOR THE MORNING

Let us lovingly draw near to the cradle of the Infant Jesus. Let us consider Him in this humble crib entirely occupied about us and our salvation. Let us thank Him and bless Him for so much love (1 John 4:19), and let us love this God who first so loved us.

FIRST POINT
✝ Gratitude to Jesus in the Cradle

The life of Jesus in His cradle was not an unoccupied life, like that of other children. In a state in which the human eye perceives nothing but a child who seems to sleep, Jesus continually occupies Himself with each one of us, and puts every moment to profit for the purpose of saving us. Zeal for our salvation absorbs Him wholly. It is this zeal which, eight days after His birth, .makes Him shed the first-fruits of His blood beneath the knife of circumcision; it is this zeal which makes Him in His cradle raise His little hands to heaven to avert the thunder which is about to be hurled against guilty earth, and which draws from Him His first tears to wash away our stains and extinguish the fire of the anger of heaven. It is this zeal which day and night brings forth from His heart such fervent prayers to call down upon us all the graces which we have received up to the present moment and we shall continue to receive, and not only ourselves but all Christians, for He embraces in His prayers all ages and all countries. It is this zeal which renders dear and precious the swaddling-clothes in which He is wrapped, the bands in which He is confined. He takes pleasure in presenting Himself in this state before His Father, to deliver us from slavery by the merit of His bonds, and before us in order to make us renounce, in presence of so great an example, the miserable liberty which will do everything that pleases it and follow its own taste and its ease. It is this zeal, lastly, which determined Him to take upon Him all our infirmities, to pass through all the degrees of weakness, to the extent of not being distinguishable in any respect from other children, and to make Himself to be looked upon with pity by the crowd as a feeble and powerless child. O my Jesus, how can we ever be grateful enough for such love? How thank Thee sufficiently for so many sacrifices, for so many prayers, for so much devotion to our salvation? Oh, that I had the heart of all the angels and of all the saints to offer Thee worthy thanksgivings! Thanks, a thousand times, my God,who hast so loved me. I will repeat it during all eternity.

SECOND POINT
✝ Confidence due to Jesus in the Cradle

When God gave His law to His ancient people, He promulgated it in the midst of lightning and thunder, because He wished to maintain this rude and disobedient people in the path of duty by means of the sentiment of fear. Under the new law, it is no longer by fear that the Saviour desires to lead us, but by confidence and love (II Tim.1:7). Fear is for slaves, confidence for children; fear discourages, and the soul that is discouraged is good for nothing.

Fear may sometimes prevent evil; confidence alone gives courage to perform a great deal of good; it multiplies its forces, and repairs past evil by present good. This is why our great God, descending upon earth to give the world a better and more perfect law than the ancient law, takes the form of a little child, as being the most suitable to inspire confidence. And, in fact, who would fear to approach a child and who would not be at ease in speaking to him? Let those tremble whom so rriuch goodness does not touch, and who will, spite of it, persevere in doing evil; but let those hope who desire to love God become a little child through love. In seeing the benignity of His face, the gentleness, the sweetness, the goodness which shine forth in all His features, may their hearts overflow with confidence, may their courage which has been cast down rise again, and may they exclaim with the prophet: "Behold God is my Saviour, I will deal confidently and will not fear"(Is. 12:2). I rejoice to see my salvation in the hands of a God so good, rather than in my own. In order to work it out I should neither have as much power, nor as much wisdom, nor as much zeal and love. Therefore I will never allow myself to be discouraged, but I will always encourage myself to live better, to repair the past by better conduct and more zeal for my perfection. *Resolutions and spiritual nosegay as above.*

Third Sunday after Epiphany

THE GOSPEL ACCORDING TO ST. MATTHEW, 8:1-13.

"And when He was come down from the mountain great multitudes followed Him, and behold a leper came and adored Him, saying: Lord, if Thou wilt Thou canst make me clean. And Jesus stretching forth His hand, touched him, saying: I will, be thou made clean. And forthwith his leprosy was cleansed. And Jesus saith to him: See thou tell no man, but go, show thyself to the priest, and offer the gift which Moses commanded for a testimony unto them. And when He had entered into Capharnaum there came to Him a centurion, beseeching Him and saying: Lord, my servant lie at home sick of the palsy, and is grievously tormented. And Jesus saith to him: I will come and heal him. And the centurion making answer, said: Lord, I am not worthy that Thou shouldst enter under my roof, but only say the word and my servant shall be healed. For I also am a man subject to authority, having under me soldiers, and I say to this, go, and he goes, and to another, come, and he comes, and to my servant, do this, and he does it. And Jesus hearing this, marveled, and said to them that followed Him: Amen, I say to you, I have not found so great faith in Israel. And I say to you that many shall come from the east and the west, and shall sit down with Abraham, and Isaac, and Jacob in the kingdom of heaven, but the children of the kingdom shall be cast out into the exterior darkness: there shall be weeping and gnashing of teeth. And Jesus said to the centurion: Go, and as thou hast believed, so be it done to thee. And the servant was healed at the same hour."

SUMMARY OF TOMORROW'S MEDITATION

e will tomorrow suspend the course of our meditations in order to consider, in the Gospel for the day, Jesus miraculously curing a leper and the servant of the centurion; and this double miracle will enable us to see; first, in the Savior, the physician of our souls; second, in ourselves, the conditions to which our cure is attached. We will then make the resolution: first, often to have recourse to Christ, as to our charitable physician; second, to study our miseries and to ask Him for the cure of them with faith, with humility, and with an ardent desire to obtain it. Our spiritual nosegay shall be the prayer of the Psalmist: "O Lord, be Thou merciful to me; heal my soul, because I have sinned against Thee." (Ps. 40:5)

MEDITATION FOR THE MORNING

Let us adore Jesus Christ as the physician of our souls, descended from heaven to cure the: human race, that great sick man who lay on the ground. (St. Augustine, Serm. 59 tie Verb. Dom.) Let us prostrate ourselves at His feet like sick men who ask to be cured. Let us bless Him for the many cures which He performed during the time He spent on earth ail d which He performs every day in the Church. Let us put all our confidence in Him.

FIRST POINT

✝ Jesus is the Physician of Souls

The hideous malady of the leper of our Gospel and the paralysis which afflicted the servant of the centurion were the figure of sin, of the passions and of the different spiritual maladies which Jesus Christ came to earth to cure. Therefore; our charitable Savior was moved with compassion for them. He touches the leper with His hand, and restores him to health. He says to the centurion: "Go, and as thou hast believed, so be it done unto thee;" and at the same moment the servant is cured. Consider how well calculated these miracles of charity and of power are to in spire us with confidence in the Savior. It does not cost Him more to cure our souls than to cure the sick who were presented to Him. On the one side He still has as much power as ever to cure us; on the other side He has as much goodwill as ever to do it. He desires, so much to see us holy and perfect. He thirsts so much for our salvation, arid He cries out to us as He did to the leper in the Gospel: "Go and show yourselves to the priests," just as you are, with the firm resolution not to allow yourselves to fall ill again, and you shall be cured, "Come unto Me, all ye who are laden" with the weight of your miseries, "and I will refresh you," that is to say, I will give you back your innocence and peace of heart. Thus it is our heavenly Physician who wills to cure us; and if He does not do it, it is because we resist His curing us. Unhappy that we are, we do not fulfill the conditions to which He has attached our cure.

SECOND POINT
✝ Conditions, on which Jesus Christ offers us our Cure

First, we must know what our malady is, and we must desire sincerely and fervently to be cured of it. The leper of the Gospel was perfectly well acquainted with his malady; he knew all the circumstances attending it, its hideousness, its shame, and its danger; and he earnestly asks the Savior to cure him. The centurion knows equally well what is the malady of his servant, he describes it in all its seriousness, (Matt. 8:6) and he conjures the Savior to cure it. Ah if we felt in the same way our spiritual maladies; if we understood all the gravity, and all the danger of them; if we desired with an ardent desire to be delivered from them; if we earnestly begged the Savior for grace, we should soon be cured and changed. Second, we must accompany our prayer with a holy faith. How admirable is the faith which inspired the leper with that beautiful prayer: "Lord, if Thou wilt, Thou canst make me clean," (Matt. 8:2) and the centurion with that other prayer: "Only say the word and my servant shall be healed. I also am a man subject to authority, having under me soldiers, and I say to this, go, and he goes; to another, come, and he comes; and to my servant, do this, and he does it." (Ibid. 8,9) Speak in the same manner to the sickness and it will depart. Oh, how so great faith in the leper and in this officer, habituated to life in a camp, ought to cover us with confusion we, who in a much better position are yet so far removed from it. O Lord, increase our faith. (Luke 17:5) Third, we must pray with humility. A great personage, a centurion humbles himself; he dares not appear before the Lord; he looks upon himself as unworthy to receive Him into his house; he prostrates himself before Him and adores Him. Why have we not these feelings of humility when we pray, above all when we repeat the words of the centurion: "Lord, I am not worthy that Thou should enter under my roof." (Matt. 8:8) Oh, then we should quickly be heard! God loves the humble so much, and listens so favorably to their prayers. (Ps. 107:6; 137:6) Let us make trial of it and we shall obtain the cure of all our miseries. *Resolutions and spiritual nosegay as above.*

Monday in the Third Week after Epiphany

SUMMARY OF TOMORROW'S MEDITATION

he Incarnate Word having come upon earth to be our Master, as we have seen in our previous meditation, we will tomorrow take from Him in His cradle a lesson of humility. We will consider: first, that in this state He teaches us humility; second that we ought to put this divine lesson into practice. Our resolution shall be: first, often to ask the Infant Jesus for courage, never to take counsel from self-love, and never to seek to attract admiration and praise. Second to perform all our actions with the object of obtaining humility. Our spiritual nosegay shall be the words of our Savior Himself: "Learn of Me, because I am meek and humble of heart." (Matt. 11:29)

MEDITATION FOR THE MORNING

Let us adore the Infant Jesus in His cradle as the great master of humility. Let us unite ourselves with the angels, who adore Him all the more profoundly because they see Him in this state of humiliation. Let us share their sentiments, and let us give our hearts to this great God who is a little child, that He may make them humble like His.

FIRST POINT

✝ The Lesson of Humility which the Child Jesus gives us in the Cradle

Humility is all the more admirable in proportion, as the person who humbles himself is more elevated by his nature, and that he places himself lower by his own free choice. Now in this cradle, the dignity of Him who humbles Himself is infinite, and His humiliation cannot be more profound. He who knows all appears as though He were ignorant; He who, can do all things appears to be nothing but powerless, He who fills immensity is reduced to the form of a little child; and He who is the Eternal Word is mute. O holy humility, how eloquently you speak to human pride, to worldly haughtiness, which desires to raise itself, to make an appearance, and to lord it over others!

If Thou, who art so great, so holy, so perfect, art so humble, what ought we to be, we who are so little, so miserable, so full of defects? It is in beholding Thee with faith, hope, and love that all the saints have learned to love humble and modest positions, a hidden life, obscure functions; to take from their exterior and their manners all that is not sufficiently simple and which is impregnated with the desire to please others; to rejoice to pass for less than others, minor, like St. Francis of Assisi; for the last of all, minimus, like St, Francis de Paul. It is still every day, when gazing on Thee in Thy cradle, O Divine Infant, that we understand the words of the Gospel: "Unless you be converted and become as little children, you shall not enter into the kingdom of heaven." (Matt. 18:3) A little child in his cradle does not esteem himself and does not believe himself to be capable of great things. If he possesses good natural qualities of body or of mind, of heart or of character, he does not esteem himself any the more for them; he feels his ignorance and weakness, his powerlessness and his inexperience, and in consequence he places himself below every one. Let him be honored or let him be despised, let him be praised or let him be blamed, it is all the same to him, he pays no heed to what is said, or what is thought, by those around him. It is true that these sentiments have no merit in him, but they ought to be found in us under the form of virtue. May we hence learn to respect Christian littleness, which preserves from so many sins and hides so much greatness.

SECOND POINT

✝ We ought to Carry into Practice the Lesson of Humility which Jesus gives us in the Cradle

God holds the proud in horror; He resists them and will not ally Himself with them. (James 4:6) On the other hand, He looks with complacence on humble hearts. (Ps. 137:6) "If you rise, He flies from you, if you humble yourselves, He comes down to you," says St. Augustine. There can no more be any solid virtue without humility than there can be a house without a foundation, a treasure which is in security without a guardian to watch over and defend it; for humility is the essential basis of the whole of the spiritual edifice; it is the guardian of all virtues, so that devoid of it the most lofty virtue is corrupted and becomes the vile nourishment of self-love, an establishing of man in himself instead of his establishment in God. *Resolutions and spiritual nosegay as above.*

Tuesday in the Third Week after Epiphany

SUMMARY OF TOMORROW'S MEDITATION

esus in His cradle not only teaches humility in general; He also teaches the different degrees of it, which are; first, to have humble ideas of ourselves; second, to take pleasure in these humble sentiments. We shall see that the Child Jesus admirably teaches us both the one and the other. We will then make the resolution: first, to bless God for all that humbles us, without troubling ourselves about it or being afflicted; second, to have recourse to Him with confidence in the midst of our miseries, knowing that He protects all those who, knowing themselves to be miserable, call Him to their aid. Our spiritual nosegay shall be the words of David: "I will make myself meaner than I have done, and I will be little in my own eyes." (2 Kings 6:22)

MEDITATION FOR THE MORNING

Let us transport ourselves in spirit to the cradle of the Infant Jesus. Let us, as far as in us lies, raise His profound humiliation by our homage, and let us beg of Him to shed the grace of it upon our souls.

FIRST POINT

✝ Jesus in the Cradle Teaches us to have Humble Ideas of Ourselves

The first lesson of Jesus, on His arrival in this world, is to teach us to substitute profound contempt for the vain esteem in which we hold ourselves. Although so little in His cradle, He humbles Himself more in His own opinion. The thought that His humanity is taken from nothingness makes Him conduct Himself in the presence of His Father with the most humble reverence and as pure nothingness. (Ps. 38:6) Now we ought to abase ourselves still more in ourselves, for not only are we nothing, (Gal. 6:3) but to nothingness we have added sin; and, because of this double title, forgetfulness, rejection, confusion, and contempt are our portion. Woe to him who does not understand this truth! The chief of the angels in heaven, because he looked upon himself as something, was lost; David, on the contrary, because he humbled himself after his sin, obtained mercy. To recognize that one is nothing in oneself, and less than nothing as a sinner, is, consequently, to despise ourselves profoundly, so as to appear vile in our own eyes, and in this true humility consists, without which we are cast off by God because of our pride. (1 Imit. 2) "I am," said St. Vincent de Paul of himself, "a monster of malice, more wicked than the devil, who did not deserve hell so much as I do." Lord, grant that, like St. Vincent de Paul, I may know myself in order to despise and hate myself (St. Augustine), and that instead of excusing my faults and defects I may ingenuously confess that I am a wretch.

SECOND POINT
✝ Jesus in the Cradle Teaches us to take Pleasure in the Low Ideas which Truth gives us of Ourselves

I take pleasure, said St. Paul, in the sight of my infirmities and my miseries, because I know that the more I abase myself in the sight of God, the more closely will He draw near to me, and will communicate to me His graces. (2 Cor. 12:10) Human pride, on the contrary, is vexed and discouraged at seeing in itself so much misery, given to so many falls and so much weakness, so many "evil inclinations, and possessed of so little talent, so little intelligence, so little distinction, so few virtues and merits. In order to correct our pride, the Divine Infant places His joy in seeing Himself in the most profound abasement, to be the last of men (Is. 53:3), a worm of the earth (Ps. 21:7), hidden in a little cradle around which people go and come without paying any attention to it; in a word, to appear as nothing but weakness and powerlessness. Mary, His Mother, sharing in these sentiments, delights to appear to be obscure and ignorant among the daughters of Juda; she loves this littleness as being the charm which has attracted towards her the eyes of the Most High. (Luke 1:4) In fact, God looks lovingly upon every soul which delights itself in the reality of what it is. He never refuses His assistance to misery which confesses itself to be miserable; He sheds His graces upon it, because it places itself at the standpoint of truth, and He cherishes this disposition so greatly that He makes of it the first beatitude of the Gospel (Matt. 5: 3). Happy those who, seeing themselves to be poor, abject, devoid of everything that is good, willingly accept their humiliations as a remedy against pride; for this remedy frees them from pride, the fruitful source of all evil, and it is in the judgment of the saints one of the most evident signs of predestination. *Resolutions and spiritual nosegay as above.*

Wednesday in the Third Week after Epiphany

SUMMARY OF TOMORROW'S MEDITATION

e will meditate tomorrow on the second degree of humility, which consists in treating ourselves with contempt and in always looking upon the lowest place as good enough for us. We shall see: first, that Our Lord teaches us this lesson by His example; second, that reason itself persuades us to follow it. We will then make the resolution: first, in everything to leave the best for others and to take the worst for ourselves; second, in our conduct, as well as in the exercise of virtue, to avoid as much as possible, and to delight in not being thought of by others. Our spiritual nosegay shall be the words of the Gospel: "Sit down in the lowest place." (Luke 14:10).

MEDITATION FOR THE MORNING

Let us adore the Incarnate Word descending from the sweet bosom of His Father and from the abode of glory, in order to come and dwell on the earth, where He is misunderstood and where He hides His divine being under the veil of humanity in its most abased condition. He there treats Himself as the last of men; in everything He takes the lowest rank as His portion (Philipp. 2:8). Let us render Him homage in this state; let us thank Him for this lesson, and let us give Him our heart that He may form therein the same disposition.

FIRST POINT

✝ **Jesus in the Cradle Teaches us to Treat Ourselves with Contempt, and always to Look upon the Last Place as Good Enough for us**

The Word of God, willing to make Himself man, might not have chosen to be born of a woman, but have shown Himself all at once as a consummate man, such as Adam was, when He was born; He preferred to pass through the stage of infancy, as being more vile and more abject. (Philipp. 2:7) Willing to be born of a woman, He might have chosen an illustrious princess: He preferred a poor work woman gaining her bread by labor. Willing to be born in Judea, He might have been born in Jerusalem: He made choice of a despised little town. In this town He chose the most abject place, a stable; the most disagreeable season and weather, winter, and the middle of the night. Having thus entered into the world, He assumes the livery of poverty; He allows Himself to be circumcised, as a slave and a sinner; at the Presentation He allows Himself to be ransomed by the offering of the poor. When Herod persecutes Him, He chooses the most abject way of escaping, which was by flight. In the temple, in the midst of the doctors, He questions them like an ignorant person who needs to learn. In the house at Nazareth, He takes the last place, which is that of obeying Mary and Joseph. Later on, upon the banks of the Jordan, He receives baptism as a sinner. In the desert He allows Himself to be carried in the arms of the devil. Amidst His disciples He is as their servant, (Matt. 20:28) and washes the feet of them all, even Judas. After such examples as these, who would not love to be below others, or to pass for a person worth nothing or of a very low condition? Who would be ambitious to occupy the first place, to be in pre-eminent and superior positions? Who would run after praise and esteem? Who would dare speak of himself, and who would not voluntarily accept reproofs and reproaches? What a subject for examination, and what a reformation to work in our sentiments, our language, and our manner of acting!

SECOND POINT
✝ **Reason Tells us to Treat Ourselves with Contempt, and always to Consider the Last Place as Good Enough for us**

First, this second degree of humility is the rigorous consequence of the first; for if we feel that we are contemptible, it is illogical to desire to be honored and not to be treated with contempt. Justice wills that to everyone should be rendered that which is his due: to nothingness and sin, rejection and contempt. God will live in us only in proportion as we do ourselves justice, according to the truth of what we really are (Jer. 4:2), that is to say, as long as we stifle in ourselves all desire for honors and dignities, for riches and praise, and thus mocking at these desires as though they were a piece of insanity, we cheerfully accept contempts and humiliations as things which are our due. Second, to treat ourselves with contempt is the means of living well with God with our neighbor, and with ourselves: first, with God, for it is to render ourselves like to Jesus Christ; it is to keep in our true place, which always attracts the complaisance and the graces of God; second, with our neighbor, for there are then no susceptibilities, no disputes about precedence, but an amiable exchange of good offices, of respect and consideration; third, with oneself, because then we have a safeguard for our humility and our peace, those two sources of happiness; we have a safeguard for our innocence and we cannot fall, for great falls are those from elevated places, and whoever is cast down upon the earth cannot fall. Let us ask God for grace rightly to understand and to put in practice these important truths. *Resolutions and spiritual nosegay as above.*

THURSDAY IN THE THIRD WEEK AFTER EPIPHANY

SUMMARY OF TOMORROW'S MEDITATION

e will meditate tomorrow on the third degree of humility, which consists in being very glad that we should be known and appreciated for what we are that is to say, little worthy of esteem; and we shall see that this degree of virtue is, first, taught by the example of Jesus Christ; second, conformable to reason. We will then make the resolution: first, never to endeavor, by means of subterfuges and lies, to hide from others our defects and our faults; second, not to justify ourselves when we are accused at any fate, unless we have good reason to do so. Our spiritual nosegay shall be the words of the Apostle: "I please myself in my infirmities, in reproaches, in necessities, in persecutions, in distresses, for Christ: for when I am weak, then am I powerful." (2 Cor. 12:10)

MEDITATION FOR THE MORNING

Let us adore the Incarnate Word delighted to allow Himself to be seen by the shepherds, the Magi, the inhabitants of Egypt, in the state of abjection to which He is reduced. Let us admire the sentiments of His heart in this profound abasement, and let us render Him, from this motive, all our homage.

FIRST POINT

✝ The Example of the Incarnate Word Teaches us to be very Glad to be Known and Appreciated as being Little Worthy of Esteem

One of our greatest weaknesses is to desire to hide from others the truth respecting what we really are, when this truth does not honor us, to take greater care to hide our faults than to avoid them; and inspite of that, they are discovered, to be grieved about it, to excuse them, to lay the blame of them now to an inadvertence on our part, and now as owing to the fault of others, whom we are not afraid of covering with shame in our place, and, in order the better to succeed therein, even to have recourse to duplicity, concealment, and lies. Such, indeed, is our weakness in this respect, that when our faults are discovered, we are more afflicted at our reputation being compromised than at the offence committed against God, and that the pardon of the least word uttered to our disadvantage, however true it may be, costs us a great deal, whilst praises, however false they may be, give us pleasure, and we are gratified with the flatterers who address them to us. Let us here admire what the Incarnate Word did in order to cure such an evil. The God of Infinite Majesty not only abases, and, as it were, annihilates Himself before His Father, by taking the form of a servant, but He is pleased to cause Himself to appear to the world in the state of abjection to which He has descended; He wills that the whole earth and all ages should know it. Long before His coming, He made known, by His prophets, His wonderful abasement; He showed it to the Wise Men of the East, that they might carry the news to the Gentiles; He caused it to be announced by His apostles and their successors to all nations; lastly, He increases and perpetuates it in the Eucharist. After that, has He not the right to say to us, woe to you, hypocrites, who desire that others should think you better than you are, and who take pleasure in falsehood and lies as soon as your self-love finds its interest therein. (Matt. 23:13-15)

SECOND POINT
✝ Reason itself Teaches us that we ought to be very Glad to be Known and Appreciated for what we Really are

Reason, in fact, tells us, first, that want of consideration or the contempt which will be our portion because we have been weighed according to our real value, is a specific remedy against our pride, justice which is rendered to us, a homage to truth, and, by all these titles, a grace of God, an infinitely desirable present from Heaven. It was this which made the holy King David say, when his officers wished to repress the insolence of Semei: "Let him curse: for the Lord hath bid him curse David." (2 Kings 16:10) Reason teaches us, second, that this sentiment of the heart is a preservation against sin, deprived of which, we should allow ourselves to give way to impatience, anger, and vengeance on the least suspicion of a want of the respect we think to be our due; we should render insult for insult, contempt for contempt, raillery for raillery; we should yield to secret animosities, to sadness, and to melancholy if we could not rise out of the humiliation caused by contempt. Alas! in order to excite us to discontent, it needs so little; it suffices that it should seem as though we were not listened to, that some little preference should be granted to another whom we fancy to be esteemed more than we are; sometimes even an idea which has no foundation completely upsets us. Reason tells us, third, that nothing is so beautiful, nothing so honorable, as frankness, which speaks the truth even when it humiliates us; which, always up right in its conduct, does its duty, and allows the world to speak without thinking of anything but doing well. He who has not a soul great enough to raise himself to such a height is base, pusillanimous, and hampered in his actions, deprived of ease and of liberty, which alone ensure success; he is false, hypocritical, and so artificial that he will tell lies in order to diminish his defects or veil his sins; a slave of vanity, he thinks only of speaking of himself, or making others speak of him and everywhere spread a good opinion respecting him. Reason tells us, fourth, that the love of truth in the soul, carried as far as the sacrifice of self-love, attracts the best blessings of God; it is even here below the secret of happiness. Raised above opinions and vain speeches, such a man lives happily and in tranquility; he prays with facility, he enjoys God, he loves Him, and he exclaims with the Apostle: "But to me it is a very small thing to be judged be you or by man's day." (1 Cor. 4:3) *Resolutions and spiritual nosegay as above.*

Friday in the Third Week after Epiphany

SUMMARY OF TOMORROW'S MEDITATION

e will meditate tomorrow on the fourth degree of humility, which consists in delighting to be treated without consideration, even with contempt, when Providence permits that we should be so treated; and we shall see: first, that Jesus Christ preaches this doctrine by His example; second, that the principles of faith confirm it to us. We will then make the resolution: first, to bear, silently and without bitterness, want of consideration, rejection, and even contempt; second, courageously to fight against all temptations to susceptibility and claims to attention, and often to ask God for grace not to descend to such littleness. Our spiritual nosegay shall be the eighth beatitude: "Blessed are ye when they shall revile you and persecute you, and speak all that is evil against you, untruly, for My sake." (Matt. 5:11)

MEDITATION FOR THE MORNING

Let us adore the Infant Jesus treated as the last of men, relegated to a stable the first day of His entrance into the world; later on persecuted and put to flight; during the whole of His life and at His death maltreated by those even to whom He had done nothing but good; and since His death, what irreverence has He not had to submit to in the Eucharist! O my Jesus, how Thou art treated in even the very sacrament of Thy love! Let us render Him our most humble homage in His profound abasement.

FIRST POINT

✝ Jesus Teaches us by His Example to Love to be Treated with out Consideration and with Contempt when Providence Permits that we should be so Treated

One of the most remarkable features of the Gospel is the fact of Our Savior flying from glory, desiring contempt in the same manner that others desire honor and celebrity. (Ps. 68:21) In His early childhood, with the exception of the shepherds and the Magi, Mary and Joseph, He is treated without any consideration as the most ordinary of children. When He grows bigger He is treated like a poor apprentice who is not yet acquainted with his trade, as ignorant alike of human and divine studies. (John 7:15) Now, who are we that we should desire to be better treated than God? If we look upon ourselves as Christians, our glory is to resemble Jesus Christ, to live in His spirit, and with His life, to love what He loved, to hate what He hated. If we look upon ourselves as men, we ought to think it well that justice should be rendered to us; now being nothing except nothingness and sin, we have no right to anything but rejection and contempt. If we consider ourselves as pilgrims passing through this life, we ought not to attach any importance to the opinion of men who will soon no longer exist, and besides which whose approbation and blame are of no consequence to us; for if they criticize and despise us, we are not worthless on that account; if they esteem and praise us, neither on that account are we worth any more. This, even, is not saying enough; if they despise us, it is a precious opportunity for us to exercise humility; whilst if they praise us, we run a great danger of being proud. Hence it was that the saints rejoiced over the imperfections or involuntary faults into which they fell, as being occasions of great gain for their humility, and they feared praise as a trial where they were afraid that pride would cause them to make shipwreck, according to the words of the sage. (Prov. 28:21)

SECOND POINT

✝ The Principles of Faith Teach us that we must Delight to be Treated without Consideration and even with Contempt when Providence Permits us to be so Treated

First, Providence has thus regulated all things: if we seek glory in this world, we shall have confusion in the next; and if, from love to Our Lord, we accept with a good grace contempt and want of consideration here below, we shall have an abundant share of glory in heaven (Rom. 8:17). What is more decisive than this reasoning? Second, it will be with difficulty that we shall find a virtue which will be in harmony with a contrary disposition, or at least which will not clash with it exceedingly. Should it be faith? One of its first lessons is that man considered in his essence is naught but nothingness and sin, and deserves nothing but contempt. Should it be religion? But it desires that all should be annihilated before God, that God alone may be great. Should it be the love of God? But love delights to render honor and glory to God alone, and to keep nothing for itself but confusion. Should it be the love of our neighbor? But love disappears if we do not know how to bear wrongs done to us, want of consideration, even calumnies and injuries; and this endurance presupposes that we willingly consent to be treated without consideration; Should it be gentleness? But the least want of consideration will change its nature; and susceptibility, with its evil temper, will take the place of it. Should it be patience? But a sweet tranquility in the midst of contempt is impossible to him who does not like to be treated with a want of consideration. Lastly, should it be penitence? But where there is penitence there is contempt of oneself and the deep sentiment that we deserve the contempt of others. Yet we are so susceptible, so ready to be angry at the least want of consideration. Let us confess our faults and correct them. *Resolutions and spiritual nosegay as above.*

Saturday in the Third Week after Epiphany

SUMMARY OF TOMORROW'S MEDITATION

After having learned humility at the cradle of the Savior, we will come tomorrow to learn there: first, meekness; second, the necessity of humbling ourselves in order to acquire meekness, for we are meek only in proportion as we are humble. We will then make the resolution: first, to watch over ourselves, in order never to allow ourselves to be carried away by outbursts of temper; second, never to speak or act when we are under emotion, but to await calmness and the self-control of meekness. Our spiritual nosegay shall be the words of the Savior: "Learn of Me, because I am meek and humble of heart." (Matt. 11:29)

MEDITATION FOR THE MORNING

Let us adore the Divine Infant Jesus so meek in His cradle; His face, His eyes, His little ways, everything in Him breathes meekness and benignity. (Tit. 3:4) Oh, how greatly He merits, in this state, all our homage and all our love.

FIRST POINT
✝ The Child Jesus in His Cradle Teaches us Meekness

The Incarnate Word, descended from heaven to earth, had nothing so much at heart as to teach men to treat one another with gentleness and charity. He proposed it to them on a certain day when He spoke to the assembled people: Learn of Me to be meek. But He would not wait so long to give the world this lesson, and, not yet being able to articulate sounds, He preaches to them by example the virtue which is the first wish of His heart. What, indeed, is meeker than an infant in the cradle? He shows neither disdain nor haughtiness to any one; he is without bitterness and malice; he does not know what it is to wish ill to others; he is accessible to all, not making any distinction between the rich and the poor, the wise and the ignorant, the powerful and the weak, the great and the little. Such are infants in general. But the meekness of the Infant Jesus is still more admirable. In Him it is not a meekness of nature but a meekness of grace, engendered by reflection and voluntary in character. Or rather it is meekness personified, gentleness and benignity impressed on all His features. Never the least outburst of bad temper, such as children often have, escapes Him, never a shade of the petulance which springs from want of reflection. It is composed of a delicate attention to avoid all that could give pain, to forestall anything which may give pleasure. Behold our model! It is thus that we ought to observe a quite divine suavity, (2 Cor. 6:6) to have nothing on our lips but sweet and kind words, (Cant. 4:11) stifling every movement of impatience or annoyance which has a tendency to appear upon our face, in our words, or in our procedure: like Samson taking the honey of sweetness out of the throat of the lion of suffocating anger. (Jud. 14:14) We ought to bear with patience and meekness all kinds of annoyances and contradictions, all that wounds our evil nature or displeases us. As long as we have not reached this degree of virtue, there is no charity possible towards our neighbor, "for all men desire," said St. Vincent de Paul, "to be where they will be treated with meekness; no one will be led by harshness, reproved with hardness, corrected with bitterness; man is made thus; we shall not be able to change him." Let us examine our conscience on this point: how many times have we not failed in Christian charity?

SECOND POINT
✝ We are Meek only in Proportion that we are Humble

Pride is essentially haughty, hard, and contemptuous; ready to take offence at the least thing to hurt its neighbor by its words, its susceptibilities, its pretensions. Consequently, with this vice no meekness is possible; with humility, on the contrary, meekness flows from its source. The humble man is essentially meek; he is never offended by anything, because he feels that, whatever may be done or said to him, he is always treated better than he deserves to be; he never offends any one, because, looking upon others as above himself, he has nothing but deference, consideration, delicate and amiable attentions for them. He is meek because he is humble; and hence those words full of justice, that meekness is the daughter of humility; it is the flower and the charm of it. When have we been wanting in meekness? Has it not been when our self-love has been touched with only the finger's end; when others have seemed to make no account of us; when someone else has been preferred to ourselves; when an insulting speech has been addressed to us? Let us humble ourselves if we desire to be meek; humility alone can lead us to meekness. *Resolutions and spiritual nosegay as above.*

Fourth Sunday after Epiphany

THE GOSPEL ACCORDING TO ST. MATTHEW 8:23-27

"At that time Jesus entered into a boat, and His disciples followed Him. And behold, a great tempest arose in the sea, so that the boat was "covered with waves: but He was asleep. And they came to Him, and awakened Him, saying: Lord, save us, we perish. And Jesus saith to them: Why are you fearful, O ye of little faith? Then, rising up, He commanded the winds and the sea, and there came a great calm. But the men wondered, saying: What manner of man is this, for the winds and the sea obey Him?"

SUMMARY OF TOMORROW'S MEDITATION

In harmony with the Gospel of the day, which shows us Jesus Christ calming the storm, we will consider: first, what are the moral tempests we have to traverse during our life; second, what is the conduct we ought to observe during these tempests. Our resolution shall be: first, to live a life of prayer and of union with God, who alone can save us in. these tempests; second, to maintain ourselves in the double sentiment of mistrust of our selves, and of confidence in God. Our spiritual nosegay shall be the cry of the apostles: "Lord, save us, we perish." (Matt. 8:25)

MEDITATION FOR THE MORNING

Let us adore Jesus Christ commanding the winds and the waves, and, by the omnipotence of His word, making a great calm succeed the tempest. Let us unite ourselves with the admiration and praise of the people who were witnesses of this triumph (Matt. 8:27).

FIRST POINT

✝ What are the Moral Tempests we shall have to Traverse during our Life?

These tempests are of two kinds: the one, public; the other, private and individual. Public tempests are those which attack the Church from one end of the universe to the other. Outside, it is inimical sects which revolt against her; within, it is bad Christians who tear her or scandalize her. In the midst of these furious waves, the Church calls on us to pity her sufferings, like a good son pitying the sufferings of his mother; to defend her by our words, to edify her by our example, to console her by our devotion. To these public tempests are to be added private and individual ones; continual tempests, which attack souls at all ages of life, by night as well as by day; horrible tempests, which often injure the vessel of the soul to such an extent as to leave it only a single plank whereby to gain the port, and which cast into eternal damnation so many miserable, shipwrecked men; tempests all the more to be dreaded because they are more invisible; we perish in them without being aware of it, and we are already at the bottom of the sea when we believe that we are still navigating towards the port. We reassure ourselves with the thought that we are acting like others; that there is nothing to fear where others do not fear; and, possessed with this idea, we live in tranquility. These tempests come sometimes from without, sometimes from within. Tempests from without: these are affairs which preoccupy us, reverses which overwhelm us, bad examples which shake us, the contradiction of tongues, the clashing of wills and of characters, embarrassments of all kinds. Tempests from within: these are the passions, pride, sensuality, avarice, which make souls perish without their having any idea of it; the senses which revolt, the desires which, torment, the imagination which is ill-regulated, the mind which dissipates itself in useless thoughts, chimerical fears, or vain hopes. O Lord, if Thou dost not save us amidst so many tempests, we are lost!

SECOND POINT
✝ How we ought to Conduct ourselves during the Tempests which besiege us

Here we have three means of salvation; prayer, confidence in God; and mistrust of our selves. First, prayer. The apostles of our Gospel, seeing their ship beaten by the waves, come to Jesus, awake Him, and implore His succor. In the same way, on seeing the assaults waged against the Church, we ought to pray, and pray all the more, the more violently she is attacked. In our private trials we ought equally to pray; therein alone is salvation. Second is confidence. The apostles, filled with confidence, strove against the tempest at the same time that they prayed. Following their example, we ought never to allow ourselves to be cast down or discouraged, but, always full of confidence in God, persevere in resistance, and never despair, either with regard to the evils afflicting the Church or our own wretchedness. God; who protects her and us, is the Almighty; He has but one word to say, and there will be a great calm. When will He pronounce that word? It is His secret; let us know how to wait and we shall be saved. "Mercy shall encompass him that hopes in the Lord." (Ps. 31:10) Whatever may be the trials of the Church, whatever may be our own, let us throw ourselves with confidence into His arms, and we shall be saved as well as His holy Church. Third, to confidence in God we must unite mistrust of ourselves. The presumptuous man, who fears nothing, does not watch over himself, and does not fly from temptation, is infallibly lost. God wills to see us always humiliated beneath His powerful hand; always mistrusting our weakness and the basis of corruption which there is in us; always on our guard against the seductions of the world and dangerous occasions. He who does not fear anything neglects himself; exposes himself and perishes; he, on the contrary, who fears, avoids even the very appearance of sin, has recourse to God, in whom he puts his hope, and is saved. Are we faithful to the means of salvation on which we have been meditating? First, do we lead a life of prayer and of recollection? Do we pray from the bottom of our hearts for the Church, for the Holy See, for ourselves, for those who are dear to us? Second, do we not mistrust the success of our prayers and the promise of Jesus Christ: Ask and you shall receive? Do we live a life of distrust in ourselves? Are we on our guard? Do we not expose ourselves to dangerous occasions of sin? *Resolutions and spiritual nosegay as above.*

Monday in the Fourth Week after Epiphany

SUMMARY OF TOMORROW'S MEDITATION

e will resume tomorrow our visits to the cradle of the Infant Jesus, and we will endeavor to fill ourselves with His purity and innocence, whilst considering that a pure heart is pleasing: first, to God; second, to our neighbor; third, to ourselves. We will then make the resolution: first, very carefully to avoid not only the slightest sins, but even the smallest voluntary imperfection; second, with this object in view, to perform all our actions with the utmost perfection possible. Our spiritual nosegay shall be the sixth beatitude: "Blessed are the clean of heart, for they shall see God." (Matt. 5:8)

MEDITATION FOR THE MORNING

Let us adore the Infant Jesus as the type of purity and innocence. Innocence is the most striking characteristic of an infant in the cradle; he does not know what evil is. Pure and without spot in his intelligence and his will, pure and without spot in his senses, pure and without spot in his heart, he teaches us to keep our intelligence always pure by repressing dangerous curiosity, and our memory by keeping it aloof from evil remembrances, and our imagination by restraining its flights, and our senses by keeping them under subjection. What the ordinary child preaches to us, the Child Jesus preaches to us better still; He, the abyss of purity, not like an infant by the powerlessness of His reason, but by the infinite holiness of the divine nature which is in Him. Let us admire this ineffable purity, and let us beg Him to make us sharers in it, so that we may avoid, as much as possible, even the slightest faults.

FIRST POINT
✝ A Pure Heart is Pleasing to God

"He that loves cleanness of heart, for the grace of his lips shall have the King for his friend." (Prov. 22:11) "Blessed," says Jesus Christ "are the clean of heart, for they shall see God."(Matt. 5:8) "How good is God," says David "to them that are of a right heart," (Ps. 72:1) that is to say, pure and innocent. "Incorruption," the Holy Spirit elsewhere says "brings near to God." (Wis. 6:20) It is of inestimable value in His eyes. (Ecclus. 26:20) A place apart, close to the Lamb, is reserved in heaven for pure souls. (Apoc. 14:4) God takes His pleasure amidst the lilies of purity. (Cant. 2:16) And even in the present life He communicates Himself quite specially to pure hearts, imparts to them His secrets, and inundates them with His graces. My God, enable me to thoroughly understand these beautiful truths, and to derive from them a horror of the least faults, with that tender appreciation of purity and innocence which embalms the heart and sanctifies the soul.

SECOND POINT
✝ A Pure Heart is Pleasing to our Neighbor

Purity of heart is so agreeable that we cannot see an innocent little child without being touched by it. This internal purity is reflected upon its face by a candor and by an ingenuousness which charms us; and, at a more advanced age, it implants in the soul a foundation of rectitude which inspires respect, esteem, and love. All our relations with these beautiful souls are delicious; in them exists no unjust suspicions, no prejudices, no hatreds, and no aversions; never any jealousies or disputes about preeminence; but, on the contrary, always constant attention, to give pleasure by their words and their actions; always a modest and amiable manner of acting and speaking. In the society of such souls we breathe an atmosphere of purity and of innocence, of humility and meekness, which edifies us, which tends to God, which disposes us to become better, and which makes us take pleasure in their company; it is like meeting an angel. Let us here examine ourselves: whence comes it that we are not always amiable towards our neighbor? Is it not that remorse for our faults makes us peevish and bad tempered; that our little passions, when they meet with contradictions, make us speak and act in a disagreeable manner that the ennui of our own conscience renders us insipid and vexatious? We make victims of those with whom we live through our ill regulated disposition.

THIRD POINT
✝ A Pure Heart is Pleasing to Ourselves

Purity is the happiness of him who possesses it; he enjoys a delicious peace which surpasses all expression. (Bar. 2:13; Phil. 4:7) His conscience, without reproach, is for his soul a bed of roses, or rather, in the judgment of the Holy Ghost, it is as a continual feast. (Prov. 15:15) Happy as it is possible to be in this world, the present offers him nothing but sweetness, confidence, and love; the future, nothing but hopes of perfect and eternal happiness. Such a man knows nothing either of the emotions of the passions which trouble the heart, nor of the desires which torment it; he reposes sweetly in God, whom he loves; finds all his pleasure in pleasing Him, and that suffices for his happiness. Oh, how badly do they understand their interests who do not endeavor to keep themselves pure and holy! They never satisfy themselves without at the same time creating remorse for themselves, and, consequently, a fund of vexation and bitterness; whilst pure souls, on the contrary, form for themselves an anticipated paradise, embellished by the joys of the Holy Ghost, the unction of grace, the peace of a good conscience, and the delight of a heart without reproach. Let us examine into all the troubles and sorrows we have given ourselves by our faults; all the graces of which we have deprived ourselves by our want of vigilance over ourselves; and let us exert ourselves by these considerations to hold in great esteem purity of heart and of the conscience. *Resolutions and spiritual nosegay as above.*

Tuesday in the Fourth Week after Epiphany

SUMMARY OF TOMORROW'S MEDITATION

We will tomorrow terminate our visits to the cradle of the Word Incarnate, and we shall bring back with us from it, as our last lesson, Christian simplicity. We shall see: first, what Christian simplicity is; second what is the excellence of this virtue. We shall then make the resolution: first, to hold in horror all concealment, all duplicity, and all falsehood; second to tend towards God wholly in all things, without any other object than the desire of pleasing Him. Our spiritual nosegay shall be the maxim of the Holy Ghost: "He that walks sincerely, walks confidently." (Prov. 10:9)

MEDITATION FOR THE MORNING

Let us adore Jesus as a child in His cradle, and let us learn from Him a last lesson, Christian simplicity. "Be simple as doves," (Matt. 10:16) He will say later on, and He says so already by His example. He allows Himself to be laid down, to be taken up, to be wrapped in swaddling-clothes, to be borne into Egypt, to be taken to Nazareth, just as those around Him will. It is a peaceful and simple abandonment to the will of others, without His desiring anything but to obey, and to make no remonstrance. Oh, how worthy such simplicity of conduct is of our homage! Let us pray the Incarnate Word to give us the understanding and practice of this virtue.

FIRST POINT
✝ What is Christian Simplicity?

Let us learn it from the ordinary child during the first months of his reason. Simple in his beliefs and his judgments, he willingly defers to the opinions of others, and never hotly maintains his own. It is thus that the true Christian prefers the judgment of others to his own, and genuinely confesses his error as soon, as he recognizes it. With still greater reason, he adheres simply to the truths of faith: the feeling of his own ignorance disposes him to believe. Simple in his conduct, a child ignores disguise and falsehood; he does not know what it is to be annoyed at a want of consideration, or to be proud of a proof of attention; he does not occupy himself with what is thought or what is said of him; he does not trouble himself about where his mother places him or carries him, nor about anything she does to him; he only knows how to abandon himself simply to her and to allow her to do with him what she pleases. It is thus that the true Christian acts in all things, without dissimulation or concealment, without duplicity or artifice, without falsehood or equivocation. He does not try to hide either his ignorance or his faults, or to excuse himself when he has failed in his duty, nor to show himself to be anything but what he is; and, caring little as to what others may say or think of him, he goes straight on his way, doing what he believes to be his duty. In his exterior he is modest without being singular; discreet without affectation; he knows nothing either of luxury in dress, or of the table, or of furniture, or of the pleasures of effeminacy or the daintiness of sensuality. In the intercourse of life, politeness is, in his case, the true expression of charity. In studying his way of action, we perceive, not that he aspires to please, but that we are dear to him; not that he aims at others being pleased with him, but that he is pleased with those with whom he holds intercourse. Lastly, in the details of his actions, he does not seek to show or hide himself, nor to appear virtuous, but to be the same in private as in public, always himself. He fears nothing with excess, he desires nothing with violence, he is poor without being humiliated, rich or honored without esteeming himself any the more for it; he knows of nothing low in what is good, nothing little in what is useful, nothing honorable in what is un-Christian. What a beautiful character, and how shall we attain to it? It will be in willing the will of God and nothing else, in blessing God always for everything and in reposing upon Him with a perfect simplicity of love.

SECOND POINT
✝ The Excellence of Christian Simplicity

It is a virtue which gains the heart of God and is the happiness of him who possesses it. First, it gains the heart of God. "His will," says the Holy Spirit "is in them that walk sincerely." (Prov. 11:20) "He will keep the salvation of the righteous and protect them that walk in simplicity." (Prov. 2:7) He loves them, (1 Par. 19:17) and beneath His guidance, which is full of sweetness, they walk in assurance. (Prov. 10:9) Therefore St. Paul recommends simplicity in all things: simplicity in alms; (Rom. 12:8; 2 Cor. 8:2) simplicity in obedience; (Eph. 5:5.) simplicity in the duties of our state; (Coloss. 3:22) simplicity in perseverance; (2 Cor. 11:3) and simplicity in our relations with one another. (2 Cor. 11:12) Second, simplicity gains our neighbor's heart; everyone likes to have relations with uprightness and simplicity, no one likes to have to treat with duplicity and artifice. Third, it is a virtue which makes the happiness of the simple soul; by its means it serves God with ease and without trouble, with the abandonment and confidence of a child who serves a very amiable father; through it we are never obliged to measure our words, or our thoughts, or our actions, nor to go back to the past, and we are content to infuse into whatever we are doing a sweet, free and cheerful attention. We have no need to be like beggars seeking our joy in outward things; we find it within us, and we have more pleasure in what passes within us than we could derive from any society whatever. When beholding the thousand frivolities of which the world makes a necessity, we are glad to be able to say, "How many things of which I have no need!" If on our path we meet with innocent pleasures, we receive them without eagerness and enjoy them without remorse. If falls or weaknesses remind us of our misery, we humble ourselves meekly, without being troubled; we rise again with confidence, and we cast ourselves with simplicity and love within the arms of God. Lastly, subjected to dryness and to trials, we accept all that God wills and are always content with God whatever He may do. At what point have we arrived in regard to this Christian simplicity which is so pleasing to God and man, and makes the happiness of all who possess it? Do we esteem it as it deserves, this beautiful virtue, and do we labor to acquire it at the expense of our self-love, if necessary? *Resolutions and spiritual nosegay as above.*

Wednesday in the Fourth Week after Epiphany

THE GOSPEL ACCORDING TO ST. LUKE, 2:22-32.

"And after the days of her purification, according to the law of Moses, were accomplished, they carried Him to Jerusalem, to present Him to the Lord, as it is written in the law of the Lord: Every male opening the womb shall be called holy to the Lord; and to offer a sacrifice according as it is written in the law of the Lord, a pair of turtle doves, or two young pigeons. And behold there was a man in Jerusalem named Simeon, and this man was just and devout, waiting for the consolation of Israel; and the Holy Ghost was in him. And he had received an answer from the Holy Ghost that he should not see death before he had seen the Christ of the Lord. And he came by the Spirit into the temple. And when His parents brought in the Child Jesus, to do for Him according to the custom of the law, he also took Him in his arms and blessed God, and said: Now Thou dost dismiss Thy servant, O Lord, according to Thy word in peace. Because my eyes have seen Thy salvation which Thou hast prepared before the face of all peoples: a light to the revelation of the Gentiles, and the glory of Thy people Israel."

SUMMARY OF TOMORROW'S MEDITATION

From the cradle of the Incarnate Word, we will go to the temple of Jerusalem, whither the Child-God caused Himself to be transported, forty days after His birth, and we shall meditate: first, on the sacrifice which He made of Himself to His Father; second, on the great love with which He made this sacrifice. We will then make the resolution: first, to seize joyfully all opportunities of mortifying and conquering ourselves; second, to perform all our actions in a spirit of love and of sacrifice. Our spiritual nosegay shall be the words of the Psalmist: "I am Thy servant; give me understanding that I may know Thy testimonies." (Ps. 118:125)

MEDITATION FOR THE MORNING

Let us transport ourselves in spirit to the temple at Jerusalem; let us beg of the Blessed Virgin to place in our arms her dear Son, as she did in the arms of the holy old man Simeon; and, pressing Him in spirit to our breast, let us render to Him our homage of adoration and of praise, of gratitude and of love.

FIRST POINT

✝ The Sacrifice which the Infant Jesus in the Temple made to His Father

Jesus Christ, from the time of His entrance into the world, had indeed said to His Father, as David and St. Paul tell us: "Sacrifice and oblation Thou wouldst not, but a body Thou hast fitted Me. Holocausts for sin did not please Thee. Then said I, Behold I come; in the head of the book it is written of Me that I should do Thy will, O God." (Heb. 10:5-7) But this sacrifice was made in the secret of His heart. Now He comes to make it public and solemn, in company with Mary and Joseph, the old man Simeon and Anna the prophetess, who were permitted to be the happy witnesses of it. Let us admire this sublime offering, destined to take the place of all the ancient sacrifices. Whilst Mary presents in her pure hands the Child-God to His Father, He abases Himself before the Eternal Majesty; He adores Him with highest esteem, with profoundest reverence; He consecrates to Him the whole of His being, and He offers Himself as the universal victim in the name of the whole creation. Oh, how glorious for God was this day and how precious for us! It is the day which the prophets foresaw across the course of ages and which they hailed from afar in these magnificent words: "Shout for joy, O daughter of Jerusalem; behold thy King will come to thee, the just and Savior." (Zach. 9:9) "Yet one little while and the desired of all nations shall come, and I will fill this house with glory, saith the Lord of Hosts." (Agg. 7-8) "And presently the Lord whom you seek, and the Angel of the Testament whom you desire shall come to His temple. Behold He cometh, saith the Lord of Hosts." (Mal. 3:1) "The majesty of the Lord went into the temple by the way of the gate that looked to the East and the house was filled with the glory of the Lord." (Ezech. 43:4-5) At the sight of this divine offering, who does not feel at the bottom of his heart that it is a duty for him to consecrate himself wholly to the Lord and to say to Him in union with the adorable Victim of today: I am wholly Thine, O my God, to serve Thee. (Ps. 118:125) My possessions, my body and soul, all is dependent on Thy sovereign power; I give them up entirely into Thy hands, I no longer belong to myself. Oh, who will enable me to understand these words: I am no longer my own; therefore I ought not to seek myself in anything; no more self-will, no more attachments, no more self-love? Whether I am placed in a high or low condition, whether I am remembered or whether I am forgotten, whether I am praised or blamed, what does it signify? I am no longer my own, I am wholly Thine, O my God! Let, then, Thy good pleasure dispose of me and of all the moments of my existence, as Thou willest; I will never complain; I will always adore and bless Thy will in regard to me, for I am no longer my own.

SECOND POINT
✝ The Love with which the Infant Jesus makes His Sacrifice

Two sentiments lead the Infant Jesus to the temple: the love of God, His Father, and the love of men, His new brethren; the love of God, because He desires to make reparation to His outraged glory, and raise up His worship which has hitherto been little worthy of His great majesty; the love of men, because He desires to save them from eternal damnation, and to give back to them heaven, which they had lost by their sins. It was on Calvary that this immortal King of ages was to fully satisfy this double love; but it was too long to wait until then: His heart could not bear the delay. (Luke 12:50) The fortieth day after His birth He caused Himself to be borne to the temple. Up to that time the offering of the first-born, according to the prescription of the law, had derived all its merit from the pious disposition of the parents, and the newborn child, who was still devoid of reason, could not add any value to it; but in this case it was quite otherwise. With what love of God Jesus offered Himself to His Father to glorify Him, and with what love for men He immolates Himself that He may save them! Oh, what a mystery! These men are a thousand times unworthy of His love; they have outraged Him, they will still outrage Him; and yet He loves them to such a degree that He offers Himself as a sacrifice for them; He foresees all that it will cost Him, of humiliations, of sufferings, of bitter sorrows, to save them; it does not signify; such is the ardor of His love that He heartily accepts all that He foresees of sacrifices; He offers His august head that it may one day wear the crown of thorns; He offers His feet and His hands to receive the impression of the nails; all His little body to be torn and wounded; all His soul to be imbued with shame and contempt, and His heart, His heart so loving, to be pierced through and through by the lance of the soldier. O Saviour God, how Thou didst love me on the day of Thy presentation! What heart, whilst meditating on these things, could help being melted with love? Oh, how well Thou dost teach me thereby what love is when it burns the heart I He who loves God and his brethren is capable of the greatest sacrifices; those only are base and pusillanimous whose hearts do not love. O love come then and consume me, so that I may live only to love! O love come and take possession of my whole being, so that all the pulsations of my heart maybe henceforth nothing but pulsations of love! *Resolutions and spiritual nosegay as above.*

Thursday in the Fourth Week after Epiphany

SUMMARY OF TOMORROW'S MEDITATION

e learnt this morning from Jesus in the temple the spirit of sacrifice; we shall learn from Him tomorrow the spirit of obedience, and in order to dispose us to enter into this spirit we shall see, first, that there is nothing more excellent than obedience; second, nothing more sanctifying; third, nothing more consoling. We will then make the resolution: first, to perform all our actions in a spirit of obedience to the good pleasure of God; second, never to do anything from impulse or natural taste for it; as well as never to omit anything from disgust or repugnance. Our spiritual nosegay shall be the words of Our Lord on the day of His presentation: "Behold, I come to do Thy will, God!" (Heb. 10:9)

MEDITATION FOR THE MORNING

Let us adore the marvelous obedience of Jesus in the mystery of His presentation. He obeys His Father, whose will He comes to perform. O my God, He says, Thy will is Mine; I have placed it in the midst of my heart, (Ps. 39:9) so that it may regulate all its movements. He obeys Moses, His servant, whose law He comes to execute. Forty days after his birth, Moses had said, the first-born child shall be offered in the temple; five shekels shall be the price of his redemption; and what Moses had said Jesus executed. He obeys His mother, to whose hands He abandons Himself, so that she may do with Him as she wills. Oh, how greatly such obedience deserves our respect and our praise!

FIRST POINT

✝ Nothing is more Excellent than Obedience

The world places its greatness in independence and liberty; to obey is in its opinion the portion of slaves, the condition of the miserable; and there is nothing finer, greater, more worthy of envy than to do our own will in everything. Jesus, the Eternal Wisdom, thinks very differently. The proof of it is to be found in the mystery of today and in His whole life, which is nothing but a continual exercise of obedience. Never does He seek Himself in anything; (Rom. 15:3) the will of His Father is always His. (Luke 22:45) In truth, there is nothing in heaven or on earth more excellent than to have, as the rule of our conduct, not the caprices of human will, but the very will of God, which is the rule and the delight of saints and angels. Then the whole of life is ennobled and rendered great; and we are no longer smaller in little things, nor greater in great, because the will of God, which is the rule, the price, and the merit of it, is always equally excellent then the least action done with the aim and for the love of this holy will surpasses the most brilliant labors inspired by self-love, and that by the whole distance which separates the divine from the human will. Thus are raised to an incomparable degree of excellence all our actions; even the most ordinary, our repasts even, our recreations and our walks, even our sleep, our silence and our inaction, when it is in the order of the will of God and when we accept it in this view. Oh, then what a great and wonderful thing obedience is! Have we, up to the present time, learned to appreciate it as it deserves? Do we esteem happy the positions in which we obey, and do we dread those in which we command and are able to do our own will?

SECOND POINT
✝ Nothing is more Sanctifying than Obedience

First, it corrects all the digressions of self-will, that perfidious and deceitful will which sees objects only through the prism of the passions and of petty interests, and changes the true color of them; inconstant and flighty, what it desires today it does not care for tomorrow; uncertain and irresolute, it often does not know to what to attach itself; capricious, its desires are devoid of reason and against all reason; it does not know how to yield, and becomes more and more obstinate in proportion to its being contradicted; haughty and imperious, it aspires to throwing off the yoke and to rule; violent and hasty, it is impatient, murmurs, rebels, if its desires are not promptly satisfied; lastly, an enemy to the law because the law annoys it, it is inclined to indulge in everything which is forbidden. To obedience alone is it given to correct so many digressions from the right way: this blind will, obedience directs; this inconstant will, it renders stable; this irresolute will, it makes determined; this capricious will, it renders steadfast; this obstinate will, it bends; this haughty will, it makes submissive; this violent and hasty will, it represses; this perverse will, it restrains or puts again in the right path out of which it has wandered. Second. After having corrected the evil, obedience enables a man to do all that is right. In it consists all perfection, humility, abnegation, patience, union with God, the life of faith, which makes all our acts supernatural; the life of hope, which is nourished by a continual succession of merits; the life of charity, of which obedience forms the most excellent practice. Therein, lastly, is the source of all graces with the most assured means of success in all good works. Is it thus that we look upon obedience? Do we entertain an aversion for self-will, and do we take pleasure in making a generous and continual sacrifice of it to God?

THIRD POINT
✝ Nothing is more Consoling than Obedience

He who follows the bent of his own will is unhappy. The past often leaves in its train repentance for what we have done, disapprobation of its false wisdom, regret for its false calculations. The present saddens us; it offers to the soul desires which are not satisfied, a discontented will, weariness and disgust. The future troubles us: What shall I do? What will become of me? But with obedience all anxiety disappears. Then there are no regrets for the past; he who has commanded may have deceived himself, he who has obeyed has always done well, and his conscience has no right to address a single reproach to him. Then there is no more sadness in the present. I am where God wills I should be; I am doing what God wills; it is paradise upon earth. Then there is no more anxiety about the future. What shall I become? What God wills. Where shall I go? Where God wills. By means of these sole words calm and peace are established in the soul, together with an ineffable joy. Good pleasure of God, where dost Thou will me to go? I hasten there, I fly there, here I am! I let myself be led by Thee as a child by the hand of its mother. O delicious life, O fore taste of paradise! What a beautiful death will follow such a life, when, looking back on the past, we shall see every day filled with the divine pleasure! How well we shall be received in heaven, which will resound with the song of victory. (Prov. 21:28) *Resolutions and spiritual nosegay as above.*

Friday in the Fourth Week after Epiphany

SUMMARY OF TOMORROW'S MEDITATION

After having meditated on Jesus in the temple, we will consider Mary, His mother, present there, and we shall admire in her, as in her divine Son, the spirit of sacrifice, for she sacrifices: first, within herself, the two objects which are dearest to us, self-will and self-love; second, outside herself, the two objects which interest her the most, she offers in sacrifice her adorable Son, and she resigns herself to extreme and unknown evils. We will then make the resolution: first, not to attach ourselves to anything in this world, and to tear courageously from our hearts

every fiber which is not steeped in the love of God; second, to sacrifice our own will in particular by obedience to our superiors, and by condescension to our equals or inferiors. Our spiritual nosegay shall be the words of the Imitation: "Empty thine heart of all which is not God and unite thyself to God alone." (2 Imit. 8:5)

MEDITATION FOR THE MORNING

Let us adore the Infant Jesus presented in the temple by the hands of Mary, and let us congratulate Mary on having, as priest of this great sacrifice, offered the adorable victim to God the Father with such pure hands and so lofty a perfection, whilst offering herself also in sacrifice together with her divine Son.

FIRST POINT
✝ **Mary in the Temple Sacrifices the two Things to which we are the most attached, Self-will and Self-love**

First, she sacrifices self-will; evidently the law of purification was not in any way obligatory upon her; for what could there be to purify in the Mother of God: in a creature purer than the angels, and who, far from having by her supernatural delivery contracted the least stain, had only through it become still more pure and more virginal? Yet she submits to the law, and does not dispense with any of its prescriptions; like ordinary women, she stays in retreat and remains secluded from intercourse with the world; like them, she abstains, during forty days, from entering within the temple; like them, she offers the victim of purification prescribed by the law. A beautiful example, which teaches us to obey without availing ourselves either of the advantage under favor of which we need not be confounded with the commonalty, nor of the pretext of dispensation with which self-love delights to cover itself. True obedience never asks the why of the commands; it performs with simplicity what is prescribed; it does not love dispensations, but accepts them if they are imposed, and solicits them only in so far as duty makes a law of them. Second, Mary sacrifices self-love. It was great glory for her to be at once a virgin mother and the Mother of God. She sacrifices this double glory, first in submitting herself to the ceremony of the purification, which made her to be looked upon in the opinion of the public as an ordinary woman, whose delivery had rendered her unclean; secondly, in redeeming her Son like a slave, and redeeming Him at the modest sum given by the poor. What a lesson of humility for us, who like to make a display of all that does us honor, and to speak to our own advantage.

SECOND POINT

✝ Mary in the Temple Sacrifices her own Son and resigns herself to extreme unknown Evils

First, she sacrifices her own Son. She loved this dear Son a thousand times more than herself; He was her joy, her happiness, her treasure, her all. Nevertheless she makes a sacrifice of Him to God His Father, for the salvation of the world. Upon the altar of her heart, still more than within her arms, she presents this adorable victim to divine justice, consenting to have Him taken from her one day for the redemption of man. In presence of this spectacle, could we call ourselves children of Mary, if we are attached to anything whatever in this world, to our vanity, to our ease, to whatever it may be which seems to us to be precious? Alas! What are all these sacrifices in comparison with the sacrifice which Mary made in sacrificing her adorable Son? Second, Mary resigns herself to extreme unknown evils. "This child," said the old man Simeon to her "is set for the fall and for the resurrection of many in Israel, and a sign which shall be contradicted; and thy own soul a sword shall pierce." (Luke 2:34-35) But what will be this sword of sorrow? Mary knows not. These terrible words, not announcing any evil in particular, gave her latitude to fear all kinds of evil. Threatened with extreme evils, without knowing what they are, her soul beholds on all parts swords suspended over her head; does not know to what side to turn for safety and dies a thousand deaths in one moment; yet Mary, although she was in such suffering, did not allow herself to be cast down; she abandons herself to all the designs of God with regard to her; what God wills will happen to me, she said to herself; and what God wills I ought also to will. O admirable calmness of Mary amidst such great sacrifices! Oh, what a beautiful example of resignation and of abandonment to God! *Resolutions and spiritual nosegay as above.*

Saturday in the Fourth Week after Epiphany

SUMMARY OF TOMORROW'S MEDITATION

After having considered Jesus and Mary in the temple, it remains for us to consider a third personage, the holy old man Simeon. We shall see, first, how he prepared himself for his happy meeting with Jesus; second, what were his joys and his sorrows during his waiting. We will then make the resolution: first, to prepare ourselves more carefully for our communions by holiness of life and ardent desires; second, to

be guided in everything by the Spirit of God, and not by the spirit of the world. Our spiritual nosegay shall be the canticle of Simeon: "Now Thou dost dismiss Thy servant, Lord, according to Thy word, in peace." (Luke 2:19)

MEDITATION FOR THE MORNING

Let us adore the Infant Jesus reposing in the arms of the holy old man Simeon, enlightening his mind with living lights and filling His heart with the sweetest consolations. Let us ask Him to let us have a share in the graces bestowed upon this holy old man.

FIRST POINT
☦ **How Simeon prepared himself to meet Jesus in the Temple.**

The Gospel tells us this in the following words: "There was a man in Jerusalem named Simeon, and this man was just and devout, waiting for the consolation of Israel, and the Holy Ghost was in him." (Luke 2:25) Let us study all the features of this beautiful portrait. First, Simeon was just and feared God that is to say, he possessed every virtue; he very carefully avoided all sin, and he spent his whole life in the love and service of God; second, he lived in the expectation of the consolation of Israel that is to say, that, detached from everything else, he desired nothing in the world but to see Jesus Christ, and die; second, the Holy Ghost was in him that is to say, that, filled with the Holy Ghost, he was in all things led by the light and the movements of this Divine Spirit; he consulted it, and the Holy Ghost answered him, directing all his thoughts, all his sentiments, all his acts, and in these pious interviews the Holy Ghost had told him that he should not see death until he had seen the Messias, the Expected of the nations. Such was the holy life which prepared Simeon for his happy meeting with Jesus in the temple. We, also are called to amiable meetings with Jesus in our churches, in our visits to the Blessed Sacrament, in communion, at holy Mass. Do we appreciate this favor as Simeon appreciated it? Do we desire it as he did? Do we prepare ourselves like him, by a pure life, by flying from sin, by the practice of virtue, by union with the Spirit of God, and our docility to His holy inspirations?

SECOND POINT
☦ **Joys and Sorrows of Simeon in the Temple**

Warned by the Holy Ghost of the day and hour when Jesus would arrive in the temple, the holy old man betakes himself joyfully there. The Spirit of God reveals to him the Messias for whom he had waited in the Divine Child, to which neither priests nor people paid any attention. He approaches and lovingly contemplates Him. At the sight of Him his heart overflows with happiness. Mary, happy to meet so worthy an adorer of her dear Son, places Him in Simeon's arms, and who could express with what ecstatic joy he receives this precious treasure, how he pressed Him to his breast, watered Him with his tears, covered Him with his kisses! In these holy embraces, his heart, inundated with the delights of Paradise, could say nothing else but what is contained in his magnificent canticle: "Lord, Thou hast until now detained my soul in the prison of my body, to allow me to behold the Saviour of Israel and the Light of the nations. Now that this happiness has been given to me, I have nothing more to desire here below. Let death come; it is my one desire." Such is, in souls well prepared, the fruit of a good communion. By it we possess Jesus, not in our arms, but, what is much better, in our hearts; and this intimate alliance of the creature with his Creator detaches the heart from all which is not God. We love God, we enjoy Him; all the world is as nothing to him who possesses so great a treasure, and we desire nothing else but to die, to love Him more perfectly and always. At the same time, however, with these ineffable joys of the holy old man were mingled also ineffable sorrows. God, enlightening him in regard to the future, showed him in the course of years: first, the Divine Infant a sign of contradiction; second, the heart of Mary pierced with a sword of suffering; third, the Savior of Israel becoming the ruin of a great number of people, and the secret thoughts of many brought to light on the last day. How greatly did these revelations afflict his loving soul! Jesus, so amiable, a sign of contradiction? What He shall have as opponents those who will not accept the austere doctrine of the Gospel respecting suffering, renunciation, the violence which alone can conquer the kingdom of heaven? What Mary shall be the Queen of martyrs? Yes; through the part that she will take in the sorrows of Calvary, and in the loss of so: many souls. What The Savior of men shall be the ruin of many, and will reveal their most secret thoughts? Yes; He will be the ruin of those who will not save themselves, and He will reveal, on the great day of His justice, their most hidden thoughts. Oh, how terrible it is not to love Jesus, and not to profit by the redemption He offers us! *Resolutions and spiritual nosegay as above.*

Fifth Sunday after Epiphany

THE GOSPEL ACCORDING TO ST. MATTHEW 13:24-30

"And Jesus proposed another parable to them, saying: The kingdom of heaven is likened to a man that sowed good seed in his field. But while men were asleep his enemy came and over-sowed cockle among the wheat, and went his way. And when the blade was sprung up, and had brought forth fruit, then appeared also the cockle. And the servants of the good man of the house, coming, said to him: Sir, didst thou not sow good seed in thy field? Whence, then, hath it cockle? And he said to them: An enemy hath done this. And the servants said to him: Wilt thou that we go and gather it up? And he said: No, lest perhaps gathering up the cockle you root up the wheat also together with it. Suffer both to grow until the harvest, and in time of the harvest I will say to the reapers: Gather up first the cockle, and bind it into bundles to burn, but the wheat gather ye into my barn."

SUMMARY OF TOMORROW'S MEDITATION

e will meditate tomorrow on the Gospel of the day, which, under the parable of the tares mingled with the corn, shows us the mixture of the wicked with the good here below, and we shall see that this mixture marvelously serves: first, to the glory of God; second, to the greater good of men. We will then make the resolution: first, patiently and meekly to suffer all that may offend or displease us in our neighbor; and never to be envious of the success of others. Our spiritual nosegay shall be the words of St. Augustine: "God leaves to the wicked the false goods of this world; He reserves for Himself alone the recompense of the good."

MEDITATION FOR THE MORNING

Let us adore Jesus Christ giving us, under the parable of the tares and the corn, the most precious lessons; let us thank Him for such great goodness; let us beg Him to enable us fully to understand His divine teachings, and to give us grace to put them in practice.

FIRST POINT

✝ God, in a marvelous Manner, derives Glory from the Mixture of the Wicked and the Good

Nothing better shows the perfections of God. First, His patience. His commandments are despised, His name blasphemed, His truths denied, and He bears it all. He might revenge Himself but He does not; He sees all and He appears as though He did not; He considers everything and He is silent. His angels only await a word in order to mow down the tares and throw them into the fire: Shall we? They ask. No, He replies, leave them time to repent. Alas! There was a time when we ourselves were these bad tares, in the field of the Father of the family. If God had abandoned us to the mowers, who asked if they might tear us up, where should we be now? At least let us imitate, with regard to others, the patience of God towards us; let us learn to bear the faults and defects of our neighbor. Second, this mixture makes the goodness of God shine forth, for not only does God bear with, but He heaps up blessings on the very men who outrage Him; making His sun to rise and shedding His rain upon the field of the sinner as well as on the field of the just; seeking them by sweet inspirations, calling them, pursuing them without ever being discouraged. Third, this mixture also equally makes the power of divine grace to show forth, preserving as it does purity in souls in the midst of corruption, keeping virtue steadfast when all is tottering around; hearts burning with charity amidst general lukewarmness; as in days gone-by He kept Daniel in the den of lions, the children of Babylon in the furnace, and made living waters spring up in the midst of arid lands. Fourth, thou dost not shine less here, O Infinite Wisdom, who knowest so admirably how to draw good out of evil, and who makes the malice of the wicked serve for the sanctification of Thy elect. Without the wicked there would neither have been, the zeal of the apostles nor of apostolic men; nor the triumphs of the martyrs, nor the courage of the confessors; nor the profound writings of the doctors, nor the solitudes of the anchorites; nor the heroism of charity suffering all arid forgiving all; nor, finally, the death of the Son of God who has saved us. Glory then be to Thee, O my God, who makes even sin, serve the sanctification of the elect and the execution of Thy designs of love and mercy!

SECOND POINT

✝ The Mixture of the Good and the Evil serves marvelously to the Good of Man

Let us suppose the good and the wicked forming two separate societies; it would be an immense evil for the one and for the other. The wicked would lose the good example and the good counsels of the just; they would lose consolation in their troubles, solace in their trials; and living only in the midst of what was evil, they would daily become more and more perverted; it would be for them hell upon earth, without any prospect of repentance or conversion. On their side the just would lose the solidity and merit of their virtues, for the virtue which has nothing to suffer is mediocre and has but little merit; they would lose the honor of being the salt of the earth and the light of the world; they would lose one of the most striking proofs of the falsity of all the goods of this world, since God gives them to His enemies as being things of vile price, sometimes even as a chastisement to blind them, so that placing their happiness in these false enjoyments, they take no heed about their eternity, and go down with closed eyes to hell; they would lose, lastly, one of the motives which stimulate them most powerfully to the love and the service of God. For it is in seeing God offended that the just feel themselves to be impelled by a greater desire to love Him more in order to repair so great an evil; to serve Him more generously in order to compensate for the homage refused to Him by ungrateful men; to pray and do penance for sinners. "Oh!" exclaims St. Teresa, "that I could hold the hearts of men in my hand in order to inflame them all with holy love," and at this thought she burst forth into holy transports, zeal inflamed her, love consumed her. Let us here examine ourselves. Do we know how, like the saints, to derive spiritual profit from the sins of others? Do we know how to make use of them as of a good opportunity for enabling us to exercise patience, endurance, humility, meekness, and as a stimulant for growing in zeal for our sanctification and the salvation of our neighbor? Do we know how to take the evil which is said of us as a warning to animate us to do the contrary? *Resolutions and spiritual nosegay as above.*

Monday in the Fifth Week after Epiphany

THE GOSPEL ACCORDING TO ST. MATTHEW (2:13-15)

"At that time an angel of the Lord appeared in sleep to Joseph, saying: Arise, and take the Child and His mother, and fly into Egypt, and be there until I shall tell thee. For it will come to pass that Herod will seek the Child to destroy Him. Who arose and took the Child and His mother by night, and retired into Egypt: and he was there until the death of Herod that it might be fulfilled which the Lord spoke by the prophet: Out of Egypt have I called My Son."

SUMMARY OF TOMORROW'S MEDITATION

e will meditate tomorrow on the flight of Jesus into Egypt, and we shall learn from it: first, to see and cherish the will of God even in the most painful trials, without ever allowing ourselves to be cast down; second, never to desire anything here below but this most holy and most amiable will. We will then make the resolution: first, to consider the good pleasure of God as the rule of our conduct and the end of our actions; second, to desire nothing beyond and to be content with our position, without dreaming of another. Our spiritual nosegay shall be the words of the Lord's prayer: "Father, Thy will be done."

MEDITATION FOR THE MORNING

Let us adore, with admiration and love, the Child-God escaping by flight and a long sojourn in Egypt from the persecution of Herod. O profound mystery! He had at His command a thousand means whereby to escape the search made by the tyrant, but He prefers flight, and He goes away not from compulsion, but from design, because His flight will be full of lessons for us. Let us bless Him in union with the angels who accompanied Him.

FIRST POINT

✝ The Flight into Egypt Teaches us to See and Cherish the Will of God even in the most painful Trials, without ever allowing ourselves to be cast down

The Holy Family were living quietly in their poor dwelling, when suddenly an angel comes, in the middle of the night, and says to Joseph: "Arise, and take the Child and His mother, and fly into Egypt." (Matt. 2:13) He does not say, make ready to set out at the dawn of day, but depart at once, in the midst of the darkness of the night. He does not say: Go, but fly; it is a shameful resource in the eyes of the world, dangerous even; for they might be discovered and arrested. It is of no consequence; fly. And whither? Into Egypt! But what will become of us in that unknown land, without help, without protection? Joseph does not reason thus; he abandons himself to Providence, without being discouraged or troubling himself about the difficulties of the road and the means; of livelihood in that distant country, and he sets off. God wills it; that is sufficient. If God wills it, He will provide for all; wherefore be troubled? Joseph starts on his journey with great calmness, with a perfect abandonment to the will of God, and traverses the hundred leagues which separate him from Heliopolis, the place of his refuge. Neither solitude nor inhabited districts disconcert him nor do privations of all kinds discourage him; Jesus is with him, He is his treasure, his providence, his consolation, his all in all. Having arrived at Heliopolis, he there pitches his tent, and by dint of labor he provides for the needs of the little family. All three are living there in content; they are where God wills them to be; they are what God wills. What more do they want? How many lessons are contained in this mystery! We learn from it: first, to detach ourselves from our country, from our relations, from our friends; to leave promptly all that is dearest to us when God orders us to do so; second, to know how to find God everywhere, and, consequently, to be content wherever we may be; third, to yield to the times; even to the extent of suffering violence and in justice, when force usurps right; fourth, to yield to our neighbor, by reserve, modesty, condescension, loving better to lose all than to lose charity, meekness, and peace; fifth, to confide in God in the midst of even the greatest reverses, to see in all things His providence, which knows better than we do what is good for us, which knows how to draw good out of evil, which knows all, which can do all, and which loves us. Let us gather together these precious lessons and place them in the bottom of our heart.

SECOND POINT

✝ The Flight into Egypt Teaches us to desire Nothing here below but the most holy and most amiable Will of God

The Holy Family sets out by night, as we have seen; it does not desire to wait for the day. It leaves in a state of absolute destitution; it does not desire to have leisure to make preparations for the journey. It goes into Egypt, a country where it knows no one; it does not desire to go to the country of the Magi, where it would be so well received. It traverses frightful solitudes; it does not desire either a better road or better caravansaries. Arrived at the place where it is to sojourn, it remains there until an order from heaven recalls it. It may suffer, be wearied, find its exile hard and long. No matter; it remains eight long years, always submissive, always content, believing that to God alone who has placed it there belongs the right to displace it. It does not say: We are here, enjoying neither honor nor glory, but are forgotten and despised, whilst others who are not worth as much as we have a great reputation and live in splendor. It says: I am where God wills me to be; where could I be better? What a lesson for men who imagine that they will always be better off in any place than the one in which they are, who are never content with their position, and are constantly dreaming about another, as if they could have roses without thorns and a position without trials. How much better advised are they who know how to feel themselves to be well off where God places them, who live in dependence upon His providence, until they pass away into the arms of His mercy! After these eight years of exile, the angel comes back and says to Joseph: "Return to the land of Israel." But where establish themselves? The angel leaves the choice to them, and the holy patriarch chooses, not a great town, but the little village of Nazareth, where the Holy Family will lead a life more humble, more tranquil, more in conformity to the simplicity of its tastes. It is thus that when we do not clearly perceive the will of Providence we ought to approach to it as closely as we can, asking ourselves: "Where shall I better work out my salvation? Where shall I be less exposed to lose myself? What decision will most console me at the hour of death?" Are these the rules of our conduct? *Resolutions and spiritual nosegay as above.*

Tuesday in the Fifth Week after Epiphany

SUMMARY OF TOMORROW'S MEDITATION

We will tomorrow reflect upon Jesus Christ at the age of twelve going to Jerusalem to give Himself up in the temple to the pious exercises which were customary during the feast of Easter: a striking lesson which teaches us that every Christian ought to have certain pious exercises to which he should be faithful. First, it is this which the example of Jesus Christ teaches us; second, it is this which the interest of our salvation calls for. We will then make the resolution: first, to draw up a rule of life which shall fix the hour and manner of each one of our exercises; second, never to depart from this rule, excepting in case of real necessity, and in that case to anticipate the exercise, if we have been able to foresee that it will be prevented, or else to resume it at the first moment of leisure. Our spiritual nosegay shall be the words of Our Lord to Mary: "How is it that you sought Me? Did you not know that I must be about My Father's business?" (Luke 2:49)

MEDITATION FOR THE MORNING

Let us adore Jesus Christ hidden, after His return from Egypt, in the retreat at Nazareth, and only leaving it to pray in the temple when Mary and Joseph took Him there. Let us follow Him in spirit during this pious pilgrimage. What holy conversations they held together while on their way; what recollection, what union with God! Let us render our homage to Jesus, Mary, and Joseph.

FIRST POINT
✝ The Example of Jesus Christ Teaches us to have certain Regular Exercises of Piety to which we are Faithful

There is no doubt but that Jesus at Nazareth occupied Himself every day with certain exercises of piety together with Mary and Joseph. We do not know what they were in detail, but we may judge of them by His journey to Jerusalem; He had no need, He who was the temple of the Divinity, to take this journey in order to honor His Father, but He was very desirous to show us by His example that we ought not to neglect any external exercises of religion and of piety, that He took no account of having to make a journey on foot of thirty leagues from Nazareth to Jerusalem. Having arrived at the temple, He there passed not only the eight days during which the festival of Easter lasted, but also the three following days; and He would have remained there still longer had not His parents come to take Him away. It is not said either where He retired during this time, or whether He took any nourishment, because, apparently, His dwelling, both night and day, was in the temple or in its environs, and His principal food was to do the will of His Father; but what we do know is that He assisted assiduously at the religious exercises. He adored there, He prayed, He listened to the divine word; and who can say with how much modesty, with what recollection, He assisted at the sacrifices and prayers; with what attention, with what respect and fervor He spoke to God; how His example influenced all those who beheld Him. He there by taught us to make of the oratory or the church our dearest dwelling, and of our spiritual exercises our principal delights; always to choose the place where we can best perform them, and never to omit them except with regret when they are impossible, and to resume them as soon as we can. Are these our dispositions?

SECOND POINT

✝ The Interest of our Salvation requires that we should have certain Pious Exercises to which we ought to be faithful

These exercises consist in reflection and prayer. If we do not reflect, we lose sight of our salvation, our eternity, our soul, our faith. If we do not pray, grace fails us, nature takes the upper hand and ruins us. If, on the contrary, we reflect seriously every day upon God, upon the means of saving ourselves, we rekindle every day the sacred fire in our hearts; and, if we pray, we draw down upon ourselves the grace which helps human weakness, the grace which makes saints. These exercises are to the soul what food is to the body; if we refuse them to it, it droops and dies. (Ps. 101:5) They are to the soul what oil is to the lamp; if it be not replenished, the light is extinguished and gives place to a black unhealthy smoke. They are what wood is to the fire: for want of wood the fire goes out; it is the same with us: without our exercises the heart becomes tepid, grows cold, and is turned to ice. They are, lastly, what weapons are to the soldier; when this sacred buckler no longer covers us, we are soon beaten and put to rout by the world and its passions. Weary of ourselves we go into society, we contract its poison, we imitate its bad examples, we allow ourselves to indulge in a life which is wholly dissipated and sensual, to take part in frivolous conversations and useless pastimes; then afterwards we permit ourselves to be carried away by the passions which ferment in the heart, by the love of self and of our own comfort, and from thence into inevitable falls and the loss of our salvation. Let us examine ourselves as to what is our fidelity to our exercises, and if we are faithful to them, in what manner we perform them. Have we a rule of life which lays down the hour and the manner of them? *Resolutions and spiritual nosegay as above.*

Wednesday in the Fifth Week after Epiphany

THE GOSPEL ACCORDING TO ST. LUKE (2:40-52)

"And the Child grew and waxed strong, full of wisdom: and the grace of God was in Him. And His parents went every year to Jerusalem, at the solemn day of the Pasch. And when He was twelve years old, they going up into Jerusalem, according to the custom of the feast, and having fulfilled the days, when they returned, the Child Jesus remained in Jerusalem; and His parents knew it not. And thinking that He was in the company, they came a day's journey, and sought Him among their kinsfolk and acquaintances. And not finding Him they returned into Jerusalem, seeking Him. And it came to pass that after three days they found Him in the temple, sitting in the midst of the doctors, hearing them and asking them questions. And all that heard Him were astonished at His wisdom and His answers. And seeing Him they wondered. And His mother said to Him: Son, why hast Thou done so to us? Behold Thy father and I have sought Thee sorrowing. And He said to them: How is it that you sought Me? Did you not know that I must be about My Father's business? And they understood not the word that He spoke unto them. And He went down with them and came to Nazareth, and was subject to them. And His mother kept all these words in her heart. And Jesus advanced in wisdom and age, and grace with God and man."

SUMMARY OF TOMORROW'S MEDITATION

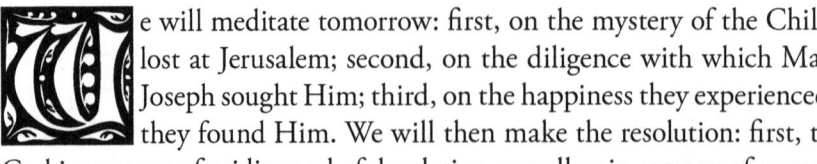e will meditate tomorrow: first, on the mystery of the Child Jesus lost at Jerusalem; second, on the diligence with which Mary and Joseph sought Him; third, on the happiness they experienced when they found Him. We will then make the resolution: first, to serve God in seasons of aridity and of desolation as well as in seasons of consolation. Second, to return to Jesus Christ as soon as we observe that dissipation has separated us from Him, and to keep Him with us by recollection and prayer

when we have found Him. Our spiritual nosegay shall be the words of the Imitation, "If you seek Jesus in everything you will assuredly find Him." (1 Imit. 7:3)

MEDITATION FOR THE MORNING

Let us adore the Infant Jesus separating Himself during three days from Mary and Joseph. Let us revere the secret reasons of this separation; let us beg of Him to enable us to understand it, and to make it serve for our instruction.

FIRST POINT
✝ The Mystery of Jesus Lost at Bethlehem

Immediately after the feast of the Pasch Mary and Joseph returned along the road to Nazareth, taking Jesus with them; but at the same time, manifesting an amiable condescension on their part, they allowed the crowd who surrounded Him to enjoy His society and His conversation. It was therefore very easy for Jesus to separate Himself from them and to return to Jerusalem without their perceiving it. When evening came and they had reached the place where they were to pass the night, they sought Him, and asked everyone about Him, but could not find Him. O Jesus, wherefore hide Thyself thus from Thy beloved parents? Let us listen to His answer from the bottom of our heart. Jesus will tell us that it is in order to teach us that many lose either Him or the feeling of His presence, at one time by mortal or venial sin, by relaxation and tepidity, and by infidelity to their exercises; at another time by negligence in doing everything well, or keeping themselves in a state of recollection, by the cowardice which prevents them from conquering and depriving themselves, watching over their thoughts, their words, and their eyes; but the example of these holy parents will also tell us that we may lose Him without any personal fault. It is true that God often sends or permits desolation and darkness, the weariness and disgust which hide Him from the soul; sometimes to keep us humble, to make us acquire more merits, to strengthen our virtue, to form us to patience, resignation, and conformity to the Divine Will; at other times to make us seek Him with greater ardor, keep Him with more assiduity, enjoy Him with more delight. For what we have the most sought and have had the most trouble to find we prize all the more, and preserve it more carefully when we have found it, and we have more pleasure in possessing it. Let us examine ourselves as to whether we have not often lost Jesus by our own fault, and when we have not lost Him by our fault, whether we have accepted such a trial without being discouraged.

SECOND POINT
✝ The Diligence shown by Mary and Joseph in Seeking Jesus

Mary and Joseph having that evening assured themselves of the absence of Jesus, return at the dawn of day along the road to Jerusalem, asking everyone whom they meet if they had seen Him whom they were seeking. Having reached Jerusalem, they make inquiries concerning Him among their friends and acquaintances, but they cannot find Him. The whole day passes in this manner, without any result. Alas! It is not in the world that the soul finds Jesus when it has lost Him. The third day they go and seek Him in the temple, and in fact they find Him there, seated in the midst of the doctors. (Luke 2:46) What a difference between the conduct of Mary and ours! Mary is inconsolable at the loss of Jesus, whilst we are insensible to it; we do not even think of it. Mary has no rest till she has found Him, whilst we, on the contrary, do not take any trouble to seek Him after we have lost Him. We ought, at such a time, to be more faithful to all our duties, to pray more, and to call upon Jesus to come to us by constant heartfelt sighs; but far from seeking Him thus, we make Him remove farther away from us by relaxing and diminishing our exercises. We pray less, or we pray badly, with less courage and less confidence and less desire to be heard. Is not this our history?

THIRD POINT
✝ The Happiness Mary and Joseph felt on Finding Jesus

To have found Jesus was, for Mary and Joseph, to have found once more the most precious of all treasures, their happiness and their life, for Jesus was both these things to them. After His loss the world had been nothing to them but a frightful desert. (2 Imit. 8:2) But with Jesus happiness had returned, and complete happiness, leaving them nothing else to desire. It was paradise on earth. (Ibid) Is it thus we appreciate the happiness of possessing Jesus? Is Jesus all in all for us? Do we count all to be as nothing without Jesus? Do we count Jesus as everything even should all else be wanting? Let us question our heart, and let us not deceive ourselves. *Resolutions and spiritual nosegay as above.*

Thursday in the Fifth Week after Epiphany

SUMMARY OF TOMORROW'S MEDITATION

e will come back tomorrow to the temple at Jerusalem where we left the Infant Jesus this morning and we will consider Him: first, in His relations to the doctors; second, in His relations to His parents. We will then make the resolution: first, always to observe perfect modesty in our language and in our relations with our neighbor; second, always to make the interests of God and His service our prior consideration. Our spiritual nosegay shall be the words of the Gospel: "Seek ye therefore first the kingdom of God." (Matt. 6:33)

MEDITATION FOR THE MORNING

Let us adore the Infant Jesus seated humbly on the bench of the disciples in the midst of the doctors. (Luke 2:46) Let us admire the humility of the eternal wisdom of the Master of all knowledge and of all light, listening to and interrogating simple men, and let us be confounded at our presumption and self-sufficiency.

FIRST POINT

✝ The Infant Jesus in the Temple in His Relations with the Doctors of the Law

First, Jesus listens to them; (Luke 2:46) there is no doubt that no one could teach Him anything, or speak better than He. But His silence was a great lesson which He wished to give us. He desired: first, to teach us thereby to keep silence; we often repent that we have spoken, and rarely that we have been silent; second, to teach us not to assume in society an air of self-sufficiency which modesty disapproves, not to interrupt persons who are speaking, to listen to others with an air of interest, that we may be instructed if we are ignorant of what they are saying, and to be still better instructed if we are acquainted with what they are telling us, for it is always profitable to listen, without taking into account that we acquire the happiness of not giving pain to those who speak, and of giving to our knowledge its most beautiful feature, which is modesty. Second, Jesus questions the doctors; (Ibid) not because He was ignorant of anything, but because He desired to teach us that truth is an inheritance which is transmitted from father to son, from the master to the disciple; (Deut. 32:7) that to wish to be our own master, without counsel and without guide, is to take the wrong path in the way of instruction; that the order of God is that we should be instructed by other men as formerly David was by Nathan and Gad, Moses by the counsels of the ancients, Saul by Ananias; that our vanity is very great, our knowledge very small, if we are not aware that we are ignorant of many things, and that it is foolish pride to prefer not to instruct ourselves by questioning others who are more clever than we are than to reveal our ignorance by asking questions. Lastly, by consulting others we avoid many faults, and we spare ourselves much repentance; and that it is always prudent to add the wisdom of others to our own wisdom. Third, after the Infant Jesus had questioned the doctors, they, in their turn, questioned Him, and He answered their questions with a modesty and wisdom which ravished with admiration all those who heard Him. We are perhaps tempted to envy the happiness of these hearers, but let us remember that Jesus Christ speaks to us by His Gospel, by all the instructions we receive from His ministers, by His holy inspirations. Let us listen, admire, and practice.

SECOND POINT
✝ The Infant Jesus in the Temple, in His Relations with His Parents

Mary, having recognized Jesus in the midst of the doctors, goes immediately to Him, and says, not by way of reproach, but animated by a sentiment of admiration and astonishment: "Wherefore, my Son, hast Thou acted in this manner towards us?" She does not say, towards me, but towards us, because true charity mingles together in a common interest the trouble others feel and our own. She does not describe her trouble, but simply says: Why didst Thou act in this manner? A general expression which includes the whole of her excessive sorrow. Thy father and I, she adds, we have been seeking Thee. She does not say, I and Thy father, but Thy father and I, words full of humility, both in the manner in which she assigns to herself the second place, and also in her speaking of herself as an ordinary mother. To these words, so remarkable in their simplicity, Jesus answers: Wherefore did you seek Me among your relatives and your friends, and not rather in the temple, which is My Father's house? Do you not know that I must give up Myself wholly to the service of My Father? This answer is more admirable even than the complaint, because: first, it gives Mary an opportunity to teach us by her example to suffer reproach in silence, even when it is not deserved; second, it reveals to us that Jesus Christ is more than a man, and that God is His Father. Third, it teaches us that we ought to give the service of God the first place, before the affection of relatives and before family interests, and employ ourselves in it at the time and in the place which He wills. Fourth, that the place of a Christian soul is much rather in the temple where he can pray, meditate, and listen to the law of the Lord, than in societies and circles which only dissipate and corrupt it. What lessons are contained in these simple words of the Child Jesus! Let us meditate upon them and conform our conduct to them. *Resolutions and spiritual nosegay as above.*

Friday in the Fifth Week after Epiphany

SUMMARY OF TOMORROW'S MEDITATION

e will meditate tomorrow on the adolescence of Jesus Christ, and we will consider: first, why the Incarnate Word willed to grow only little by little like other children. Second, what we must understand by these words of the Gospel: "Jesus advanced in wisdom and age, and grace with God and men." (Luke 2:52) We will then make the resolution: first, often to encourage ourselves to make progress in Christian life; to live better today than yesterday, during the present hour than during the one which preceded it; second, often to say to ourselves: I have done nothing yet for God; I must begin now for good and all to serve Him better. Our spiritual nosegay shall be the words of the Gospel: "Jesus grew in wisdom and age and grace with God and men." (Luke 2:52)

MEDITATION FOR THE MORNING

Let us adore Jesus, arrived at the age of adolescence, increasing every day in wisdom and in grace; not in the sense that He acquired some fresh degree of knowledge and holiness, because, from the first moment of His conception, He was consummate wisdom and infinite holiness; but in the sense that He permitted to appear outwardly little by little and by degrees His wisdom and holiness, not showing signs of either the one or the other except in accordance with His progress towards manhood. Oh, how adorable He is, how amiable He shows Himself to be in this delicate attention, springing from His love, only to let us see, little by little, what He was in Himself. It is thus that, instead of showing us all at once the sun at its meridian, which would dazzle us, He brings it little by little above the horizon, after having begun with a dawn which is almost indistinguishable from night, in order to humor our delicate eyesight. Let us render to Him our homage of praise and love.

FIRST POINT

✝ Why the Incarnate Word would only Increase in Age Little by Little, like other Children

There is in this succession of growth in the Savior, until He arrived at adolescence, at the state of complete manhood, a profound mystery. Jesus, hiding Himself at the beginning of His career, willed two things: first, to prepare minds, little by little, for the splendor of His miracles and of His divine mission; second, to give a great lesson to our self-love and our ignorance: to our self-love, which cannot bear to see its own miseries, its weaknesses, and its temptations; to our ignorance, which cannot comprehend that a man does not become perfect all at once that perfection is a work which takes a long time, which is only consummated by dint of tearing out and replanting, of destroying and building up, things which are not done in a day; and that, lastly, a perfect life resembles a mysterious ladder, the top of which is not reached by a bound, but only by painfully climbing all the rungs, one after the other. It is this intemperate zeal, this impatience springing from self-love, that our amiable Savior willed to correct, by showing less perfection outwardly, less knowledge and less holiness during His childhood than during His adolescence, and during His adolescence than when He had arrived at manhood, (Luke 2:40-52) as we read in the Holy Scriptures. Let us learn from hence: first, to have patience with ourselves, to bear with a meek and humble spirit all our weaknesses, and to make them the foundation of solid humility. Second, to grow constantly in a better life; to persuade ourselves thoroughly that we are still far from attaining our object; to repair past sin by present well-doing, continually to correct our defects, and ceaselessly to press forward, following therein the example set us by St. Paul. (Phil. 3:13)

SECOND POINT

✝ What we must Understand by the Words: "Jesus Grew in Wisdom and Age and Grace."

To increase in grace is to grow in the knowledge of God and of His infinite perfection, in the knowledge of ourselves and of our wretchedness, in the knowledge of all that concerns our salvation and the duties of our state. Intelligence has been given us for that alone. To grow in age is to put away the spiritual miseries of another age, such as the frivolity which does not reflect, vanity, inconstancy, malice, all the weaknesses from which St. Paul esteemed himself happy to have been freed, when he said: "When I was a child, I spoke as a child, I understood as a child, I thought as a child. But when I became a man, I put away the things of a child." (1 Cor. 8:11) Lastly, to grow in grace is to grow in holiness; and herein we lie under a daily obligation until we have arrived at the fullness of grace of the perfect man in Jesus Christ, which will take place only in heaven. Such is the holy life in which Jesus, when He was adolescent, allowed exterior progress to show itself every day before God and before man: (Luke 2:52) before God by His interior life and before man by means of the edification of His divine example. We ought to act in the same manner, because not to advance is to go back; we ought at least to desire it ardently, because we advance only in proportion to the desire we have for it; the desire excludes the thought of acting wrongly, and gives to the soul courage and energy to do well. Let us examine ourselves as to whether we have this great zeal for our spiritual progress; whether every day we heartily desire to become better, and if, in order to be so, we make serious and constant efforts, accompanied by fervent prayers and holy desires. *Resolutions and spiritual nosegay as above.*

Saturday in the Fifth Week after Epiphany

SUMMARY OF TOMORROW'S MEDITATION

After having seen Jesus adolescent, growing at Nazareth in wisdom and in grace, we will consider Him tomorrow as arrived at manhood, and we shall see that: first, He led a very laborious life in His poor dwelling; second, how He sanctified His work. We will then make the resolution: first, not to lose our time, but to employ it assiduously in work; second, to offer our work to God, praying Him to bless it and enable us to perform it well; third, to unite our work and our intentions to the work and the intentions of Jesus Christ. Our spiritual nosegay shall be the words which Jesus Christ said of Himself by the mouth of the Psalm, "I am poor and in labors since My youth." (Ps. 87:16)

MEDITATION FOR THE MORNING

Let us transport ourselves in spirit to the poor dwelling of Nazareth. Let us there contemplate with admiration and love a God subjecting Himself to labor. He who created the world, raised the vault of heaven, sowed in the firmament planets and stars, does not disdain to handle the tools of a hard trade; to make Himself the aid, the companion, and the servant of a poor carpenter. Let us unite ourselves to the homage of the angels ravished by this marvelous spectacle.

FIRST POINT
✟ The Life of Jesus at Nazareth was a very Laborious Life

Jesus in His poor dwelling was never idle. "I am in labors since My youth," He said by the mouth of the prophet David. With the exception of the Sabbath, all His days were employed in labor, and in hard labor; He made use of the saw and the plane like a poor workman; He gained His bread by the sweat of His brow. It was not enough for Him not to lose time doing nothing; every moment of His life, excepting the interruptions which nature requires, were employed in hard labor for the body, which the mind could not enjoy, and for which the heart had no attraction; for the law of labor imposed upon the first man, and which He accomplished in His person, is not limited to a pastime which amuses us; it prescribes a penance which annoys, which fatigues, which makes the sweat burst forth: "In the sweat of thy face shalt thou eat bread," (Gen. 3:19) the law had said. Have I thoroughly understood this law until now, and how have I observed it? Have I not sought only to kill time, as we say, by doing nothing, or doing nothing but frivolities, by amusing myself, by occupying myself with reveries having no object, by useless conversations, by frivolous reading, by needless walks, by work which leads to nothing? Have I not allowed myself to be disheartened by all serious and useful work, because it troubles or wearies me? That is to say, because it is the condition which is the most appropriate to the object of the law, which is expiation of sin by penance.

SECOND POINT
✟ How Jesus at Nazareth Sanctified His Labor

Let us consider this divine Artisan at His trade: how holily He performs everything! First, He does not Himself choose His kind of labor; He does with simplicity all that St. Joseph prescribes, and He does it at the time and in the manner St. Joseph directs. (Luke 2:51) He does not examine whether it is work which will be pleasing to Him. He says to Himself: The work pointed out to Me by Joseph is that which is in the order of God My Father, since it is in the order of obedience; therefore it is pleasing to Me, and I devote Myself wholly to it. He does not examine whether the work is suitable for His condition, His rank, His age, His strength: God My Father wills it. What can I do better than that which God wills? Second, the work is not of His own choice, but the choice of Providence. He performs it in the best possible manner, without the slowness which is the sign of idleness, and also without the haste which springs from want of reflection; without the negligence which is not careful about what it does, without the effeminacy which is afraid of fatigue; and already it may be said of Him what the people said later on, "He hath done all things well." (Mark 7:37) Third, He accompanies His work with interior sentiments which ravish the heart of God. Very different from those Christians who in their work occupy themselves solely with what is exterior, and do not keep God in view. Jesus, on the contrary, without taking away from the exterior action the attention which it requires, occupies Himself principally with His interior, which He always keeps present before the eyes of the Divine Majesty. There exists within Him an intention of pleasing God even in the most trifling details, an offering so perfect of His whole being and of all His moments to the sovereign dominion of His Father, a union so intimate, so constant, so devoted with His whole soul to His Creator, that God considers Himself to be infinitely honored thereby, and takes His pleasure therein, as He declared upon the banks of the Jordan. (Matt. 3:17) Let us examine if our work bears the three characteristics of holiness which we have been admiring in Jesus Christ. Do we always perform the work which is most in the order of Providence, and do we not prefer that which amuses us? Do we perform everything in the best manner possible, and do we perform it solely with the desire of pleasing God thereby? *Resolutions and spiritual nosegay as above.*

Sixth Sunday after Epiphany

THE GOSPEL ACCORDING TO ST. MATTHEW 8:31-35

"And Jesus proposed this parable unto them, saying: The kingdom of heaven is like to a grain of mustard seed which a man took and sowed in his field, which is the least indeed of all seeds; but when it is grown up it is greater than all herbs, and becomes a tree, so that the birds of the air come and dwell in the branches thereof. Another parable He spoke to them: The kingdom of heaven is like to leaven, which a woman took and hid in three measures of meal until the whole was leavened. All these things Jesus spoke in parables to the multitudes: and without parables He did not speak to them that it might be fulfilled which was spoken by the prophet, saying: I will open my mouth in parables, and I will utter things hidden from the foundation of the world."

SUMMARY OF TOMORROW'S MEDITATION

e will meditate tomorrow upon the Gospel for the day, which shows us a grain of mustard seed changed into a great tree, and a little leaven fermenting the whole three measures, first, we shall admire, by means of this parable, the mercy of God, which, abasing itself

down to our littleness, works by it great things, when it so pleases Him; second, we shall learn from the example given us by God to become ourselves merciful men, who do not disdain any kind of misery nor any kind of littleness. We will then make the resolution: first, to banish from our hearts thoughts of discouragement and sadness, as being an offence against the Divine Majesty; second, to bear the faults of our neighbor in a spirit of patience and charity. Our spiritual nosegay shall be the words of Our Lord: "Be ye therefore merciful, as your Father is also merciful." (Luke 7:36)

MEDITATION FOR THE MORNING

Let us adore the heart so tender and so compassionate, so merciful and so kind, of Our Lord. In presence of His infinite majesty we are less than a grain of mustard seed, which is in itself only a grain of dust, less than a little leaven mixed with the dough, and yet, however little we may be, His mercy lowers itself down to our baseness, to raise us up as high as the skies, as high as His angels and saints, in the midst of whom He has prepared a throne for us. Can we ever sufficiently admire, sufficiently praise, and sufficiently love so much mercy?

FIRST POINT

✝ Amongst all the Attributes of God, we ought Especially to Honor His Mercy

Doubtless all the perfections of God are excellent, seeing that they are infinite; but mercy possesses this special characteristic: first, that it is better known to us, it shows itself in all its works; it is that which has done everything. (Ps. 32:5) Second, that it possesses a very special charm for our hearts; we admire greatness, we fear justice; but we can do nothing except love mercy and delight in it: it is so suitable to our misery! Third, that it brings God near to us and unites us to Him. The other perfections of God seem to remove Him to an infinite distance from us; but His mercy, precisely because it is infinite, descends to us and places its throne on the very abyss of our wretchedness. It is there that the Holy Spirit teaches us to honor Him. (Ps. 102:8) Let us praise the Lord, He says, because He is good, because His mercy is everlasting. (Ps. 105:1) Jesus Christ also presents God to us in the form of a father full of tenderness, or of a good shepherd who hastens after a wandering sheep, and the apostles show Him to us principally as the Father of mercies and the God of all consolation. (2 Cor. 1:3) In fact, we owe everything to the mercy of God, whether it be in the order of nature or in the order of grace, the being we enjoy, the air which enables us to live, the sun which lights us, nourishment that sustains us, our redemption, the Church and the sacraments, and the blessing of a Christian education. Mercy precedes us and loves us even when we do not love it; it seeks for us when we fly from it, (Ps. 58:11) it accompanies us when we desire to do good (Ps. 102:4) and it crowns us after we have done it. It is a mother which accompanies us everywhere, sustains and raises us when we fall, feeds us sometimes with the milk of consolation, sometimes with the solid bread of tribulation. Oh, what good reason the Prophet King had to sing the divine mercies continually in his psalms, and finding the time of his life too short to satisfy his heart with so beautiful a subject he promises himself to compensate for it throughout eternity. (Ps. 88:2) Let us imitate him and let us have a special devotion to the mercies of God. Let us throw ourselves wholly, and with our eyes closed, into this abyss of mercy, with unlimited confidence. It is there that the heart is dilated, that courage is renewed, and that hope with its peace and sweet joys inundates the heart.(Ps. 31:10; Ibid 5:8)

SECOND POINT
✝ We ought ourselves to be Merciful Men

First, the first object of our mercy ought to be our own soul. Let us have pity for it, and do not let us lose it by our negligence in working out its salvation. Let us have pity on its miseries, and do not let us aggravate them and render them incurable through spiteful self-love, which cannot bear to see how miserable it is. Do not let us be astonished that we have fallen, being as miserable as we are; let us rather be astonished that we have not fallen still more, let us thank God for it, whose grace has restrained us, and let us set ourselves once more to do well with the calmness of confidence, and a great desire to repair the past by the present. We ought, second, to be merciful men in regard to our neighbor; the poor, the sick, the afflicted, the widow, and the orphan, ought always to find in us bowels of mercy, a voice to console them, a hand to solace them. (Coloss. 3:12) The wrongs done to us, and the faults of others ought still more to find in us mercy which not only bears them with meekness, with patience, and with compassion for human weakness, (Gal. 6:2) but which also endeavors to bring them back to what is good, by treating them with gentleness and prudence. Oh, how greatly are these poor sinners to be pitied, what compassion we ought to have for their blindness, for their evil nature, for their prejudices and their passions! Merciful men are blessed by God and men. (Ps. 22:9) Let us examine our conscience: are we really merciful men? *Resolutions and spiritual nosegay as above.*

Monday in the Sixth Week after Epiphany

SUMMARY OF TOMORROW'S MEDITATION

e will continue to study the life of Jesus at Nazareth, and we shall see, first, that it was a life of poverty; second, how we ought to imitate it. We will then make the resolution: first, always to take for ourselves what is least and most in convenient, leaving the best to others; second, to Jove to be poor in everything, in clothing, in food, in lodging, and everything else. Our spiritual nosegay shall be the first of the beatitudes: "Blessed are the poor in spirit, for theirs is the kingdom of heaven." (Matt. 5:3)

MEDITATION FOR THE MORNING

Let us transport ourselves in spirit to the poor dwelling at Nazareth; let us there contemplate the eternal Son of God in a state of poverty. He is clad in poor clothes, His food is poor, His bed poor, His home poor, and He gains His bread, like the poor, by the labor of His hands. Let us render Him our homage in the state to which He has been reduced by love.

FIRST POINT
✝ Marvels of the Life of Poverty led by Jesus at Nazareth

Poverty must indeed be a very great thing, in order that a God living upon earth should have chosen it as His portion. He might have been rich, had He so willed; it depended only on Him to live in the splendor of opulence, to have a palace for a dwelling, to surpass in riches all the princes of this world He who had given such great treasures to the earth, to the sea, to the firmament, and who could derive the richest tributes from them. But, O holy poverty, your excellence ravished His heart; He preferred you to all else. You appeared to Him as the sister of humility, for riches often render men proud and haughty; they think themselves worth more than others because they have more servants, more splendid clothes, a more magnificent dwelling, more extensive estates; whilst you, holy poverty, inspire quite other sentiments; on account of you men are less considered, more forgotten, often even despised, and then they easily humble themselves. You appeared to Him as the companion of meekness; for the rich man feels himself to be inclined to domineer and to command with harshness; whilst the poor man, who sees everyone to be above him, makes himself as gentle as he can in his words and his manners. You appeared to Him as the mother of holy love; for by disengaging the soul from all earthly solicitudes, you leave it more free to raise itself to God. Like the bird when its cage is opened, it takes more easily its flight to heaven, to God alone, whilst riches bind the heart; their possession is an embarrassment which preoccupies and distracts it; the administration of them causes anxiety, the loss of them brings bitterness, the enjoyment of them is a danger in a word, he saw in you the secret of holiness. In cutting off from the heart earthly helps and consolations, you dispose it to have recourse to Him who is called the Father of the poor, to pray with confidence to Him who has promised to listen to the prayers of the poor, (Ps. 10:17) to unite itself to God as the surest of friends, the most devoted of protectors, and thus to enter into the life of divine union, which is the consummation of all virtue. O holy poverty, how excellent thou art! I am no longer astonished that a God should have made choice of you; may I appreciate you as He did!

SECOND POINT
✝ How we ought to Imitate the Poverty of Jesus Christ

There are two kinds of poverty: interior poverty and exterior poverty. Interior poverty consists in having the heart detached from earthly possessions and riches; that is to say, when we do not possess them, not to blush at being destitute of them, not to desire them, not to seek after them; and when we do possess them, not to take advantage of them to make ourselves more esteemed, not to think of them with complacence, not to place our confidence in them or lean upon them; to bear the loss of them without sorrow; not to give to the administration of them the time which other duties claim; to show ourselves to be disinterested, to give alms willingly, to lend easily, to contribute to all kinds of good works, regarding ourselves only as the steward of the wealth God has given us, and disposing of it as seems most in accordance with the will of Providence. Let us examine our hearts and see if such be our dispositions. Exterior poverty consists in suffering, without complaining, privation and destitution, heat and cold, fatigue and labor, all that the poor suffer; to content ourselves with common furniture, with simple clothing, with plain food; to lend ourselves cheerfully to the performance of the most humble offices, such as sweeping out our room and making our bed; not to imitate those who desire not to want for anything, to enjoy themselves at their ease and satisfy their vanity by the richness of their clothes or their furniture, luxurious food and superfluous expenses. If we are born poor, we show ourselves to be content. If we have become so through reverses, we suffer them without murmuring; and we are delighted to be thought poor, thereby to be conformable to Jesus Christ, who was poor. Are these our dispositions? *Resolutions and spiritual nosegay as above.*

TUESDAY IN THE SIXTH WEEK AFTER EPIPHANY

SUMMARY OF TOMORROW'S MEDITATION

e will still continue to study the life of Jesus at Nazareth, and we shall see that His life there was, first, a life consisting wholly of obedience; second, how we ought to imitate it. We will then make the resolution: first, to live by rule, without yielding in any way to caprice, to likes or dislikes; second, often to offer to God the sacrifice of our own will, through deference to His good pleasure. Our spiritual nosegay shall be the words which the Holy Spirit uttered respecting the life of Our Saviour during thirty years, "He was subject to them." (Luke 2:51)

MEDITATION FOR THE MORNING

Let us return to the holy house at Nazareth, that we may there contemplate the eternal Son of God obeying Mary and Joseph. Let us adore, praise, and bless Our Lord for this great mystery; let us beg Him to apply the grace of it to us.

FIRST POINT
✝ Obedience of Jesus at Nazareth

The Holy Spirit has summed up in one single sentence the history of the thirty years of the life of God made man, He obeyed Mary and Joseph. Let us search into this profound mystery. Who is He that obeys? It is the supreme Monarch of heaven and earth; no one had a better right to command than He, since commandment supposes power, maturity, wisdom, and no one possessed these qualities in a higher degree than Uncreated Wisdom and Sovereign Power. Whom did He obey? Mary and Joseph, doubtless two holy souls, who could command nothing but what was wise and just, but who, after all, were two of His creatures who derived from Him being, life, and movement. In what did He obey? Mary and Joseph had nothing great to command Him to do; they could only ask of Him, the one to practice His mechanical trade, the other to perform little domestic duties. Up to what age did He obey? Up to thirty years, that epoch of life in which a man believes himself to have a right to command and to govern himself. Nevertheless Jesus obeys, as a servant obeys his master; He executes instantly all that is commanded Him, all that is hinted to Him to do, and all that is desired of Him, repeating meekly in the bottom of His heart His favorite words, "The Son of man is not come to be ministered unto, but to minister." (Matt. 20:28) He has no will except to sacrifice it to obedience, He does nothing for the sake of His own satisfaction, (Rom. 15:3) and He dispenses Himself from nothing, either from displeasure or repugnance. All His enjoyment consists in allowing Himself to be guided by the authority of His holy parents, and to abandon Himself in all things to their direction, in a spirit of humility and meekness. Oh, how great, then, in the eyes of God is the virtue of obedience, since it was the life of a God during thirty years, and since it is the sole characteristic of this life during thirty years which the Holy Spirit has revealed to the world. We may give to God all our wealth, all our labors, the sweat of every moment, but it is all as nothing, if we do not add to it the sacrifice of self-will; without it, there may be devotion, but there is no virtue; or else it is a varnish only of virtue, a phantom, an appearance of virtue; it wants the foundation, the reality, the seal of the life of Jesus Christ, which is obedience. Have we up to the present time rightly understood the excellence of obedience?

SECOND POINT
✝ How we ought to Imitate the Obedience of Jesus at Nazareth

First, by always seeing God in those who command us a marvelous secret, whence results an obedience without sadness, without murmurings, always gay, always ready to do what is desired of us; without delaying a single moment, without reasoning or discussing commands laid upon us; a courageous obedience in difficult things as well as those which are more easy, in the most advanced age as well as in childhood; lastly, an obedience which wills and desires nothing but the good pleasure of God, by which the soul allows itself to be molded like clay in the hands of the potter. Second, the example of Jesus Christ ought to inspire us with aversion for employments where it is necessary to command; as well as for a certain kind of life, in which from morning to night we do what we like. We ought, above all things, to fear to do our own will, we ought to love to take advice, to obey, and to submit ourselves to the representatives of God, in the persons of our superiors. To live a life of obedience is the supreme happiness of a soul animated by the spirit of Jesus Christ. Third, we ought to obey God in all things by the complete abandonment of ourselves to the dispositions of His Providence, by submission to His commandments and to those of Holy Church, by acquiescence with His inspirations, by our deference towards the superiors He has set over us, by our condescension to our equals and inferiors, in so far as duty permits and charity demands; lastly, by the resigned acceptance of everything that creatures may make us suffer, cold and heat, ill-health, reverses, and all the contrarieties of life. True obedience submits to all, is tranquil in the hands of God, like a child in the arms of the best of fathers. Are these the characteristics of our obedience? *Resolutions and spiritual nosegay as above.*

WEDNESDAY IN THE SIXTH WEEK AFTER EPIPHANY

SUMMARY OF TOMORROW'S MEDITATION

We will terminate tomorrow our meditations on the life of Jesus at Nazareth by considering Him from two new points of view: first, it was a life of retreat, or of separation from the world. Second, it was a hidden and obscure life. We will then make the resolution: first, to love retreat, and to mingle with the world only in so far as the duties of our position demand; second, never to say or do anything through self-love, and from the bottom of our hearts to renounce all desire to attract attention and to make others speak of us. Our spiritual nosegay shall be the words of the Imitation: "Love to be ignored and counted as nothing." (1 Imit. 2:3)

MEDITATION FOR THE MORNING

Let us adore Jesus at Nazareth, leading a life separate from the world, hidden and unknown during thirty whole years. Let us thank Him for having thereby given so necessary a lesson to our self-love, to our desire to see and be seen, and let us beg Him to enable us to understand it.

FIRST POINT

✝ The Life of Jesus at Nazareth was a Life of Separation from the World

After His return from Egypt, Jesus remained shut up in the poor dwelling at Nazareth, content to be with God His Father, to behold Him and to be seen by Him, to love Him and be loved by Him. God alone was sufficient for Him, and He had no need of anything else to be happy. He enjoyed this divine society, delighted in its charms, and from them looked with pity on the world with its pleasures, which render men effeminate and corrupt; its fears, which dissipate the mind; its glories, which nourish pride; all its vanities, which leave after them nothing but weariness and satiety, sadness and sin. Happy retreat! It is therein that we learn to know ourselves, and consequently to be humble. As the passions are more tranquil there, and the heart more at peace, we are able to penetrate more deeply into our inner self; we discern better what we are. It is there that we learn to know God, and, consequently, to love Him. Far from the noise of creatures which amuse and dissipate, we study better the loving kindnesses of the Creator, and we are penetrated with His love. It is there that we learn to know the world, and consequently to detach ourselves from it. Seen near at hand, its vain splendor dazzles and deceives; seen from a distance, we feel better how deceitful and insane it is, how little its judgments are to be feared, how little desirable are its praises. It is there, lastly, that we enjoy God; that the soul, being freer and more recollected, enters with Him into those intimate communications which sanctify and console. There, say the saints, the air is purer, the sky more open, and God speaks more familiarly to the heart. (Os. 2:14) O happy retreat! O sole happiness of life! said St. Bernard. Let us examine our dispositions with regard to this subject. Do we place our happiness in family life and a life of retreat? Do we not love the world, its society and its amusements?

SECOND POINT
✝ The Life of Jesus at Nazareth was a Hidden and Obscure Life

There are illustrious retreats; men of genius have immortalized their solitude by learned works or marvelous discoveries. But it was not so with Jesus Christ. He spent thirty years in the most profound obscurity. "I am become," He says by the Psalmist "as a vessel that is destroyed;" (Ps. 30:13) "like the slain sleeping in the sepulchers, whom thou remembers no more." (Ps. 88:6) He who could have shed such great brilliancy over the world by His wisdom, His knowledge, His power; He who could evangelize the whole world, and make all the nations of the earth fall down before Him, He is scarcely known in the little town of Nazareth. And, again, how is He known? He is a humble carpenter, the son of a carpenter as poor as Himself. (Matt. 13:55) There were at that time upon earth princes, kings, famous conquerors, who were praised by every mouth; everywhere their great deeds were spoken of, but of Jesus not a word was said. The world was ignorant of His dwelling, of His name, of His birth; He was there in His poor home, as much ignored as though He had never existed. There were at that period geniuses who wielded learned pens, and made themselves an immortal name by their writings; and during that time the Eternal Son of God was hardening His hands with handling rude and rough tools. What was the reason for such a life? Ah, it was because Jesus

Christ saw that this stern, strong lesson was necessary to man to disabuse him of the desire to make an appearance and attract attention; to take from him the passion for honor and glory, and the thirst for reputation which devours him. He saw that if three years were sufficient to preach His religion, thirty years were not too much in which to teach humility alone; and, as though even that were not enough, He adds to it the three years of His mission, in which He hides Himself where it is not necessary that He should be seen, and submits to the calumnies of His enemies; He joins to it His passion, His death, His eucharistic life, the perpetual mystery of a hidden life. In presence of such examples, all ambition, all vanity, ought to disappear, and every Christian ought to be content with the position in which God has placed him. Let us here examine our hearts. Do we love to be counted as nothing, to do good in secret, content to be seen by God alone; not to desire that others should speak of us, and to enjoy God alone, without any mixture of the creature? *Resolutions and spiritual nosegay as above.*

Thursday in the Sixth Week after Epiphany

SUMMARY OF TOMORROW'S MEDITATION

After His long years of solitude spent at Nazareth, Our Lord, before beginning His apostolic ministry, betook Himself to the banks of the Jordan, and there received baptism from St. John. We will meditate tomorrow on this touching mystery, and we shall gather from it: first, a lesson of humility; second, a lesson of zeal for our perfection. We will then make the resolution: first, always to treat our neighbor with consideration, and humble ourselves willingly in order to do him honor; second, to pursue without abatement the work of our sanctification as being the principal business of our life. Our spiritual nosegay shall be the words which the heavenly Father said of Jesus Christ: "This is My beloved Son, in whom I am well pleased." (Matt. 3:17)

MEDITATION FOR THE MORNING

Let us transport ourselves in spirit to the banks of the Jordan. Let us there consider Jesus Christ receiving baptism from St. John. The heavens open above His head, the Holy Spirit appears under the form of a dove, and our heavenly Father proclaims that Jesus is His well-beloved Son in whom He is well pleased.

What a magnificent spectacle! Let us adore the Holy Trinity which thus reveals itself in this mystery, and let us beg Him to make us profit by the lessons therein contained.

FIRST POINT
✝ The Baptism of Jesus Christ is a Lesson of Humility

Can there, in fact, be a more profound humiliation? The Saint of saints confounded with sinners, the Son of God at the feet of a man, claiming his ministrations, as though He needed to be purified! St. John shrinks from baptizing Him: "I ought to be baptized by Thee," he said "and comes Thou to me?" Jesus answering said: "Suffer it to be so now, for so it becomes us to fulfill all justice." (Matt. 3:14-15) John obeys with profound confusion; the great God of heaven humiliates Himself beneath the hand of His servant, and receives from him the baptism of penitence. Let us admire this debate of humility. Neither John is proud of the honor done to Him, nor is Jesus jealous of the confidence of the numerous disciples which crowd around John; both of them live in perfect harmony, rendering to each other honorable testimony, never any debate between them except as to which shall yield and humiliate himself the most. I must efface myself, said John, that He alone maybe in sight. I must retire into my own nothingness that He alone may appear. (John 3:30) "The same is He that shall come after me, who is preferred before me, the latchet of whose shoe I am not worthy to loose," (John 1:27) so greatly is He above me. O admirable humility of John and of Jesus, which teaches us not to prefer ourselves to others, willingly to praise them even when they do less will than ourselves, to respect our competitors, and to be always kind and obliging with regard to them; to hide ourselves on occasions of notoriety, and to leave the honor to others. Are these our dispositions?

SECOND POINT
✝ The Baptism of Jesus is a Lesson of Zeal for our Sanctification

First, Jesus, who is holiness itself, wills, before commencing His mission, to purify Himself in the eyes of the creature, by the baptism of John, to teach us that we ought never to esteem ourselves as being sufficiently pure; that, subject to daily venial faults, we ought to neglect no means of purifying ourselves still more. We do not always see our faults, but they are only all the more deplorable on that account; sometimes they consist in oblique intentions which are perhaps good in their beginning, but which degenerate when carried into action; sometimes they are sentiments of self-love; sometimes indulgence in vanity, of impatience towards some persons and of too great indulgence towards others; then a thousand snares are laid for our innocence by the world and the devil. Oh, what great need we have to purify ourselves more and more by frequent confession, by general and particular examinations, and by assiduous recourse to God. Second, at the moment when Jesus comes out of the Jordan, heaven opens, and a voice descends from it which says to the world, "This is My beloved Son, in whom I am well pleased," (Matt. 3:17) to show us that the more we humble ourselves the more God is glorified. A voice from heaven adds, later on, upon Mount Tabor: "Hear ye Him," (Matt. 17:5) a sentence which includes in it the whole Christian life. Listen to Jesus: these words say everything; listen to Him, not only in His Gospel, His doctrine, and His example, but listen to Him also when He speaks to us by His grace and makes us to be led by His holy inspirations. Therein is the secret of perfection. Unhappy the soul which is too dissipated to hear Him, too cowardly to obey Him, slave enough to self to be carried away by its likings and pleasures, the love of the world and its comfort, by the caprices of pride, and by a sensual life! How happy the soul which attentively listens to Him within, in a spirit of recollection and of prayer, and which is generous in obeying Him! If it be constant in its obedience it will make rapid progress towards perfection. Do we recognize ourselves under these characteristics? *Resolutions and spiritual nosegay as above.*

Friday in the Sixth Week after Epiphany

SUMMARY OF TOMORROW'S MEDITATION

ntil now we have considered Jesus Christ from the moment of His Incarnation down to His baptism by St. John. Everywhere we have beheld suffering and sacrifice. We will tomorrow meditate upon the profound reason underlying this fact. It is: first, that to suffer is a necessity; second, that to suffer is a happiness. We will then make the resolution: first, to detach our hearts from the love of enjoyment and of pleasure, and to make a sacrifice of both to God when an opportunity presents itself; second, cheerfully to accept all the trials of life, without murmur or complaint. Our spiritual nosegay shall be the words of the Gospel: "Blessed are they that suffer." (Matt. 5:10)

MEDITATION FOR THE MORNING

Let us adore Jesus Christ making of His life, until he was thirty years old, a life of suffering, of privations, and of martyrdom. Let us admire this profound mystery, and let us bless the Divine Savior for it; for it is for our good that He freely chose this kind of life; it is to console and encourage us in our trials; it is to merit for us the grace of patience, it is to teach us the excellence of suffering and of sacrifice. A thousand praises, a thousand thanksgivings to our good Saviour, who for love of us devoted Himself to so painful a life.

FIRST POINT
✝ To Suffer is a Necessity

First, it is a necessity of nature: "Go where you will," says the Imitation, "seek on high, seek below, seek to the right, seek to the left, everywhere you will find the cross, you cannot escape from it." (2 Imit. 12:3-4) The cross in your body, through infirmity; the cross in your soul, by anxiety, sorrow, weariness which makes you a burden to yourself, without being able to understand it; the cross in the contrarieties of characters, of wills, of interests, of ideas of those with whom one lives; the cross in possessions, through the fear of losing them, and of embarrassment in administering them; the cross in privation, through the distress which is the consequence of it; the cross in labor, by the fatigue it engenders; the cross in idleness, by weariness of oneself; the cross in the loss of relatives and friends; the cross in reverses of fortune; the cross in the contradiction of tongues; the diminution of reputation, the "What will they say?" Lastly, the whole world is one great Calvary, where each, whether he likes it or not, is attached to the cross. Now human things being thus, is it not unreasonable of man not to wish to submit to what is inevitable, to lose the merit of that which, borne in a Christian spirit, maybe so meritorious for him in regard to heaven, and to aggravate his troubles in bearing them with a bad grace? How much more wise is he who makes of necessity a virtue, and bears his cross courageously. Second, to suffer is a necessity of salvation. If we had nothing but enjoyments here below, we should attach our hearts to them; we should take this earth to be our home, we should forget heaven. Sorrow brings a man back to God. The proverb has its foundation in experience. Struck by adversity, man says to himself that his home is not then here below; that on leaving this world he will find himself in a better place, where justice is rendered to all, to true Christians by an eternal recompense, to sinners by an everlasting punishment; (Matt. 25:46) that, after being unhappy in this world, he must take precautions not to be still more so hereafter. Then he puts his conscience in order and begins to lead a Christian life. God refused Solomon the grace of suffering, and his salvation is, to say the least, very doubtful; He granted it to David and it was that which enabled him to be numbered amongst the saints. The cross, the author of the Imitation tells us, is the royal road to heaven; it was only by it that Jesus Christ Himself arrived there; we must not hope to go there by any other way. In order to be glorified with Jesus Christ in heaven, we must suffer with Him here below. (Rom. 8:7) Do we thoroughly understand this truth? Have we really determined to suffer without murmuring and with cheerfulness all the crosses of this life?

SECOND POINT
✝ To Suffer is a Happiness

Doubtless these two words seem to contradict each other, and outside religion they do contradict each other. For him who has in his heart neither faith nor love, suffering is an evil which irritates, which distresses, which often casts a man into despair. But for him who believes and loves it is quite otherwise, and he feels the words of Christ to be true: "Blessed are they that suffer. Blessed are they that mourn. Come to me all you that labor, and I will refresh you." (Matt. 5:1-5; 11:28) It is because the soul which believes and loves sees in all its trials the hand of God which strikes it; and in this hand of God, the hand of a Father who is infinitely loving, who disposes all things for its greatest good. From that time it loves and kisses with emotion this hand, always kind, even when it afflicts it. It is the love of my God, which sends me this cross, it says to itself; how could I do otherwise than love it and esteem it above all thrones? The soul which believes and loves remembers that there is no proportion between the trials of this world and the joys of glory. For a moment of privations, an eternity of enjoyments; for a drop of bitterness, an ocean of happiness; for each moment of suffering borne in a Christian manner, an increase of ineffable and eternal joys. At these thoughts, the soul is overwhelmed with joy in the midst of all its sufferings. (2 Cor. 7:4) The soul which believes and loves looks at the crucifix, and it understands that Jesus, innocent, having suffered for it, it is just that it, guilty, should suffer for Him. Jealous to render in equal measure love for love, it desires to suffer as much as Jesus suffered, and if the divine crucified Savior has suffered much more than it, at least it accepts with a good grace lesser sufferings. It then kisses the crucifix, it presses its lips and its heart to it and it repeats with delight the words of St. Peter: "If you partake of the suffering of Christ, rejoice, that when His glory shall be revealed you may also be glad with exceeding joy," (1 Pet. 4:13) or those of St. Andrew, "O good cross, thou art welcome!" Thus, where souls who have neither faith nor love find only unhappiness and despair, it finds happiness and enjoyment. Is it thus that we regard and receive suffering? Let us assume with respect to these things more Christian sentiments than those which have guided us up to the present time. *Resolutions and spiritual nosegay as above.*

Saturday in the Sixth Week after Epiphany

SUMMARY OF TOMORROW'S MEDITATION

s tomorrow at the first vespers, the season of Septuagesima will begin, we shall consider, first, the reason for passing in a holy manner this season of the year; second, the manner of passing it holily. We will then make the resolution: first, to give ourselves specially up to a spirit of recollection and prayer; second, to mortify ourselves in something or other in regard to eating and drinking. Our spiritual nosegay shall be the words of the Apostle: "Behold now is the day of salvation." (2 Cor. 6:2)

MEDITATION FOR THE MORNING

Let us adore God, addressing to us at the beginning of the holy season of Septuagesima the parable of the good father of a family calling laborers to his vineyard, that is to say, to the care of their salvation. Thanks, O my God, for the appeal which Thy love makes to me in the Gospel of tomorrow; I present myself before Thee in order that I may be encouraged to reply to it, by meditating, beneath Thy eyes, on the reasons for passing this holy season holily. Help me to be penetrated with them, and to conform my life to them.

FIRST POINT

✝ **The Reasons for Spending in a Holy Manner the Season of Septuagesima**

First, the Church in her offices takes back our thoughts to the creation, in order to remind us that we are born of God, made for God, and consequently that we ought to be wholly given up to God. From thence she transports us to the fall of Adam, followed by our original degradation, in order to tell us that sinners as we are by nature, we ought to devote ourselves to penance. In order the better to inculcate in us this disposition, she suppresses at Mass the vestments of the deacon and sub-deacon, retrenches from all her offices the Alleluia and the Gloria in excelsis, which are canticles of gladness; she recounts in the epistle of the day the sufferings of the Apostle in his combats against the flesh, and in the Gospel the invitation of the father of the family to the laborers he summons to his vineyard, followed by the terrible declaration of the small number of the elect. Now, what can possibly be better calculated than are all these holy things to animate us to pass in a holy manner the season on which we are about to enter? Second, in the same proportion as the Church acts in order to excite us to pass in a holy manner the days which separate us from Lent, the world acts in order to induce us to pass them in disorder, in the enjoyments of the table, profane amusements, dances and theatrical entertainments. Now, the conduct pursued by the world, of leading us into what is evil, ought to make us tend to what is good. A heart which loves God feels itself to be urged to love Him still more in proportion as others love Him less, and to make to Him reparation for the sins of others by redoubled love. A heart which loves its neighbor suffers at seeing its brethren losing their souls, and it does penance for those who do not perform it for themselves; it loves for those who do not love, and prays for their conversion. Third, if by employing this season holily we prepare ourselves worthily for the holy season of Lent, God will recompense by special graces the zeal we show to enter into the spirit of the Church, to repair its outraged glory, and to save our brethren who are losing their souls; and later on, we shall receive an abundance of: the: graces attached to the blessed season of Lent. Let us penetrate ourselves with these holy considerations.

SECOND POINT
✝ How to Pass in a Holy Manner the Season of Septuagesima

First, we must give ourselves up during these days to a spirit of recollection and prayer. Since the world is entirely occupied with exterior things, seeking after nothing but material enjoyments, we, children of the Church, called upon to repair the errors of the world, ought to be wholly given up to interior things, united to God to adore Him, to love Him, to pray to Him, to thank Him, to offer to Him all our actions, and to do everything for love of Him. Let the world ruin itself by dissipation and forgetfulness of God; we will meanwhile better perform our prayers and our ordinary actions, offering them to God as so many expiatory hosts for the sins of the earth, and we will repeat the cry of the saints: "Pardon me, my God, for not loving Thee. I would that I could hold the hearts of all men in my hand in order to cast them all into the brazier of Thy holy love." Second, we must mortify ourselves in regard to eating and drinking. The luxury of the table is one of the principal follies of the world at this season. In order to expiate and make reparation for it, it is just to retrench something from sensuality, and to oppose some privation or other to this rage for enjoyment. Third, we must, above all, apply ourselves to the chief of mortifications, which consists in making war against our besetting sin. Let us fix upon it precisely at the beginning of this holy season, and let us fight against it every day by contrary acts. *Resolutions and spiritual nosegay as above.*

SAINTS DAYS

WHOSE FEASTS, BEING ON FIXED DAYS, DO NOT FOLLOW THE VARIABLE COURSE OF THE LITURGY

November 30th

ST. ANDREW THE APOSTLE

See the meditation on the saints at the end of the fifth volume, where we have placed the meditation on this saint, because his feast frequently occurs before the first Sunday in Advent.

December 3rd

ST. FRANCIS XAVIER

SUMMARY OF TOMORROW'S MEDITATION

e will meditate tomorrow upon St. Francis Xavier, and we shall see that he had: first, the zeal of the greatest among the apostles; second, the virtues of the greatest among the anchorites. We will then make the resolution: first, to revive in ourselves zeal for the salvation of souls and for our own salvation; second, to practice during the day,

certain acts of humility and of mortification. We will retain as our spiritual nosegay the two ejaculatory prayers of St. Francis Xavier: "O holy Trinity! Jesus my love!"

MEDITATION FOR THE MORNING

Let us adore Our Savior Jesus Christ, the author of all holiness. Let us thank Him for having given to His Church a saint so admirable as St. Francis Xavier, an apostle who united in his person, to so great a degree, a life which was exteriorly so wonderfully laborious and interiorly so holy. Let us ask Him for a share in the double grace of this great saint.

FIRST POINT

✝ St. Francis Xavier Possessed the Zeal of the Greatest among the Apostles

Appointed by his superior to the mission of the Indies, Xavier sets off immediately, and from the time of his arrival at Goa, he evangelizes the children, the sick in the hospitals, and the prisoners. They are converted, and the whole town follows their example. Thence he passes to other places, and performs the same miracles; traverses the Indies, uprooting idolatry, reforming morals, bringing over kings and peoples to the Gospel. He flies, like the clouds, from one place to another; it might be said that the winds carry him on their wings. He crosses vast seas, full of rocks and of tempests; he visits desert islands and lands peopled by barbarians, where hunger and thirst, nakedness and persecutions await him and a thousand perils of death; and in ten years he evangelizes more than three thousand leagues of country, converts fifty-two kingdoms, and baptizes more than a million idolaters. His devotion to the glory of God and the salvation of souls knows no limits. He visits the sick, dresses and kisses their wounds, receives all the sinners with gentleness, and patiently bears all their obstinacy; he knows that souls are to be gained only through kindness. His life is hard and austere; he knows it is that which most touches the hardest hearts. After having thus taken the Gospel from Goa to the last of the nations of our hemisphere, Xavier turns towards the North, plans the conquest of China, then of Tartary; thence he proposes to return to Europe by way of the North, in order to convert the heretics there and to reform their morals; then into Africa to seek new kingdoms to evangelize. Thus his great heart dilated in proportion as he extended the kingdom of Jesus Christ, without his ever saying, "It is enough." What apostle had ever greater zeal than this? And how far are we from imitating him? Have we even a single spark of that great fire by which he was consumed?

SECOND POINT

✝ St. Francis Xavier had the Virtues of the Greatest among the Anchorites

"It would serve me nothing to convert the whole universe if I were to lose my own soul," he often said; and consequently, he occupied himself before all things with his own salvation. Beginning this great work with humility, he was filled with the most humble sentiments of himself. Although surrounded by the veneration of a whole world which he had converted, although he was honored with the gift of miracles, he esteemed himself to be nothing but a useless servant, a vile and contemptible creature, an abominable sinner, who, by his infidelities and his sins without number, placed an obstacle to the progress of the Gospel, spoiled the work of God, and made the intentions of the divine mercy towards the nations of no avail. He attributed his successes to a design of God, who willed to make His power to show forth by choosing, in order to perform the greatest prodigies, the most unsuitable of instruments. He is so penetrated with the necessity for humility, above all in a minister of the Gospel, that on a certain occasion he, throwing himself, with tears, on the neck of one of his fellow priests, conjures him to despise himself and to despise the esteem of men. "O human esteem, what evil you have done and what evil you will do! It is through you that the preacher opens hell for himself, whilst he opens heaven to others." As mortified as he was humble, Xavier loves suffering in the same way as others love pleasure. From the time of his entrance upon his mission, God shows him all that he will suffer there. "Still more, Lord" he exclaims, "still more!" And in the course of his mission he walks with naked feet over burning sands; he has no other bed than the bare ground; no other relaxation in the midst of his fatigues than attendance upon the sick in the hospitals; no other food than the bread he begs for, he who often might have been seated at the tables of the great; no other clothing than poor garments. More mortified still interiorly than he was exteriorly, he maintains always perfect tranquility of mind, an unalterable equality of temper, a sweet gaiety which renders intercourse with him delightful; and in this mortification his happiness consists. "Oh, how stupid men are," he said "not to understand that by refusing to mortify their natural desires, their tastes, and their inclinations, they deprive themselves of the sweetest pleasures of life." How shall we give expression to the greatness of faith and the ardor of love of this holy apostle? Filled with superhuman courage, he travels alone to unknown shores, amidst barbarous nations, in the midst of a thousand perils and a thousand obstacles, even to the courts of powerful sovereigns, where he is not afraid of preaching the truth and of condemning vice. "The more human succor fails me," he wrote" the more I count upon the help of God." No danger affrights me, for God holds in His hand the tempests of the seas; rocks and abysses are subject to His power; the rage of enemies and of persecutors, as well as that of devils, is submissive to His guidance. Why then, should I fear man or the fury of the elements let loose? In the midst of the greatest dangers I am overwhelmed with joy, and I know of nothing sweeter in this world than to live in continual peril of death for the honor of Jesus Christ and the good of souls." And he who thus spoke had seen himself, during three days and three nights, upon a plank, exposed to the mercy of the winds and the waves, and had fallen a hundred times into the hands of his enemies, who had subjected him to the most cruel torments. But when we love nothing costs us aught, and Xavier loved Jesus Christ to such a degree that often, not being able to bear the flames of charity which consumed him, he cried out: "Enough, Lord, enough!" His face was inflamed, his breast on fire, and from his heart burst forth, as though they were sparks, these burning words: "O Most Holy Trinity! O Jesus, my love! " Sometimes, when looking at the crucifix, he would burst into tears, break forth into sighs, and he would burn with the desire to give his Savior life for life; sometimes, beneath a beautiful, clear sky, sparkling with stars, in the silence and calmness of night, with both his hands crossed on his breast, he would rise to the most sublime contemplations; at other times he passed in presence of the Blessed Sacrament a portion of the night, overwhelmed with love; lastly, always, even in the midst of the difficulties of his immense ministry, he kept himself always recollected in God. May such beautiful examples confound without discouraging us, and may they lead us to enter upon a better life. *Resolutions and spiritual nosegay as above.*

December 8th

THE IMMACULATE CONCEPTION

FIRST MEDITATION

SUMMARY OF TOMORROW'S MEDITATION

e shall see tomorrow in our meditation: first, that Mary, for the sole reason that she was to be the mother of God, must have been immaculate in her conception; second, that her immaculate conception was the generating principle of all her virtues. We will then make the resolution: first, to thank God, and to congratulate the Blessed Virgin on so glorious a privilege by frequent and fervent elevations of the heart; second, to invoke Mary, under her title of Immaculate, in our difficulties and trials. Our spiritual nosegay shall be the well known invocation: "Mary conceived without sin, pray for us who have recourse to Thee."

MEDITATION FOR THE MORNING

Let us bless the Holy Trinity for the privilege of purity and innocence with which it embellished the first moment of the existence of Mary in the womb of her mother. Let us congratulate the divine Virgin, saluting her in the very words of the Holy Spirit: "Thou art all fair, O my love, and there is not a spot in thee." (Cant. 4:7)

FIRST POINT

✝ **Mary, for the sole Reason that she was to be the Mother of God, must have been Immaculate in her Conception**

Was it not, of a truth, evident that God, willing to become man in the womb of a virgin, could not employ, for the execution of so great a design, anyone except a person who had been pure from the first moment of her existence? Would it have been possible that the blood which was destined to flow in the veins of a God should be soiled at its source? Could the Word have allowed the devil to have the first fruits of its sanctuary, and have taken for

Himself only the leavings of the impure spirit? Would it have been suitable that she who was to crush the head of the serpent should have been once under his empire? No, evidently; the sole idea of the mother of a God implies the idea of a creature who had always been pure and endowed from the first moment of her entrance into life with a holiness in proportion to her lofty destiny. It was necessary that the heavenly Father, in order to associate Himself in the generation of His Word, and make her the mother of the same God of whom He is the Father, should have a person who, far from having been for a single moment soiled, should have been, from the very origin of her existence, enriched with more purity and innocence than there is even in heaven, amidst the angels. It was necessary that the Word should find, in the creature who was destined from all eternity to be His mother, perfect original purity; from the moment that He incarnated Himself in this daughter of Adam to make her one day His mother, He ought to have the heart of a son towards her, and of a son who desires to do his mother all the good he can, and who admits her to participate in his treasures and his riches; therefore it was requisite He should adorn her with purity from the first moment of her life, and be her Redeemer, not by effacing a stain already contracted, but by preserving her from all stain. It was, lastly, necessary that the Holy Ghost, in order to form in Mary a Man-God, and thus raise her to the dignity of His spouse, should have a person who had always been perfectly holy, and it was not too much that she should have all the virtues which a creature can have. Consequently, from all eternity, it was decreed, in the counsels of God that Mary should be pure from the very first moment of her existence, that she should be enriched with all the graces and all the prerogatives of original justice, and be raised to a holiness greatly superior to that of all the saints and angels put together. It is thus that the divine maternity bestowed upon Mary the honor of the Immaculate Conception, and that the definition of it given to the world by the great Pontiff Pius IX, amidst the acclamations of the whole Catholic world, is proved to be perfectly legitimate. Let us congratulate Mary on this fresh gem added to her crown, and let us love to ad dress to her the salutation of the Universal Church: "Thou art beautiful and there is no stain in thee."

SECOND POINT

✝ The Immaculate Conception was the Generating Principle of all the Virtues of Mary

Mary, so holy from the first moment of her existence, saw in this privilege only a reason for raising herself still higher and progressing every moment from virtue to virtue; thus this star, so radiant at its rising, ascended ceaselessly towards its meridian, casting around itself a constantly renewed brilliancy of holiness. In ordinary souls, grace is subject to annoyance by the opposition to good, and the tendency to evil, which we have with us from our birth. But in Mary immaculate grace, far from meeting with any obstacle, finds all the channels of the soul open to receive it; it spreads itself in them without reserve, flows in them like a flood, and makes all the virtues expand therein. Hence that purity of conscience, of mind, of heart, of the body which made Mary appear in the eyes of heaven like a beautiful lily of dazzling whiteness; hence that humility which renders the poverty of a cottage dear to the daughter of kings; that patience which was invincible under suffering; that sweetness which was never affected by opposition; that tranquility of soul in peril; that lively faith which does not only transport mountains, but makes the Eternal Word descend from heaven; that hope, more heroic than that of Abraham after the death and burial of the real Isaac; that charity, O charity of Mary, what a burning furnace, what a vast conflagration, what a torrent of divine flames! O holiness of Mary, how thou dost ravish my heart! "Many daughters have gathered together riches. Thou hast surpassed them all." (Prov. 31:29) "The Most High hath sanctified His own tabernacle." (Ps. 45:5) Therefore what most rejoices the heart of Mary is not her title of Queen of heaven, nor that of earthly sovereign: it is much rather her immaculate conception. That which has regard to herself is nothing, the consent of God is everything to her. This is why, when she was asked what was her name by the humble virgin of Lourdes, she replied: "I am the Immaculate Conception." Let us hence learn: first, always to be making progress in the path of virtue without ever saying: It is enough; second, to place the happiness of pleasing God above all other considerations. *Resolutions and spiritual nosegay above*

December 9th

THE IMMACULATE CONCEPTION

SECOND MEDITATION

SUMMARY OF TOMORROW'S MEDITATION

After having meditated upon the graces bestowed upon Mary through her immaculate conception, we will tomorrow consider the great advantages we ourselves ought to derive from it, and we shall see: first, that this mystery is for us a treasure of graces; second, a precious lesson. We will then make the resolution: first, often and with full confidence to invoke Mary conceived without sin; second, to prepare ourselves better for our communions, to watch more over our senses and our thoughts, and always to keep them pure; third, to apply ourselves to perform the present action better than the one which preceded it. We will retain as our spiritual nosegay the words which the Church applies to Mary: "Thou art all fair, my love, and there is not a spot in thee."(Cant. 4:7)

MEDITATION FOR THE MORNING

Let us adore God for giving Mary Immaculate to the world, to be its hope and its salvation. Let us afterwards address to this divine mother the hymn of the Church: "Hail, holy Queen, Mother of mercy, our life, our sweetness, and our hope. To thee do we cry, poor banished sons of Eve; to thee do we send up our sighs, mourning and weeping in this valley of tears. Turn, then, most gracious advocate, thine eyes of mercy toward us, and after this our exile show unto us the blessed fruit of thy womb, Jesus. O clement, O loving, O sweet Virgin Mary!"

FIRST POINT

✝ **The Immaculate Conception a Treasure of Graces**

Inasmuch as nature has placed in the hearts of mothers a certain kind of weakness, by which children obtain from them more than they ask, there exists also in the heart of Mary a more loving feeling towards those who honor her under the title of the Immaculate Conception. Mary conceived without sin has been invoked by tempted souls, and they have triumphed over temptation; by afflicted souls, and they have been consoled; by troubled hearts, and they have recovered peace; by courage ready to fail, and it has been fortified. Besieged cities, threatened with pillage, have been known to inscribe on the doors of their houses, "Mary was conceived without sin" and they were preserved; buildings in the act of being consumed by a conflagration, individuals menaced by a thousand perils, have been saved by the inscription, or by pronouncing the same words. The medal bearing the effigy of Mary conceived without sin has filled the whole world with marvels; it has driven away misfortunes, brought down graces, converted sinners, and it has deserved to be acclaimed everywhere by the title of the miraculous medal. The sanctuary of Our Lady of Victories at Paris, at one time almost entirely forsaken, no sooner dedicated itself to the Immaculate Heart of Mary, than it became the most celebrated sanctuary in the world, the one most frequented, and where miracles have been multiplied. Pius IX, lastly, when exposed to the attacks of his enemies raging against him, recommended himself to Mary conceived without sin, and in tranquil Rome, surrounded by furious enemies, he was able to hold an ecumenical council, the freest and the most independent of the powers of the earth which has ever been held. The accomplishment of this great fact is a guarantee to us that whatever trials may happen, the Church will triumph over them all, as she has done over the preceding ones, through Mary Immaculate. Is anything more required to show that the mystery of the Immaculate Conception is a treasure of graces to which we ought to have recourse with full confidence in our temptations and trials?

SECOND POINT
✝ The Immaculate Conception a Precious Lesson

This mystery, in fact, teaches us: first, the purity of conscience which it is necessary to bring to holy communion; for if it was requisite that Mary should have been so pure in order to receive into her womb the Word Incarnate, how reprehensible would those be who did not bring to holy communion a conscience without reproach, seeing that the God of the Eucharist is the same as the God of the Incarnation. How pure ought those to be who receive this Incarnate God, not once only, as Mary did at the Annunciation, but so often during their lives! Second, this mystery teaches us to watch over ourselves, our imagination, our mind, our hearts. For if Mary, in whom all was upright, pure, innocent, exercised the most active vigilance over her virtue, how carefully ought we to watch over ourselves, and mistrust ourselves, we who are so fragile, so inclined to evil, so easily seduced. Third, this mystery teaches us ceaselessly to progress towards perfection; for if, as is certain, Mary, although eminently holy, ceaselessly aspired, during her whole life, to a still higher degree of holiness, if she labored without a pause to become more holy by means of a constant correspondence with grace, how shall we, so imperfect as we are, dare to place limits to our perfection, remain always the same, which is the same thing as going back, according to the maxim of the saints, "Not to advance is to retrograde." How, continually receiving, as we do, graces from God, shall we allow them to remain sterile in us, without being determined to break off our attachments, without advancing there where God calls us? Let us keep this lesson of the Immaculate Conception in the bottom of our heart, and let us conform our conduct to it. *Resolutions and spiritual nosegay as above.*

December 21st

ST. THOMAS, APOSTLE

SUMMARY OF TOMORROW'S MEDITATION

We will meditate tomorrow: first, upon the impression which the wounds of Jesus Christ made upon St. Thomas; second, the impression which these same wounds ought to make upon us. We will then make the resolution: first, often to look at and lovingly to kiss the crucifix; second, to excite ourselves by the sight of it to zeal for our perfection. We will retain, as our spiritual nosegay, the words of St. Thomas: "My Lord and my God!"

MEDITATION FOR THE MORNING

Let us admire and bless the infinite goodness of the Savior, who is willing, by a special apparition, to show to St. Thomas the wounds with which His adorable body was pierced upon the cross. Oh, how greatly does this charity of a God for the salvation of a sinner deserve our adoration and our love.

FIRST POINT

✝ **The Impression which the Wounds of Jesus Christ made upon St. Thomas**

First, they cured him of his infidelity. He had been obstinately resolved not to believe unless he could touch the wounds of the Savior. Jesus Christ condescends to his weakness, appears to him in the midst of the apostles, shows him His wounds, and invites him to put his finger into them. Behold, Thomas, behold these hands which have cured so many sick and bestowed so many blessings, how they are pierced through and through! Behold these feet which have walked on the sea, and have hastened after so many wandering sheep, how the nails have gone through them. I Behold this side opened by the lance, this sanctuary of love and of grace! Thomas has no sooner touched these adorable wounds than his eyes are opened, his voice makes itself to be heard, and he lovingly confesses, not only the resurrection, but also the divinity of Jesus Christ, by those beautiful words: "Thou art my Lord and my God." Second, these wounds of the Savior in flame his zeal. In the sacred side of Jesus, where the heart beats with love, he imbibes an ardent love for the Savior and for His Church. The wounds in the feet inspire him with a marvelous agility which makes him push his conquests farther than any other apostle; from the wounds of the hands he receives the zeal for good works which so greatly honored his apostolate. There we see him go with intrepidity and amidst all kinds of perils to evangelize the Parthians, the Medes, the Persians, the Scythians, the Hyrcanians, and even to the uttermost parts of the Indies. Third, the wounds of the Savior inspire his heart with a thirst for martyrdom. Penetrated with what this good master had suffered for the salvation of man, he rejoices to be shut up in prison, to be thrown into a deep ditch, torn by scourges, and stoned; he triumphs at being made to suffer hunger, thirst, nakedness, fatigues, long journeys. Provided that at the end of his course he finds the martyrdom which the wounds of the Savior have taught him to love, he is content. In the end, he finds at Calamina, a town in the Indies, that which he had longed for. The king of the country condemns him to death, and the holy apostle expires, his body pierced with arrows, happy at heart at bearing the stigmata of the wounds of the Saviour. What a beautiful apostolate, and how truly have the wounds of Jesus Christ been lively sources of grace for St. Thomas! What have they done for us up to the present time? Let us profit better by them in future.

SECOND POINT

✟ The Impression which the Wounds of Jesus Christ ought to make upon us

If Jesus Christ has willed to preserve on His body, even in heaven and in the Eucharist, His adorable wounds, it is in order to nourish our faith, our confidence, and our love. Let us meditate then upon these sacred wounds. Let us gaze upon them, let us fix our lips on them, and we shall feel our faith becoming more lively, our confidence more entire, our love more ardent. The wounds in the feet will teach us to walk without being afraid of fatigue, wherever duty calls us, wherever there is good to be done, troubles to console, sinners to bring back, the sick to visit. The wounds in the hands will teach us to say like St. Augustine: "Lord, do not despise the work of Thy hands. The wounds which Thou hast in them beg of Thee grace and mercy for me; listen to them and save me." Lastly, the wound in the sacred side, a true sanctuary of love, of graces, and of benedictions, shall be to me like the mysterious cavity wherein the dove loves to retire in order to be sheltered from the attacks of the bird of prey, (Cant. 2:14) that is to say, we shall find a refuge therein against the assaults of the world and of the devil. We shall rest there in safety, lays St. Augustine; there we shall derive fruit from our meditations; we shall pray with fervor; there we shall love and we shall sanctify ourselves. O adorable wounds, how dear you are to me! May I learn from Thy example, O my Savior, always to make a holy use of my hands to do Thy will, of my feet to go whither Thou wiliest, and of my heart to love Thee, to will all Thou wiliest and nothing else whatever! *Resolutions and spiritual nosegay as above.*

January 17th

ST. ANTHONY

SUMMARY OF TOMORROW'S MEDITATION

e will tomorrow meditate upon this patriarch of the solitaries, and we shall see him: first, as a finished model of perfection; second, as a master eminent in the science of the saints. We will then make the resolution: first, not to love to mingle with the world,

remembering that God showed the world to St. Antony as a place wholly covered with snares, where many souls perish; second, on the contrary, to love solitude, as being more favorable to recollection and to prayer. We will retain as our spiritual nosegay the saying of the saints: "In solitude the air is purer, and heaven more open, God more communicative and more familiar."

MEDITATION FOR THE MORNING

Let us adore God, assisting St. Antony to give to the world the spectacle of the most sublime virtue, and through him creating the monastic order which has given so many saints to heaven, and so many beautiful examples to the earth. Let us honor in St. Antony the first institutor of this kind of life, the patriarch of the anchorites, the father of the solitaries, and the star of the desert.

FIRST POINT

✝ St. Antony, a Finished Model of Perfection

St. Antony was only eighteen years old when, entering into a church, these words of the Gospel, spoken from the pulpit, fell upon his ears: "If thou wilt be perfect, go sell what thou hast, and give to the poor, and thou shall have a treasure in heaven, and come follow Me." (Matt. 19:21) Immediately he sells all his possessions and distributes the price of them to the poor, in order to buy the rich treasure which had been shown to him; then he retires to the desert, that he may occupy himself thenceforth solely with his perfection. He fasts every day on bread and water, he wears a hair shirt, he has no other bed than the bare ground, no other roof than heaven, of which the meditation absorbs his thoughts to such a degree that he complains when the sun, rising in the morning, distracts him from it. The devil, jealous of so much holiness, tempts him in all kinds of ways. The saint resists, and triumphs by dint of humility and of prayers. The devil recommences his cruel war, the saint complains to Our Lord: "Where wert Thou, then, O good Jesus?" he asks. "I was here, Antony. I saw you fight, I rejoiced in your victories, and because you have fought so well, I will make your name famous throughout the whole earth." So much holiness, in fact, soon attracted numerous disciples; they came from all parts to place themselves under his guidance, believing that there could not be a better guide to lead souls to heaven. And, what is most admirable, surrounded by so many testimonies of esteem, the saint looks upon himself as the last of all; he studies whatever is good in each one of his brethren; the humility of this one, the meekness of that one, the mortification of one, the patience of another, the recollection and the union of God of such and such among them. Through a holy emulation he endeavors to imitate them and to collect together in himself the perfection of all, and then, by imitating them, he becomes, in his turn, the model of all. Is it thus that we act ourselves? Instead of seeking in others what there is of good, that we may imitate it, do we not often seek for what is evil or for what is less perfect, in order to criticize it?

SECOND POINT
✝ St. Antony, a Master Eminent in the Science of the Saints

"Blessed is the man whom Thou shalt instruct, O Lord, and shalt teach out of Thy law." (Ps. 93:12) This happiness was that of St. Antony. Without the means of study and without books, and solely through his communications with God, this man became a light of the Church. He enchanted the most able doctors by his conversations, and even emperors esteemed themselves honored to receive a letter from his hand. Having on a certain occasion come forth from his desert to defend religion attacked by heretics, he confounded them by the wisdom of his words and the solidity of his reasonings. Being asked to expound the doctrine of perfection, he explained the maxims of it with a good sense and a precision which excited astonishment. "In order soon to attain perfection," he said "think that it is today you are beginning to serve God. Think that today may be the last of your life. If you are tempted, remember that the devil can do nothing against prayer, fasting, and the fervent love of Jesus Christ. Discretion is the mistress of all the virtues. Humility is the greatest of all miracles. Whoever esteems God alone never loses peace and the joy of the spirit. Confidence in God and a perfect dependence upon His Providence render man, so to say, all-powerful. The world is to him who sees in it God only, a voluminous book which renders him wise in the science of the saints." Let us be penetrated with some of these holy maxims, and our soul will derive great profit from them. *Resolutions and spiritual nosegay as above.*

January 25th

THE CONVERSION OF ST. PAUL

SUMMARY OF TOMORROW'S MEDITATION

e will meditate tomorrow upon the conversion of St. Paul, and we shall see: first, that it was a magnificent confirmation of the faith; second, the model of a perfect conversion. We will then make the resolution: first, to be converted to a better life, and to come forth, at last, out of the life, always the same, in which we have been languishing for so long a time; second, to follow in all our actions the good pleasure of God, as being the compass which will lead us into the port. We will retain, as our spiritual nosegay, the words of St. Paul: "Lord, what wilt Thou have me to do?" (Acts 9:6)

MEDITATION FOR THE MORNING

Let us adore Our Lord Jesus Christ appearing to St. Paul upon the road to Damascus. Let us admire Him descending from heaven to convert the apostle who was destined to convert so many others; let us praise Him for this miracle, one of the greatest He ever worked, and let us beg Him to convert ourselves.

FIRST POINT

✝ **The Conversion of St. Paul is a Magnificent Confirmation of the Faith**

In order to understand it, let us recall the facts of it. Paul, a furious enemy of Christianity, sets out from Jerusalem, and, full of rage, goes to Damascus to imprison and put to death the Christians in that town. Half-way on his road thither, at noonday, he is stopped by a dazzling light, which environs him and his companions by an invisible force, which throws him to the ground, and by a voice from heaven, which cries out: "Saul, Saul, wherefore dost thou persecute Me?" "Who art thou, Lord?" he answers. "I am Jesus, whom thou persecutes!" replies the heavenly voice; and immediately his eyes are closed to the light of day, his mind is opened to receive the truth, his heart is changed; he is led by the hand to Damascus; Ananias baptizes him. Three days afterwards the scales fall from his eyes; his blindness ceases, and, behold he is an intrepid apostle of the faith he had come to destroy. Now, whosoever recognizes Thy intervention here, O my God, can easily conceive that these facts took place. Thou dost command the tempest, and immediately there is a great calm; Thou dost command the heart which is the most carried away by passion, and immediately it allows itself to be molded according to Thy good pleasure. But without Thy intervention, O Lord, how would it be possible to see anything else in these things except a mass of impossibilities and of facts which are contrary to nature? It was impossible and against nature that Paul should have passed, all at once, from a furious hatred of Christianity to a passionate love of it; that he should have separated himself from the nation he loved so dearly, of which his epistles are a proof; from the princes and the magistrates, whose man of confidence he was, in order to associate with poor boatmen, who had no education and no credit. It was impossible and contrary to nature that he should have renounced the brilliant future which awaited him among his own people, in order to devote himself to persecutions, to contempt, to a kind of life of which he himself says that if we had hope only in this world, we should be the most miserable of all men. (1 Cor. 15:19) It was impossible and against nature that he should thus have sacrificed all his interests, all his national prejudices, to espouse the cause of a crucified man, and of a religion which offered him so few chances of success. It was impossible and contrary to nature that in the recital which he himself makes of this event in the book of the acts of the apostles, he should have wished to deceive. His noble character, his virtues, his miracles, his writings, the prejudices of his education, his dearest interests, are opposed to such a supposition. It is not less impossible and contrary to nature that he should have been the dupe of an illusion or of an exalted imagination. The facts happened at midday, upon the high road, in presence of several witnesses; the blindness lasted three whole days, and everyone saw the scales fall from his eyes when he recovered his sight once more. Lastly, the whole of his life and the whole of his miracles protest against all supposition of falsehood in such a recital. Therefore, O my God, it is very true that the conversion of Thy apostle is a magnificent confirmation of the faith. Augment in me that faith so splendidly proved, and may I be in my whole conduct, and in all my sentiments, a man of faith.

SECOND POINT
✝ **The Conversion of St. Paul is the Model of a Perfect Conversion.**

For a perfect conversion there must, first be confidence in the divine mercy, which, through the assurance of pardon, animates us to act rightly and disposes us to love. Now nowhere does the divine mercy show itself better than in the great miracle of this conversion of St. Paul. There is in it matter to encourage whoever may be tempted to grieve over his wretchedness and to mistrust the divine mercy. There must be, second, a perfect abandonment to the will of God, an abandonment which leaves the government of our whole being to the divine pleasure. Now what more beautiful example of this abandonment could be found than St. Paul on the day of his conversion. "Lord, what wilt Thou that I should do?" said the great apostle. In that one sentence is contained the sum total of a perfect life: not to have any desire but that of pleasing God, no other will than that of the divine will; that is the beginning, the middle, and the consummation of all perfection. There must be, second, a complete detachment from all that passes away, so as no longer to hold in estimation anything except eternal possessions, and all that leads to them. Now this is what the blindness of St. Paul, with which he was visited during three days, also teaches us. He kept his eyes closed to everything on earth; heavenly graces were all in all to him. There must be, fourth, a humble docility in allowing ourselves to be guided. "Whoever confides in himself is a fool," says St. Bernard. (Ep. 87) Now, this is what is taught us by St. Paul being sent to St. Ananias. There must be, fifth, entire devotion to the glory of God and the good of our neighbor. Now it is useless to say that St. Paul fulfilled this condition. But how do we fulfill the five conditions of a perfect conversion? Let us examine and judge ourselves severely. *Resolutions and spiritual nosegay as above.*

January 29th

ST. FRANCIS DE SALES

SUMMARY OF TOMORROW'S MEDITATION

e will consider tomorrow: first, that St. Francis became a saint only by dint of renouncing himself; second, that by renouncing himself he found both happiness and sanctity. We will then make the resolution; first, heartily to embrace all the opportunities which present themselves of mortifying our desires, our will, our attachments; second, to impose on ourselves voluntary mortifications, such as certain privations, certain sacrifices, which do not in the least compromise health, but which do great good to the soul. We will retain as our spiritual nosegay the words of Our Lord: "If any man will come after Me, let him deny himself." (Luke 9:23)

MEDITATION FOR THE MORNING

Let us adore Our Lord Jesus Christ, imposing on all who desire to be His disciples the law of abnegation or of renunciation of themselves. "If any man will come after Me, let him deny himself. Every one that doth not renounce all that he possesses cannot be My disciple." (Luke 9:23; 14:33) "He that loveth his life shall lose it, and he that hateth his life in this world, keepeth it unto life eternal." (John 12:25) Let us adore Him who Himself gives us an example of this renunciation, (Rom. 15:3) and who inspires all His saints with the same dispositions, especially St. Francis de Sales, and let us beg of Him to give us also this grace.

FIRST POINT

✝ St. Francis de Sales was a Saint only by Dint of Renouncing Himself

It would be a great delusion to imagine that virtue cost nothing to St. Francis de Sales. Like all the children of Adam, he had a predisposition to temper which is vexed with what wounds it, which revolts against what annoys it, which pursues enjoyment and glory, and desires to have neither pain nor humiliation. This great saint acquired virtue only through mortifying his passions and by means of this struggle he obtained over them so absolute an authority, that they obeyed him like slaves obey their master, so that, towards the end of his life, says St. Chantal, they hardly ever showed themselves. On a certain occasion he was insulted, and threats were added to injuries. Nevertheless he remained calm and tranquil. His friends reproached him with his insensibility: "You believe," he answered, "that I am insensible; put your hand upon my heart, and you will see, by the quickness of its pulsations, how greatly it feels the storm, and that it would break out into anger if I did not restrain it. But would you wish that by allowing a quick and impatient word to escape I should lose in one moment all the meekness that, by dint of efforts over myself, I have endeavored to acquire during four and twenty years?" "Whatever you may do to me," he said to another who abused him, "I will hold my heart in both my hands, and you will not succeed in making me angry. You might tear out one of my eyes, and I should still look affectionately at you with the other." Nor was it without doing greater and more continual violence to himself that he had succeeded in acquiring such a perfect mastery over self that he was never seen to be unduly elevated by joy, or cast down by sorrow, or carried away by haste, or embittered by opposition, and always to be under such self-control that, whatever happened, nothing could shake his confidence, trouble his serenity, or disturb his peace. He had such a placidity of mind, of heart, of the face, in his manners, that he was always the same; and there was such a regularity and orderliness of the whole of his interior, which was made visible by the regularity and orderliness of the whole of his exterior, in a manner so supernatural and so divine, that St. Vincent de Paul and St. Chantal looked upon him as a living picture in which Our Lord had delineated Himself, and that in seeing him, even in the most secret part of his private life, was like seeing Jesus Christ on earth. "When he came to see me at my house," says the Bishop of Belley, "I looked at him, alone in his room, through secret holes which I had had purposely made, and I saw that there, as in public, he maintained a placidity of manner similar to that of his heart; a way of standing up, of sitting down, of rising, of lying down, so pious, so edifying, that you would have said he was in the presence of the angels and of all the saints." Oh, in presence of so great an example, how we ought to be confounded that we put ourselves out of the way so little, that we allow ourselves to do just what pleases us, that we allow ourselves to be subject to temper, to pusillanimity, to effeminacy, to self-love, to our own will! It is not in this way that we become holy.

SECOND POINT
✝ St. Francis by Renouncing Himself found both Happiness and Holiness

The whole secret of happiness upon earth lies in having no desires and no attachments exterior to God. However few may be our desires or our attachments, they render us unhappy. Desires are opposed, and they engender bitterness of heart; attachments are wounded, and they become a painful laceration of the soul. By his spirit of renunciation St. Francis de Sales rendered himself superior to all these causes of pain. To desire nothing, to ask nothing, to refuse nothing, was his favorite device. "I desire very few things," he said, "and the little I desire I desire very little; and if I could be born again, I should will to have only one sole desire. I desire God only, and the God whom I desire is all to me. All that is not God is nothing to me, and what is there in heaven or on earth for which I care, except God only and His good pleasure?" In this holy disposition of his heart he saw all events, great and little, issue from the order of Providence, in which, even in the midst of the most boisterous tempests, he reposed with the tranquility of a child on the breast of the most tender and the most amiable of mothers. "Like the pilot," he says again, "who guides himself over the sea by keeping his eyes steadfastly fixed on the pole star, so I guide myself across the sea of life by keeping my eyes uninterruptedly fixed on the good pleasure of God; and as this divine good pleasure is infinitely amiable in all that it permits or ordains, I am always content, always placid amidst the vicissitudes of human affairs. If the whole universe were to be turned upside down," he adds, "I should not be troubled; I am, I shall, and I desire always to be at the mercy of Divine Providence, in presence of which I desire that my own will should hold no other rank than that of servant." Now what can be happier upon earth than a soul with such dispositions as these? *Resolutions and spiritual nosegay as above.*

February 2ⁿᵈ

THE PURIFICATION OF MARY AND THE PRESENTATION OF OUR LORD

See meditation for Wednesday in the fourth week after Epiphany and the following.

HAMON, A. J. M. BQ

Meditations for All the Days of the Year.

Reprinted by Valora Media 2011

www.ingramcontent.com/pod-product-compliance
Lightning Source LLC
Chambersburg PA
CBHW061954180426
43198CB00036B/922